Sustainable IT Architecture

Sustainable IT Architecture

The Progressive Way of Overhauling Information Systems with SOA

Pierre Bonnet
Jean-Michel Detavernier
Dominique Vauquier

Jérôme Boyer and Erik Steinholtz

First published in France in 2007 by Hermes Science/Lavoisier entitled *Le système d'information durable : la refonte progressive du SI avec SOA* © LAVOISIER, 2007
First published in Great Britain and the United States in 2009 by ISTE Ltd and John Wiley & Sons, Inc.

ISTE Ltd
27-37 St George's Road
London SW19 4EU
UK

www.iste.co.uk

John Wiley & Sons, Inc.
111 River Street
Hoboken, NJ 07030
USA

www.wiley.com

Library of Congress Cataloging-in-Publication Data

Bonnet, Pierre, 1967-
 [système d'information durable. English]
 Sustainable IT architecture : the progressive way of overhauling information systems with SOA / Pierre Bonnet, Jean-Michel Detavernier, Dominique Vauquier.
    p. cm.
 Includes bibliographical references and index.
 ISBN 978-1-84821-089-9
 1. Service-oriented architecture (Computer science) 2. Information technology--Management.
 3. Business enterprises--Computer networks.
 I. Detavernier, Jean-Michel. II. Vauquier, Dominique, 1962- III. Title.
 TK5105.5828.B6613 2009
 658.4'038011--dc22

                                                                                    2008045287

British Library Cataloguing-in-Publication Data
A CIP record for this book is available from the British Library
ISBN: 978-1-84821-089-9

Printed and bound in Great Britain by CPI Antony Rowe, Chippenham, Wiltshire.

FSC
Mixed Sources
Product group from well-managed
forests and other controlled sources
Cert no. SGS-COC-2953
www.fsc.org
© 1996 Forest Stewardship Council

Table of Contents

Acknowledgements

The modernization project of our information system that we carried out took five years to complete. During these five years many different employees from an insurance company, the SMABTP (a mutual insurance company in the construction sector), worked together with external IT specialists. This experience will be used as a case study to illustrate the concepts and procedures that are described throughout this book.

This project could not have been successful without the support of the general management of the SMABTP, and without the support of Mr. Emmanuel Edou as well as Mr. Bernard Milléquant, throughout the entire project. It is impossible to completely restructure an existing information system over a one- to two-year period. A project that takes longer than this cannot be maintained only by the IT department but the whole company needs to support it.

All the users of the information system as well as the business executives took part in the project. They re-examined their business processes, their products and offerings, their business letters and mail, etc. that were already in place. In other words an enormous task was carried out.

As far as the project of overhauling the claims management system is concerned, the settlements' manager, Daniel Lemaître, and his deputy, Jean-Luc Buisson, put their trust in us and monitored the changes that our work (related to the business service) brought to the company. The introduction of the business service led to the creation of a new process-based approach as well as improving the ergonomics of the user interfaces.

As soon as this new concept was adopted, it was then sold to all potential users of the concept.

Each of the different IT teams worked extremely hard on the project:

– the architects provided the ideas, the methodology and the different tools required for the project such as the service-oriented development framework;

– the EAI team, which later became the ESB team, worked on connecting the different components that exist within information systems. This team also worked on connecting the different domains together, as well as connecting the different platforms, and the different internal and external information systems together;

– the teams who worked on the MVS or AS400 platforms produced surface components with the aim of enabling all of the users of the information system to have a unified access to the information system;

– the claims project team worked non-stop in order to change their methodology and their tools with the aim of generating reusable business components;

– the activity of IT production teams was largely modified due to the fact that the monolithic MVS system was replaced by a multi-platform system made up of asynchronous connections, which enables communication to be carried out in XML with other parts of the information system.

This project could not have taken place without the innovative ambition of Jean-Claude Lebois, the CIO. His advice and experience are greatly appreciated.

We would also like to thank the project's external auditor for the advice and the recommendations that were given to us.

Special thanks also go to all those people who proofread this book as well as those people who contributed to the creation of this book in other ways: Jean-Pascal Ancelin, Christophe Barriolade, Jean Baudrin, Frédéric Bonnard, Fabrice Chevrier, Philippe Gire, Marc Jérome, Jean-François Labro, David Lapetina, Didier Mamma, Jérôme Marc, Joël Milgram, Didier Pujol, Nicolas Regnier, Fabien Villard, and the Research and Development team from Orchestra Networks.

The illustrations of the UML models were created by UML modeling case Objecteering. This tool was used in SMABTP's SOA overhaul project for the modeling and management of the Model Driven Architecture (MDA) chain.

Foreword

In this time of profound questioning of our economy, Pierre Bonnet, Jean-Michel Detavernier and Dominique Vauquier raise the question of sustainable information systems. Can we indeed continue to endlessly reproduce the same applications re-developments each time changes occur in the technical, organization or business context? Can we continue to lose and re-discover the business knowledge at the heart of these applications, at each re-development time? Do we have no other choice than to reproduce the difficulties encountered when integrating new systems into existing ones?

The answer to these recurring problems is a set of solutions, above all methodological, organizational and architectural. Furthermore, technologies are here to help us, and the latest developments – MDM (Master Data Management), SOA (Service Oriented Architecture), BRMS (Business Rules Management Systems), MDA (Model Driven Architecture) – provide undreamt of means of building agile and sustainable systems.

An information system is an asset for companies, who must recognize, preserve and consolidate its value. Companies rely on their IS and cannot function without it. They have no choice but to evolve, improve their functioning and transfer more and more requirements to the IS. But how can the IS evolve more quickly and provide more and more services other than by radically revising practices and techniques, unless we suppose that the IT service can regularly assume ever-increasing loads and requirements without a glitch? Many companies are confronted with this dilemma: radically revising practices and techniques means taking difficult risks, notably risking the unknown. And then there is the question of which practices and techniques to go for? The choice is vast, and too many commercial "off-the-shelf" solutions only tend to orient us towards proprietary solutions, resulting in consistently incomplete coverage of the necessary set of solutions. This aversion to risk and to the unknown incites us to continue with earlier practices and to fiddle with the IS, at the risk (this time well-known) of making it too complex, thereby taking the current situation to suffocation point.

The ever-renewed promise of new techniques to resolve recurring IS problems, which is inevitably followed by a phase of disillusionment, has made more than one IT director cautious when it comes to new technologies. To remedy this, this book recommends an approach centered on models whose initial parts are technology-independent, and on the implementation of architectures providing a high level of separation: the separation of reference data from the usual management data, the separation of process orchestration from business entities management, the separation of business rules, the break-down into autonomous service components, etc. The link between model and architecture is provided by the now mature MDA technology, enabling models to be instrumented, in order to check them and automate the production of applications on the target architecture.

A great number of practices, methods, tools and technologies are available nowadays, each of which contributes as part of the solution. The real challenge is to federate and organize these techniques, in order to have a solution adapted to the context of each individual company. The open source Praxeme approach used in this book meets the method requirement by federating tried and tested practices, basing itself on modeling standards (UML, MDA). It provides content by describing how to model each level of the approach, and provides rules enabling the MDA approach to be put in place.

This book is built on an example of how the approach is put into practice and how architecture combining technologies ensuring agility and separation is set up. All set up aspects are dealt with, along with sociological IT team aspects, company organization in terms of business owners and IT services, budget preparation aspects enabling these evolutions in the organization, methods, techniques and IS to be taken on, and finally the planning strategy taking into account increasing team competence, architectural studies and the migration of what already exists.

The authors provide here a summary of these techniques and approaches. The real value of this book is that it describes implementation on a real company IS, with its inherent pitfalls and keys to success. This is therefore a precious source of information on both theory and implementation, independent of all commercial off-the-shelf solutions, but not hesitating to cite choices where this is necessary.

I know and like Pierre, Dominique and Jean-Michel, who are renowned professionals in their fields. The association of their skills has enabled the realization of this book, rare in the field of IT literature.

Philippe Desfray
VP for R&D at SOFTEAM
OMG Contributing Member

During the last ten years, globalization has exacerbated competitive battles for the conquest of market shares. Domination of the market segment is the condition that makes it possible to reach a critical size and benefit from lever effects, competitive barriers and consequently, continuity. Pressure applied to the company by the market, legislation, competition and shareholders demands high levels of performance in a fluctuating, uncertain and aggressive economic context. Corporate bodies in general and companies in particular have no other choice but to rethink their organisational methods, their economic models and all underlying systems. The recent economic crisis is a perfect illustration, even if its systemic nature shows an imbalance of forces acting on the current growth model.

Before going any further in search of solutions, it is necessary to have a full understanding of the issues, the forces in action, their effects and their directions. Globalization is not a new phenomenon. Ever since mankind emerged from the cradle of Africa, it has never ceased to extend its territory, its "procurement" sources and its exchanges. This trend remains a constant and the increased volume of relations between nations and companies continues in all dimensions: politics, military, cultural and social. These exchanges have generated ruptures with which companies have had to cope, with more or less success or damage. It is important to isolate the determining factors, thus making it possible to change the "company" system to give it the capacity to co-develop with its environment as well as varying factors of the physics of the information system.

The first determining factor is the exponential acceleration of commercial transactions. Acceleration is maintained by the increase in the power of computers, network capacity and the number of Internet users. This convergence has produced a break in the way in which business is conducted and services are provided. A study conducted by the Gartner Group shows that in numerous industries we have moved to the provision of services within a single day (same-day service); i.e., only 24 hours between the customer's order and delivery of the product or service. In industries where products are intangible (video, music, e-books, surveillance, banking, telecommunications, stock exchange, etc.), consumption is on request and immediate.

The second factor is complexity, which has exploded under the effect of globalization. The modern company's value chain has adopted more varied forms capable of integrating with greater and more complex value aggregates. This polymorphism has destabilised both organisational methods and the underlying structure of the information system. Company value chains must move towards a composite form and be capable of rearranging themselves and co-developing with their ecosystem in a federated macro-entity. The advent of "cloud computing" will intensify the trend towards polymorphism and the pervasivity of the information system within the next three years.

Acceleration and complexity are the two factors that push information systems to the brink of infarct, caused by a digital atheroma phenomenon affecting flows, data and processes. Under such conditions, information systems are incapable of meeting the requirements of the driving organs, which are the business lines. What is observed in the field is the opacity of systems, their illegibility, their rigidity and their fragility. Mediocre speed and inadequate efficiency/cost performance can be added to this non-exhaustive list. All these elements have a significant impact on the competitiveness of companies and the efficiency of organisational methods.

It is essential to be aware that complexity and speed can only increase. This is a reality that cannot be ignored and revitalisation of the IS cannot be postponed without risk. Why are we seeing a situation approaching total breakdown of today's information system?

Information technology is a new industry; information systems were constructed using the organisational and economic models of the 1970s. In order to develop them, companies weighed them down with ever-increasing layers of software in partitioned bunkers, thus saving on a consolidation that, for all the wrong reasons, has always been put off until tomorrow. The mistake would be to believe that it is still possible to continue along this path. The relatively well designed "encapsulation" and patches applied to historic systems is no longer acceptable, while the complexity and speed of economic models have jumped up to a new level. In this context, the information system must also jump up to another scale to be able to meet the challenges of the 21st century and a globalized economy. For IT engineers and for business lines, the new challenge is nothing less than a conceptual leap such as when mankind discovered that the Earth was round not flat, from Aristotle to Darwin, from a static universe to an expanding one and from determinism to indeterminism. This type of leap is not easy to negotiate because it requires changes in mental representation and understanding of the world.

The initiative of the "Sustainable IT Architecture" community is to propose a conceptual and practical location and framework capable of addressing these problems. When I first met Pierre Bonnet and the "Sustainable IT Architecture" community, I immediately noted our agreement on the diagnosis of the situation and the challenges to be met on the way to establishing a new vision of a sustainable information system. The Agility Chain Management System (ACMS) concept, advanced by the community and explained in this book, is an approach that makes perfect sense when placed in the dynamic situations generated by "trade" issues. It offers a range of tools and experience and a reference architecture that will allow companies to embark upon an in-depth but progressive transformation of the information system in a guided and structured manner.

The following illustration is largely inspired by the ACMS to which Progress Software has added three transverse components. Firstly, the integration semantic layer located at the level of data processed by the new BUS generation (see chapter 14). This integration approach at semantic level allows maximum capitalization on MDM input in the procurement and distribution of reference data throughout the entire information system, productivity, transparency, security and reduced complexity and costs are the benefits provided by this approach. Secondly, governance, which ensures 360° visibility of the performance of IS components, operating processes and regulatory and security policies; transparency and control of complexity are at the forefront. Finally, Business Activity Monitoring is coupled with the Complex Event Process (BAM-CEP), the new event-oriented BAM generation, the principal function of which is to synchronize the speed of the company with its economic model, i.e., the capacity to react before prejudicial effects become apparent.

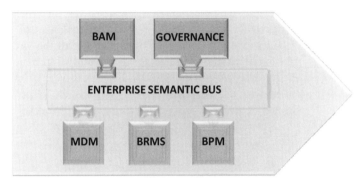

AGILITY CHAIN MANAGEMENT SYSTEM

I recommend careful reading of the innovative concepts developed by the authors, Pierre Bonnet, Jean-Michel Detavernier and Dominique Vauquier, which are based on real experiences in the field. The authors have made this conceptual leap, which is bold, imaginative, sound and full of good sense, so that the sustainable information system may become not only a reality but also an integral part of company strategy.

Didier Mamma
Europe Director for Strategy and Development, Progress Software

Preface

It is not an easy task to explain in simple terms what service-oriented architecture (SOA) is. IT experts sometimes get lost when trying to give a simple definition of it, and their explanations can sometimes be incomprehensible for the users of this type of architecture. It is now time to provide a summary of how SOA actually works, since this type of architecture will radically change the way in which information systems are produced and used. There are both functional and technical advantages to using SOA. It is not only the IT specialists who need to understand exactly what the approach involves and what the consequences of this approach might be on the company, but also the general management of the company as well as the users of the information system.

That is why we decided to write this book. This book is a compilation of the expertise of the three authors whose main aim is to modernize information systems. Their fields of expertise range from the business aspect of the information system right through to its technical aspect.

Pierre Bonnet is an expert in the field of information system architecture based on modern technology. In 2002 he was one of the first people to publish work on the uses of service-oriented architecture (SOA) and XML Web services. He has a lot of experience in IT consultancy as well as in project management. He has managed many large SOA projects such as the one that was carried out at the SMABTP. With two partners, he created the company Orchestra Networks in 2000. Orchestra Networks is a software development company that specializes in the field of Master Data Management. In 2004 he became the co-author of the Praxeme enterprise method and took part in the creation of the Praxeme Institute, which works towards the production of an open source enterprise method.

Jean-Michel Detavernier is a business consultant and information system manager. His area of expertise lies in the functional dimension of the information system. He also creates decision models for the general management of companies who are having their information system modernized. He was also in charge of organizing the SOA project that took place in the SMABTP insurance company.

Dominique Vauquier is a recognized methodologist and is the creator of the Praxeme enterprise methodology. His area of expertise lies in the methodological dimension of the information system, and in the change management approach. He was in charge of many modeling and methodology projects while he was working as a consultant at Logica Management.[1] Today he works for the Group Information System Department at Axa Insurance.

The creation of a LEGO-style company

In 2002 the chief executive of a large finance company told us that his job consisted of creating financial packages that were made up of a combination of services that were managed by his company, subsidiaries and partner companies. These offers were produced and marketed under their own brand names and also as white label products in different distribution networks. Each time a new deal was made with a brand name, with a subsidiary or with a partner company, the following processes needed to be slightly changed: the production process, the distribution process, as well as customer relationship management, to name but a few. This meant that these processes had to be able to adapt quickly to new marketing situations. Creating a process that can adapt quickly to new marketing situations is not possible if traditional information technology and software are used. If traditional information technology and software were used it would mean that the processes would not be able to adapt quickly enough to the changes that take place in the market. It is therefore necessary to create more advanced modern technology, which would make it possible to create new processes (within the quickest timescale possible) from existing services. This type of information technology would be easier to use over and over again; in other words, it would become sustainable.

This vision was named the lego-style information system by the chief executive of the company. At the time, the company's existing information system was nothing like the chief executive officer's description of a Lego-style information system. The existing information system of the company was

---

1. Logica has been a member of the Praxeme Institute since it was first created. Logica has supported several events and has been in favor of making the Praxeme method more accessible to everyone.

organized into inflexible functional silos, which could not be easily adapted to any changes in marketing contexts. The silos had to be redesigned in the form of services that were more aligned with the company's business activity. This issue led to the creation of an SOA project within the company. Using the SOA approach means using services that favor the agility of the information system and in particular using a Business Rules Management System as well as Master Data Management. Back in 2002 the chief executive officer had understood what was involved in the SOA approach, and even encouraged other companies to use it. Today the company is benefiting from a more agile information system, which is more aligned with its business needs.

The creation of a sustainable information system

In order to understand why SOA is so important nowadays, we need to take a closer look at the history of information technology and place SOA in the timeline of IS approaches. We also need to have a closer look at the state of our existing information systems. The IT industry is approximately 50 years old. The programming language COBOL, which was invented in 1960, remains the language that is most used because it can support the largest information systems that exist all over the world. Since the 1960s lots of methodological and technological innovations have come and gone, and very few of these innovations have been used on a large scale for at least two reasons. Firstly, it took a long time to build the original information systems and their ability to absorb new technological innovations was limited. The most profound advances in modern technology were the arrival of the PC, the Internet and software packages (ERP, CRM, etc.). Modern object-oriented approaches (the first object language, Smalltalk, dates back to 1972) and the Unified Modeling Language (UML), whose first version was released in 1997, are not used very much. It takes time to learn how to use all of these different approaches, and the different techniques and methods that are available need to reach a certain level of maturity before they can be used on a large scale.

Assessing the information technology that is available to us nowadays is a complicated process. Today's information systems are in a state that could be compared to an inflexible industry, which does not recycle; in other words, it is wasteful. The term "inflexible" is used because it is more difficult for the information systems to accept functional evolutions. Information technology maintenance costs and the complexity level of the information technology that is available limit any modernization work that IT specialists can carry out on the existing information systems. Users of these information systems believe that information technology is actually slowing down their companies' business activities. A large number of IT specialists work in the larger companies; however, they tend to work more on the maintenance of the information systems. There is not much scope for restructuring the information systems. Modifications that are to be carried out on the information systems are then stacked on the old systems and software packages, which in turn progressively increases the inflexibility of the information system. By contrast, the aim of SOA is to reduce the inflexibility of the information system.

The term "wasteful" is used because the ability of the information technology to recycle components and services is largely reduced. It becomes difficult to reuse the software in different contexts, such as using it with different partners, using it in places where legislation is different or using it in different communication channels. All of these components and services are duplicated, which leads to the creation of unnecessary data and processes. This unnecessary information uses development resources, machine resources, network resources and production resources, as well as generating multiple data keying. This type of information technology is not easy to manage and creates strategic problems for the company. These strategic problems, which have undoubtedly increased since the arrival of the Internet, have also increased the communication needs of a company. These strategic problems have undoubtedly increased due to two business effects: firstly, with the arrival of the Internet, which has increased communication needs; secondly, the number of acquisitions and mergers that have taken place, which in turn leads to an increase in the number of information systems being restructured.

The aim of SOA is to take control of the existing information technology by adopting a more rational IS governance. This aim of SOA can be compared to the idea of sustainable development in the world of ecology. The ambition of building information systems today without limiting actions that can be carried out by future generations is a key principle of SOA. Contrary to the real ecology field, this generational cycle does not take decades but can take years or even weeks due to the rapid change in functional requirements and IT solutions.

A strategic view of information technology

SOA makes it possible to share certain IT developments as well as improving the way in which information technology is reused. This information technology is organized in the form of services rather than in the form of monolithic applications. The service is smaller than the traditional IT module. The service is created in such a way that it can be used in many different processes. The applications still exist but they become compositions of services. Thanks to these compositions of services, it is not only possible to reuse the same services in several applications, but it has also become possible to remove some of the boundaries that existed between the traditional applications when it comes to creating more integrated and better optimized processes. SOA removes the barriers of functional and technical silos existing with the traditional IT modules.

It is in adopting the SOA approach that a company can create a sustainable IT architecture which is capable of integrating any new advances in modern technology. In other words, the IT architecture can easily adapt to any technical or business changes which take place. There is not much point in rebuilding an information system that cannot adapt to new needs whenever they arrive. It is necessary to create information technology in a different way so that it can adapt more easily to any future evolutions that will take place. A service which has been used before can be reused with the aim of enhancing or completely changing the information system that is in place, and all of this is possible without affecting the other services and processes that exist within the information system. For this to happen we need more than an approach that produces reusable services. We also need an enterprise method that is responsible for organizing the many different disciplines that exist within the IT world. The number of these disciplines has rapidly increased over the past few years. This enterprise method will state the design procedures and needs analysis procedures that must be considered when it comes to restructuring the information system. This method will also re-establish a better level of communication between the users of the information system and the IT specialists.

The construction model which is created from a composition of services is a strategic model. It is used not only to guarantee the agility of an information system, but also to make services available to other tools and devices outside the information system in which they are found. This construction model is the only method that a company can use if it wants to integrate services from other partner companies or from other software component vendors into its own information system. A company that does not have a service-oriented information system runs the risk of cutting itself off from its own market.

Guide for the Reader

Aim of this book

This book shows that it is now possible to carry out projects that deal with the progressive overhaul of a company's information system. The methods and techniques that are used to control risk management are proven and can be used throughout the entire information system. In this book we introduce the foundations of SOA and also list the advantages of adopting the SOA approach when it comes to restructuring an information system. We also show that SOA cannot be used on its own if a company's aim is to successfully restructure its information system. The SOA approach needs to be accompanied by the use of an enterprise method, which models the company's needs.

This book will have achieved its objective if it can make IT departments and companies in general understand that SOA is an architecture that should be used for the progressive overhaul of a company's information system. Another aim of the book is to make them aware of the methods and techniques that are available so that they can undertake such an overhaul project.

Who is this book for?

This book has been organized into four parts, which will enable readers to read a topic that they are particularly interested in:

– For the decision-maker, "Part I – Why a Sustainable Information System?" looks at the strategic reasons why a company might want to carry out a progressive overhaul of its information system.

– For the architect of the information system, "Part II – The Principles of SOA" defines SOA and lists all of the concepts that are part of the SOA approach.

– For the project manager and the project team, "Part III – The Need for an Enterprise Method", shows that it is necessary to use a methodology during the restructure of an information system. Part III also shows how this methodology can control the risks linked to renovating the information system.

– For the technical architect, "Part IV – Mastering Existing Techniques" introduces the technical components that are available and the way in which they should be used in order to carry out a successful SOA project.

Organization of the chapters

Chapter 1 – Initial Perspectives – is an assessment of the current state of information systems and an introduction to an SOA type of architecture.

Chapters 2 to 4 (Part I – Why a Sustainable Information System?) provides decision-makers with an understanding or a better understanding of SOA as well as providing information on the different SOA maturity levels:

– Chapter 2 – Company-oriented Services – looks at the strategies of the service-oriented approach and lists guidelines which help the decision-makers see how the SOA approach can benefit the company in which they work.

– Chapter 3 – SOA Maturity Levels – describes the main phases of the SOA approach. This chapter deals first with cosmetic SOA; this level of SOA does not change the IT that is in place. This is followed by a description of extended SOA and overhaul SOA, both of which work harder towards increasing the agility of the information system as well as the rationalization of the information system.

– Chapter 4 – Economic and Social Aspects – provides important information on what people expect from SOA. This enables us to judge the importance of the SOA approach as well as judging how it will be used in the future. In this chapter we also explain why it is important that both junior and senior IT specialists work together, as well as explaining why the rationalization of a company's production process is more important than offshoring, and finally we explain the role of software editors etc.

Chapters 5 and 6 (Part II – The Principles of SOA) give more precise information on the properties of SOA:

– Chapter 5 – The Properties of SOA – reviews all the criteria that an information system must adhere to if SOA is to be integrated within the information system.

– Chapter 6 – Orchestration (BPM and SOA) – provides information on the concept of orchestration and shows that this concept can be found on all levels of the information system's architecture.

Chapters 7 to 9 (Part III – The Need for an Enterprise Method) deal with the methodologies that need to be used while the services are being designed:

– Chapter 7 – The Discovery of Services (Reference Framework and Urbanization) – highlights the importance of having a reference framework that is capable of organizing an information system. The reference framework should possess a topology whose structure can place all of the services in their rightful position in relation to the modeling of organization and business needs. In this chapter we introduce the Anglo-Saxon reference frameworks of Zachman, TOGAF by the Open Group and Herzum. We also introduce tools and processes such as UML, MDA and functional enterprise architecture, which leads us on to the Praxeme enterprise method.

– Chapter 8 – The Praxeme Enterprise Method – introduces the origins of this method as well as enterprise system topology, which is divided into eight aspects that deal with the design needs of the information system and which integrates the SOA approach into the information system.

– Chapter 9 – Modeling with Praxeme – provides information on the design process. This starts with the upstream models that are used to express the company's needs and continues right through to the procedures that are used to design the services. In this chapter a detailed description of the SOA approach is also given.

Chapters 10 to 14 (Part IV – Mastering Existing Techniques) introduce the technical aspects that need to be considered when restructuring an information system:

– Chapter 10 – Tools for Industrializing the Method – describes what tools are to be used with the methodology. The following principles are described in detail: virtual machine (which is used for the execution of services), pseudo-code, modeling CASE tool and Model Driven Architecture (MDA). A detailed description of the tools that are used to increase the agility of the information system is also given, including the Business Rules Management System and Master Data Management.

– Chapter 11 – Systems Integration and Common Information Language – details the tools that are necessary and which it make it possible to interconnect remote and heterogeneous information systems. The components of the Enterprise Service Bus (ESB) are described in this chapter. A description of the procedure that is used to create the common language (unified data structure relying on XML), which is necessary for the information systems to communicate with one another, is also given.

– Chapter 12 – SOA Platform – lists the different technical constituents that need to be adopted in the SOA approach beyond the level of the ESB. This chapter also deals with different technical themes such as performance management, security and how the technical constituents should be used. The audit tool, which works out the maturity level of the information technology that is available, is also introduced in this chapter. The SOA test card, which is divided into eight key areas and three maturity levels, lists the technology that is required for the traditional SOA approach to become platform SOA.

– Chapter 13 – Rules Management at the Scale of the Whole Enterprise – details one of the major components of ACMS (Agility Chain Management System): the Business Rules Management System (BRMS). We will also cover how BRMS brings agility for developing a Sustainable Architecture, thus deploying it at the enterprise level within an extended SOA.

– Chapter 14 – Semantic Integration – tackles how to reuse the semantic modeling to streamline interconnections between systems. In other words, the semantic modeling is useful to set up MDM but also to streamline systems integration in a sustainable manner.

Introduction to the SOA Project at SMABTP

Throughout this book we will use examples from the SOA project that was undertaken at the SMABTP. The context of this project is described in this section.

The beginning of the project

In 2001 the SMABTP, a French mutual insurance company in the construction sector, decided to restructure its information system. After an unsuccessful first attempt to change its information system to a market software package, the IT department of the company, in agreement with the general management of the company, decided to modernize its information system and launched its restructuring plan. The company's plan for restructuring its information system took into consideration all the needs and expectations of the members of the SMABTP. The company wanted to provide a range of insurance deals, which could be easily adapted to the needs of the company's customers. The creation of such a product offer was a complicated process due to the large variety of activities that the members of the SMABTP worked on. In other words, the product offer would have to cover all areas of the construction industry in which members of the SMABTP worked. These different areas include civil liability, building contracts and insurance. For example, they provide insurance cover against the breakdown of machines and heavy goods vehicles.

The decision to restructure their information system led the insurance company to focus the overhaul of their information system on its main business activities. The company also wanted to focus on creating a modern information system which would be capable of managing all of the company's insurance contracts, collecting the company's insurance premiums and paying out any claims. All of this would be carried out in a rather customer-oriented market. In focusing the overhaul of their information system on its main business activities, the SMABTP has been able to create fruitful partnerships with other mutual insurance companies who are leaders in the private insurance market (companies that deal with car insurance, comprehensive home insurance, etc.) or in other very competitive markets, such as providing insurance for fleets of vehicles. The SMABTP has also worked in collaboration with other distribution networks with the aim of selling its construction insurance products.

Innovative decisions had to be made with the aim of creating an information system that could meet the following requirements of the company: how would it be possible to provide services that could be used for the processes of pricing, drawing up and consulting contracts, as well as providing services that could deal with claims management and the collection of insurance premiums. These services would function differently at the presentation level (user interface) or at the authorization level of the information system depending on whether they were used by the creators of the contracts, the company's customers or the company's partner institutions. This complete redesign of the company's information system, which focused more on the business needs of the company, had been planned several years in advance and started with the automation of the most important points of the old information system. Such a complete redesign meant that the company had to try to get the old and new information systems as well as the internal and external information systems to exist side by side for a long period of time. This was made possible by using a particular infrastructure that meant that the different systems could exchange data securely with one another in real time.

The first task the IT department had to deal with was to structure the information system into high-level functional domains and technical components, such as publishing, presentation (UI) or rights management. Inter-domain communication was carried out by using a standardized flow of data thanks to the use of an application integration tool or Enterprise Application Integration (EAI) with XML messages. This type of investment required the use of a lot of hardware and software. It also required a lot of work to be carried out by the people working on the project since they continually questioned the work methods that they were used to and were always learning new ones. The business advantages of this first phase of the project were significant:

– the double entry of data in different applications was removed, there was an improvement in the exchange of data between partner companies, and there was also an increased fluidification of the different processes;

– desktop publishing was integrated within the work process;

– applications became increasingly integrated into individual work stations.

Other important work carried out in this project increased the agility of the original information system and made the information system more reactive to the requests made by the users of the system, such as: product rules could now be parameterized; it became possible to outsource business rules to an external business engine used by reusable services; and it also became possible to manage certain processes in a workflow tool. This first approach is a tool needs to be used in order to prepare today's society for the revolution of evolutionary processes and reusable services that is going to take place in the future. This first approach is only a step towards a stronger shared vision that everyone within the company will have.

The business services which were obtained from the original information systems could only partly adapt to change and were therefore only partly reusable. The next phase would be to create new agile business services and then to orchestrate them. The search for an effective methodology was essential at this point. This methodological approach facilitates the communication that takes place between users of the information system, analysts and developers. It also seems to be the keystone that was missing in previous overhaul projects.

After having spent five years working on the project it can be said that the SMABTP now has an information system that can be placed in one of the higher maturity levels of the SOA approach. However, it has still not reached the maximum level possible. Only some of the company's IT specialists and some of the users of the information system actively participated in the process (20% of the company's IT department). The concepts of SOA and the advantages of using them need to be shared with everyone working on IT projects within the company. The good thing about any future projects that may take place in the company is that the workload will be lightened. Not all of the different phases of the project were completed at the same time and the company's employees who were involved in the project began to understand what technology and what methods were required so that such a project could be a success. All of this was made possible thanks to continuous support from the company's general management and managers.

More agility

The modernization of the SMABTP's information system started with an SOA approach that did not have any impact on the company's original information system. Connectors were then created and added to the old systems and these improved the data exchanges that took place between the different platforms. The exchanges of data flow were standardized in XML in order to improve the clarity of the flow of data being exchanged. Very soon after this, the users of the information system requested that the portal (UI) be improved so that the data coming from other information systems could be presented in the same way. The objective of modernizing the company's information system was for the company to have an overall view of their customers and contracts, claims and premiums files.

We benefited from the introduction of the company's new contract management system to complete another phase of the modernization process. This was achieved by outsourcing the business rules, which were part of the ILOG company's business rules management system known as ILOG JRules. It was possible to outsource the business rules thanks to the exchange of XML messages using the EAI tool. The interactions between the contract management application (AS400 software) and the business rules engine occurred thanks to the use of XML messages, which completely separated the two systems from one another. We also outsourced the different editions of the two systems with the help of a desktop publishing tool, which was also managed by flows of XML data that were sent from the contract management tool.

The project that was undertaken to digitize the claims management application gave us the opportunity to carry out more research as far as the SOA approach was concerned, especially after we made the decision to completely rewrite the application. We naturally adopted the overhaul SOA approach for the project, as this would let all of us use our own experience from other projects. EBX Platform, which is the Master Data Management tool that (Orchestra Networks), was added to the overhaul SOA project. Depending on authorization rights, the functional and technical users of the information system, as well as the users involved in the production of the claims management systems, could all have access to the Master Data Management tool. This tool managed the codes, the reference data, and the functional and technical parameters used by the different services, processes and rules.

After analyzing the users' needs, which was accompanied by a comparative study of the two claims management systems (gap analysis), and after studying the new processes with the users of the systems we noticed that the reusability level of the business components was low. For anyone who understands what is involved in this type of management they should be aware of the fact that many different processes affect the same management rules, such as: verifying the existence of the customer and the contract; verifying the existence of the insurance policies; evaluating policy; settling policy; consulting policy; and possibly canceling policy. In a reusable business service approach, it is expected that these different management rules are shared with other domains in the insurance industry.

The old methodologies do not highlight this fact. UML notation and the creation of object components do not make it possible to share these different management rules with other domains in the insurance industry. This is why that we felt that it was important to create a methodology that would easily facilitate the implementation of an overhaul SOA project. After some unfruitful research we finally found a methodology that existed and was used, in part, in the SAGEM company. This methodology generally corresponded to what we were looking for: we wanted a methodology that would highlight all of the company's business services so that we could create our claims management application.

We improved the quality of this methodology with the aim of creating an agile information system when we carried out the overhaul SOA project at the SMABTP. Our work has also contributed to the creation of the public Praxeme method.

This huge effort on our part enabled us to create a piece of software which meets the requirements of having highly reusable and agile business services, i.e. the creation of agile data and agile parameters, the creation of processes through the outsourcing of business rules as well as the creation of processes by isolating the business rules in orchestration services. All modeling procedures that were used to achieve this end result are mentioned in this book.

Chapter 1

Initial Perspectives

1.1. 50 years of computing – an overview

We begin this book almost 50 years after the creation of the computing language COBOL (1960), which corresponds to first generation computing. During this long period, numerous languages, methods and techniques have been created but not many of them have been used by companies on an industrial level. More often than not, the lifecycle of a new innovative product is shorter than the time needed for such a product to become widely available within an organization. It can take a period of 15 years or more for product evolution to take place on a large scale. We are going to focus on three of these evolutions, which have taken place over the past five decades.

The first of these evolutions spans a 20-year period from 1960 until the end of 1980. Companies use information systems that are specific to each function within the company. The design of the information systems is organized around the data and functions of the company, with the use of methodologies such as Merise (1974), Warnier (1977), Yourdon (1979), AXIAL (1986), etc. Towards the end of the 1980s certain key innovations appeared but these innovations were not used at that time; they turned out to be an important asset in the world of computing much later. With this in mind, we can make reference to the proposal made by John Zachman who developed the first framework for enterprise architecture (1987), which organizes the different disciplines necessary for the construction of information systems. There is also the example of Bertrand Meyer [MEYER, 2000] who formalized the work undertaken in the field of design by contract and programming by contract (1988). This is an approach, which, today, is not foreign to the new practices of service-oriented design. Information technology from this period can be outdated because it is not flexible in terms of evolution. The rigid structure of information systems that were structured around functions means that it is quite difficult to reuse and compose new processes. Furthermore, problems linked to the ergonomic integration of the workstation (which at that time was passive and only available in character mode) reinforce the idea of complexity that was associated with information technology of that time.

From the beginning of the 1990s, companies saw the arrival of the PC as the way to modernize information technology by building on client/server structures that were less cumbersome and more ergonomic than mainframes. The graphic interface of the intelligent workstation had to be capable of interacting and cooperating with multiple servers in a revamping mode. In practice, the subjacent technical structure of the client/server model turned out to be too complex, in particular due to the lack of standards of interoperability and the difficulties related to the management of the workstations. To make matters worse, this technological vision of the sharing of programs between the servers and microcomputers implied the notion of ownership of all of the machines. The beginning of globalization, supported by the Internet, has forced more and more businesses to open up to the outside world, which will increasingly expose the companies' business to exterior workstations (thanks to the Internet): this has meant that more and more companies are working together and there is also more collaboration between the company and its clients.

At the same time, it was the arrival of Jacques Sassoon's approach (1990), which is based around the functional enterprise architecture (in France this is called "urban planning"), that tried to provide a better understanding of the information system thanks to cartography, and then through the use of interconnection solutions of heterogenous systems, in other words EAI (Enterprise Application Integration). The equipment used in the functional approach with EAI was not successful in establishing itself as an efficient model for updating information systems. In practice, there were too many dissimilarities between the functional approach that was used in architecture with EAI and the initial design of the applications. The functional approach was too far removed from the object-oriented approach, which was increasingly integrated and used within companies during the 1990s; as a result of this the computing language Java was born in 1995.

The increasing number of software packages that were available at the time established themselves as ready-to-use solutions to overcome problems such as those mentioned in the previous section. Such packages prevented certain developments from taking place within information systems (developments that would take place in an unstable methodological and technical context). Such software packages that are used in information systems include ERP (Enterprise

Resource Planning) for the back office and CRM (Customer Relationship Management) for the front office. After using the software packages for some years, companies commented on the fact that the software packages were unable to evolve efficiently with the modern technology of that period; this is similar to what happened with the first generation systems. The use of integrated solutions would rectify the problem; however, this in itself can pose several drawbacks, since the room for maneuver to make such software packages evolve is often limited, costly and remains in the hands of the software editors and integrators of the software. Along with this lack of efficiency in evolving with modern technology, there is also a loss in autonomy. The company's information system is unable to conform closely enough to the company's needs.

Thus far in our overview we have been rather unkind to the world of information technology: the organization of software packages, EAI and older systems that produce considerable functional and technical silos on the level of the information system. This existing information system brings a lack of quality regarding reference data (or master data), the integration of organizational processes within companies, the general security of systems and the companies' ability to open up to new markets, etc. Even if the process of the functional enterprise architecture (IS cartography or IS maps) enables IT specialists to better understand what needs to be done to help current information systems evolve with modern technology (by looking at the current information system and following strategic guidelines), the systems pile up one beside the other without any real perspective of rationalization. This becomes more complicated because the maintenance costs of such existing IS assets are extremely high, which does not leave much leeway for working on the progressive restructuring of information systems in great depth.

After the unfruitful years of the client/server period, the arrival of the year 2000 and the passage to the Euro prevented companies from modernizing their information systems. Critiques of information technology have continued to be published up to as recently as 2004, as can be seen in the famous book written by Nicholas G. Carr, *Does IT Matter?* [CARR, 2004], in which the author sees information technology as a strategically valueless commodity for a company. This is a crisis period for information technology. In addition to these critiques, and since the bursting of the Internet bubble at the end of the year 2000, the computer industry has been taking initiatives to improve the interconnection capabilities of heterogenous systems thanks to the use of XML and Web services which are transported on Internet networks (Intranet).[1] For the first time in the history of information technology, standardization organizations such as W3C and OASIS

---

1. In order to find out more technical information on Web services, it is recommended that the reader consult [MONFORT and GOUDEAU, 2004].

have progressively encouraged and succeeded in getting their editors to work together to establish the standards for the next generation of information technology.

Based on this idea of standardization, it was towards 2002 that the concept of service-oriented architecture (SOA) appeared. SOA is a type of architecture that aims to bridge the gap between functional enterprise architecture and object-oriented design. It is an important link when it comes to acting upon existing systems and design practices. Rather than exchanging distributed and heterogenous objects (as was the case in the client/server period), the idea is to retain a standard communication in service mode which makes use of interfaces that mask the existence of objects on both a logical and a technical level.

SOA only deals with service interfaces and flows of information, not objects. In addition, a service can be implemented into non-object-oriented technology, for example in COBOL, which allows for the integration of old systems within the most recent information systems thanks to the latest developments and advances in modern technology. SOA makes it possible for companies to make the strategic choices that are necessary to help information systems evolve efficiently and simultaneously with the advances in information technology.

SOA is a combination of the best practices of the following: the functional enterprise architecture, the Enterprise Architecture Framework, design and programming by contract, UML notation, and the object-orientated approach. SOA is being implemented more and more in all areas of the computing industry such as in the industry's methodological framework, the development and tools used in information technology, software packages, etc. In addition to the free software community, SOA is also being increasingly defined and used by industrialists, standardization organizations such as W3C, OASIS, OMG, etc. It is estimated that the lifecycle of SOA will not be short. Rather, the opposite is true because SOA absorbs other historical advances in computing, and should be available in the long term, at least for the next generation of information technology, which is approximately for another 15 years. This is only the beginning.

VOCABULARY NOTE: FUNCTION AND SERVICE

A function responds to a requirement which has several different hidden factors within it. For example, the function "order entry" may also include another function such as "change of address", which can only be used when an order is being taken. A service also responds to a requirement but it deals with only one factor. For example, for the taking of an order several business objects such as order and person can be identified. There will therefore be a service that is attached to the object person who will deal with the management and upkeep of the address. The address service can be used in other processes, not just in the process of order taking. The order taking function can thus call upon the use of other services, in other words it is an orchestrator.

If the information system is made up of several dozen business objects, it is therefore possible to identify a catalog of services which can be reused in multiple processes. This reuse of services is much more efficient than adapting the services to the different contexts in which they can be used is possible. For example, the service that deals with the management of changes in address will be used differently depending on the language of the user and on the format of the postal address.

1.2. What remains today?

Computing systems that have been inherited from projects carried out during the 1980s are still present in the workplace today. The systems are often updated and improved by adding numerous software packages to them from the 1990s, and also by carrying out some restructuring of the systems, a process which does not occur very often. Such information systems are made up of multiple heterogenous silos, for both the functional structure and technical platform of the system. This inheritance of systems is quite difficult to operate (significant maintenance budget) and also because the systems have problems in keeping up with the evolution of the business. Therefore this raises the question of the agility of the information system and its ability to adapt to the needs of a business. How is it possible to overcome these problems? We will answer this question in the next part of the book with the concept of extended SOA (extended service-oriented architecture). On the basis of the analysis that was mentioned at the beginning of this section, there are two strategic problems that arise when it comes to managing the evolution of an information system:

– The people who worked in the teams, and who had an in-depth knowledge of the systems that were created in the 1980s, are now beginning to retire. This is a new phenomenon for the computing industry, as this is an industry that is relatively young. Such a generational cycle has never been experienced before. Before the members of these teams retire, they have to take back control of the existing systems, which are, more often than not, not well documented and they must also be at the forefront in the transition of knowledge to the teams of the new generation. This leads to the creation of a position that deals with knowledge management in relation to the information systems, and in particular deals with semantic modeling. Semantic modeling is an actual practice that is used for appropriating knowledge related to the business side of the information system.

– Software packages have led to the creation of additional silos, which make it difficult for the systems to evolve. Local decisions that were made for using the software packages have increased, sometimes without sufficient control and supervision from the companies' IT departments.

The renovation and restructuring of systems takes time. In the meantime, a company must make sure that they have the means necessary to ensure that their current information system can evolve despite the constraints that have been identified above. If a company regards agile computing as a strategic advantage for its business, it will therefore have to overhaul its information systems in a progressive manner. It is in this context that we see the appearance of SOA, at the beginning of a generational transition. We also see the appearance of SOA when experts realize and accept that a particular information system is obsolete; this acknowledgement occurs during maintenance work on the systems.

We know that SOA can be applied to an existing information system but only in small quantities to expose, in a non-intrusive manner, the services that the system's applications provide: this is known as cosmetic SOA. This is not the main purpose of SOA; however, it is a useful step in the restructuring and evolution of information systems. SOA provides an appropriate type of structure, which is used in the restructuring of information systems. It is a type of structure that takes into consideration the existing applications that an information system possesses, and which therefore makes it possible to run successive and progressive operations to overhaul the information system. This approach is different to those that were launched during the 1980s, yet the main objective, that of restructuring the system, has remained the same. It is therefore a question of renewal, with the notion of completely restructuring the information system. It is this idea of completely restructuring the information system that will make the generational transition process run as smoothly as possible, limiting the risks of failure. What will the maintenance costs of our old systems be once the experienced team members have retired?

Part I

Why a Sustainable Information System?

Chapter 2

Company-oriented Services

2.1. Consequences of the Internet revolution

Consumers have changed their shopping behavior in the space of several years, by exchanging or trading goods on auction websites, ordering books online, booking holidays online, purchasing toys and even financial services online. Consumers also do their shopping online, and even declare their taxes online. In addition to all of this, the freedom that the Internet provides enables users to remain in close contact with current affairs and allows them to be aware of what is happening around them. Thanks to the Internet, potential consumer power is great and will only increase in the future. Internet user communities are able to exchange their consumer experiences on products and services in real time. A company that markets questionable products and services will be the subject of many visible critiques on the Internet.

These Internet communities will progressively supervise and take control of the products. They will force suppliers to conform strictly to their commitments and agreements. They will also make the products evolve in certain directions. It is still not clear today, but future generations of consumers will be able to share their purchasing experiences online thanks to the Internet. In any case, is it possible to imagine a company without a website, the support of online users or the idea of mobility for its sales representatives? On its website a company offers its own products or services but also displays offers from partner companies.

Internet and electronic commerce technologies connect companies to the center of a value chain in real time, starting with the supplier of products and services and finishing with the final customer. This opening of companies to the outside world has made them think about their information technology in a different way to that of the silo mode. The silo approach was sufficient for specialized managers and administrators who worked with divided processes; in other words, they worked on different parts of a process. It should not be forgotten that the computerization of companies began by taking into consideration the administrative needs and everyday management of a company (order entries, stock management, billing, etc.). These needs were computed by software, which created the famous silo applications. Silo applications were not designed to communicate easily with other internal software, and even less so to communicate with the software of partner companies. In the current competitive environment, companies are faced with tight deadlines due to customer expectations and silo applications prevent the company's information system from evolving with the company's needs. New concepts in information technology, and in particular SOA (service-oriented architecture), are now able to tackle this problem.

Let us take an example that everyone among us can experiment with, the services provided by Google Earth. Google Earth provides services that make it possible to view terrestrial maps thanks to a collection of satellite images. From these satellite images, Google offers numerous other value added services. For example, it is possible to display air traffic in real time. Users also have access to the instrument panel of an air traffic control tower. The service can be personalized to filter the air traffic around an airport, calculate the air distance between two airports, etc. Google is a service-oriented company and this can be seen at both the lower and the higher levels of the company's hierarchy. It can be seen at the lower level because such a service is offered to all Internet users, and at the higher level because Google connects to multiple services and databases, which provide it with information in real time about air traffic. The technologies that these databases use are undoubtedly very heterogenous and are not under the control of Google. Nevertheless, thanks to SOA the interoperability of the systems functions at a lower cost and the system is quick to use. This represents a considerable evolution in the flexibility of information technology, which was never experienced in the past.

This example can be adapted to many other activity sectors. The value potential from connecting different services is infinite, and increases each day as and when companies provide new services. A company that adopts this type of structure is capable of responding very quickly to frequent changes, irrespective of the cause of the change. The example of Google is interesting but is not representative of a company that already has a long history of information technology inheritance, i.e. a history of several decades. We will see that the new computing structures allow for the reuse of a part of old applications that are connected to other, more recent, applications or to partner applications.

For some years now the IT departments of companies have been rapidly interconnecting existing information systems to respond to business needs. Some of these IT departments have been urbanizing their information systems to respond to the business demands of the companies. The IT departments have also added connectors to the front of the silo applications to provide data to the users of the companies' websites. This data is then brought together before it is made available to the users who will have access to it. With the arrival of XML, exchange standards have also developed on a global scale and editors of software have added to this approach by creating or by improving infrastructure tools, development tools or assembly tools of software components. Additional tools, such as business rules management systems and tools that allow for the management of data and parameters, are currently being added to increase the agility and the ability of the components to adapt to future business needs. What all these different computing concepts are seeking to do is to organize the information system around the business concerns of a company to respond to the needs in the shortest time. All of these initiatives have been summarized under the abbreviation SOA by the Gartner Group.

SOA goes beyond the traditional technical and functional frameworks that are associated with information technology and includes the business needs of companies. SOA is synonymous with an intelligent restructuring of the information system, focusing on meeting the business needs of a company, enabling the old and new applications within an information system to exist together. This technological way of thinking merits the attention of leaders at the highest level because it favors rapid changes in the way employees work within the company and with company partners in the wake of the Internet. As far as the entire information system is concerned, SOA must be placed within the company's strategic IT plan, within the framework of the management of information technology and even the management of the company. COBIT (Control OBjectives for Information and related Technology), an IT management approach for company leaders and auditors, recommends that the technology is governed by the best practices possible to guarantee that a company's information and associated technologies are oriented towards the company's business objectives, the resources are used responsibly and the risks are managed as they should be. These practices form a basis for the management of information systems with the double aim of managing risks and making profits. With these aims in mind, SOA is one of the best approaches available on the market today.

The difficulty for general management is being able to manage their information technology by understanding the opportunities that are available today and how these will help the company in the future. This demands a strong personal investment from leaders with the aim of integrating all of the concepts that are part of SOA. The views of software editors only cover a small part of the large subject that is SOA. The many different views that the software editors have do not help general management and the business as a whole in visualizing the overall picture of the future information system that the IT departments have to create. Large consultancy firms have understood this lack of vision and have positioned special SOA consulting and support dedicated to the general management of companies.

2.2. What do the leading market players say?

The entire IT industry is adopting the SOA approach but, in general, is not using it in a global context. The proposed approaches focus too quickly on aspects related either to the first implementations or to marketed software. According to certain experts, there is a lot of fuss about nothing, while others have been thinking of adopting SOA for a long time. Articles in newspapers describe a particular IT creation, sponsored by this supplier or that supplier; however, explaining the information technology of tomorrow in a few pages is an impossible exercise. If we take a closer look, it can be seen that some articles give a more global analysis of SOA by including the business problems that a company might face, the essential involvement that is needed by general management if such company projects are to succeed, as well as stating that there is a lack of methodology in the SOA approach. As a result of this lack of methodology, not everyone can see clearly what is happening when it comes to working on the progressive overhaul of an information system.

As for the large consultancy firms, many of them have now adopted the SOA approach after the Gartner Group described SOA as a major innovation in 2002. The McKinsey Group see SOA as a trend for global chief information officers towards the end of 2007 (survey carried out in October 2006 among 72 senior IT executives on the subject of their main investments). The aim of these chief information officers is to insure a quicker and cheaper evolution of the information systems, to favor the opening of the systems to the outside world, customers, partners and suppliers thanks to the standardization of exchange protocols. In 2005 the McKinsey Group had already predicted a revolution in information system design, through the complete revision and simplification of the systems' infrastructure.

In 2006, in an article entitled "The next generation of in-house software development", the McKinsey Group talked about the industrialization of the supply of business components so that companies can develop applications with reusable software components for all functions of a sector. These components are assigned to business processes, which reuse them as efficiently as possible. The method used consists of identifying identical functions (from the entire set of business processes) by concentrating on the future needs of the business. In a few years a portfolio of standard components can be created. Of course, not everything has to be restructured at the same time and the old applications have to be updated (by adding connectors) to be seen as a component that is part of the business process. From this article, it can be clearly seen that the redesign of the systems must be carried out by mixed teams (made up of business and IT specialists) who have a clear view of the business needs of the company that is standardizing its activities. Business sponsors must also be a part of a project like this and the running of such a project falls within the competences of the general management of the company.

Another large consultancy firm goes beyond what the McKinsey Group did. In July 2006 Accenture said that it was going to invest $450 million over the next three years in new approaches that are based on the reuse of components. Accenture's aim is to equip itself with the expertise and business solutions necessary to assist companies in the architecture process of their information systems. Accenture, who noticed that this important concept for the evolution or restructuring of information systems was not well accepted by the general management of companies, decided to commit itself to its cause by offering to assist large companies who were willing to urbanize their information systems. Accenture also launched a global research and development program to provide ready-to-use business services with the aim of accelerating the rate of implementation of SOA in certain sectors, such as health and finance. The approach involves the collaboration of businesses for the specification of the business processes and the subjacent activities which can be understood by the end user. These different specifications are then converted into IT components, which leads on to the MDA (Model Driven Architecture) approach. This approach is described in the next part of the book.

Large IT software vendors such as BEA, IBM, Oracle, Microsoft and SAP structure their solutions around SOA. Numerous other, more specialized companies, are working towards their own evolution so that they can benefit from this new approach: workflow tools, business process management tools, and tools that deal with the exchange and transfer of data between systems are examples of what these companies offer. Other companies offer tools that make it possible to outsource the business rules management process or business components to increase the companies' agility. They also offer tools that allow for the management of data and parameters (Master Data Management), and many more. All these tools have a role to play in the restructuring of information systems with SOA. Some of these tools have to be installed in the new information system even before the first IS business project. The first designs of the services should not have to deal with any problems relating to the lack of any technical infrastructure within the system, for fear of penalizing work being carried out to establish functions within the system. If this lack of technical infrastructure turns out to be significant in terms of the restructuring of an information system, it could call into question the whole SOA approach.

The general management of a company is not always aware of any previous technical investment that has been injected into the company's information systems, and why such investments had been made. They also tend to make snap decisions when a project is to be undertaken by the IT department. As a result, they do not pay sufficient attention to the project. The capacity of the information system's infrastructure to adapt rapidly to and consider new business needs is part of the strategic management of the company.

2.3. What do the chief information officers think?

Recent studies have shown that the majority of large global companies have already adopted an SOA type project by 2007. In France, a survey published in February 2007, which surveyed 85 companies, shows that 74% of chief information officers believe that the idea of SOA is a new way of designing and modeling the information system. Some 14% of chief information officers believe that SOA is a new generation of integration platform and 11% see SOA as simple buzz marketing. Of the companies interviewed, 79% said that they believe that SOA affects potentially every company. However, only 21% have already undertaken one or more projects using the SOA approach.[2]

Some IT departments, even those which have not adopted an SOA-style project, have benefited from the mergers of companies, partnership programs, companies opening towards the client and many other programs. In benefiting from such activities, these IT departments have been able to renew and redevelop their infrastructures and set in place all or some of the tools necessary for the creation of the first service-oriented information systems. As far as the other IT departments are concerned, they need to convince the leaders of their companies to invest progressively in the necessary architecture if they want their companies to be able to respond to the increasing needs of the business.

2.4. The issues faced at general management level

Businesses, pushed by competition, the opening of markets, new regulations and new customer needs, expect their information technology to respond to the company's needs. Unfortunately, the reality of the business world provides examples every day of just how difficult the maintenance cycle of information technology can be. The addition of a new product, the acceptance of a new partner, the modification of an organization rule or the addition of a single piece of

---

2. Study published in February 2007 with the participation of Microsoft and the SQLI group.

information to the database and its on-screen presentation all require development and test work which takes a lot of time and energy to complete.

Why does it take so long? This has already been explained earlier in the chapter. The existing information systems are oriented too much around silo applications, which eventually make software and data redundant. These silos are so poorly or so little urbanized that each time there is a demand to make the system evolve there is the risk of regressing the entire system, which is sometimes identified several months later, for example during the execution of processing at the end of the year. If the systems were to evolve from silo-architecture to service-architecture then any demand to make the system evolve would involve modifying an identified component only once, which would limit the costs and risks of regression. There has been a marked decrease as far as the deadlines of functional evolutions are concerned, thanks to the integration and organization of a well-constructed SOA. Deadlines of several weeks can be shortened to a few days.

The information presented in the section above explains why businesses have several main priorities. Some of these priorities include: an improvement in the provision of products and services that a company has to offer (either internally or thanks to partner companies), the general flexibility of the information system to deal with varying changes such as the merging or acquisition of other structures, an increase in the range of products or sales of others through other channels of distribution, etc. Businesses have not carried out enough research to check whether or not the information system is able to help with the issues that exist in the modern business world, even though it is these same businesses that diagnose and deal with any problems the company may face.

Not all the promises that have been made regarding information technology have been kept, and this has been the case for almost 20 years. A large number of projects have failed or have not given the expected results. However, the rapid development of SOA is rising in the IT industry and any delay that is experienced today will be very difficult to make up. Companies have everything to gain from this approach, which gives a business meaning to the IT components. SOA drew its inspiration directly from the needs of businesses: opening up to customers and partners by the intermediary of a seamless processes and components that are capable of working in several different contexts such as country, language, organization, etc. SOA enables businesses once again to become players in the evolution of information systems. The evolution of information systems is a continuous process and will become easier for companies to deal with over time, and this evolution process will not be affected by successive IT revolutions, as was the case in the past. We can refer to this as sustainable computing.

To be considered as sustainable computing, the integration of SOA must be part of a company project which mobilizes all sectors of a company to redesign the new horizontal processes beyond the traditional IT silos. This long-term plan should take into consideration the issue of the renewal of different generations of collaborators within IT, and also within the business as a whole. These past few years have seen a decline in the quality of documentation of IT tools, which can lead to the creation of two strategic problems:

– If the IT specialists who created the old systems retire before they hand responsibility over to the new generation of IT specialists, this will create tensions as far as the maintenance of the information system is concerned. The absence of experienced IT specialists at a time when a restructured system is about to be launched means that a company loses the experts who have considerable knowledge of the system. Companies also need these experts because they can make sure that a project can be successful for a reasonable budget.

– If the functional teams see their job primarily as working with IT tools then their knowledge is limited and innovation is slowed down.

To overcome these problems, companies should take advantage of the SOA approach by setting up project teams that are made up of both business and IT specialists, and among these specialists there should be both experienced and less experienced members. The younger members of the teams will be aware of new methods and technologies that are available, whereas the more experienced members of the teams will be able to provide knowledge and experience on the existing systems and on the business as a whole. Mistakes that were made in the past should not be repeated, notably with the younger members specializing in the object approach and the more experienced members specializing in the functional enterprise architecture of information systems. The object approach without the functional process has remained too local, whereas the functional approach on its own has remained too global and bears no relation to the projects that are undertaken. One of the objectives of the SOA approach is to bring the two together.

2.5. Levels of maturity

The majority of large consultancy firms are interested in the SOA approach for the progressive restructuring of information systems. For them, the first step to be considered is the drawing up of a business case so that they can determine the level of maturity of their firm in relation to the SOA approach. They recommend evaluating the business needs of the company, evaluating the company's ability to execute such a business plan, and they finally establishing a master plan. In the stages that follow – in other words after the first implementations of the business process using the services of a pilot project have taken place – the companies consider the organization of the technical infrastructure that will enable them to generalize the SOA approach. After this has been completed, there is the industrialization phase for which the production of business services becomes part of the day-to-day functioning of the company.

In reality, the evaluation of budgets is not as simple and as clear as first thought, since the original costs and cost of ownership of the infrastructure have to be determined. When assessing and evaluating the profits, both quantitative and qualitative factors must be taken into account. Determining the financial commitments and expected returns is an unavoidable task, and everything must be justified. The main problem lies in communication within a domain (information technology), which people outside IT departments know very little about or do not understand. It is a considerable asset for a company if it has an auditor working for it; an auditor who has experience of managing information systems and the full support of the general management.

The maturity model described by consultancy firms becomes valid as soon as the contracting authorities of businesses, the general management of businesses and the businesses as a whole have understood the concept of restructuring the information systems in terms of processes and services, which is far from being the case at the moment. In reality, companies generally start with tactical phases that are driven by the IT departments. The strategic plan adopted by businesses only comes into force after the first signs of a profit. As explained earlier in the chapter, IT departments have problems in estimating the profitability of the first phases of investment made in hardware, software and methodological infrastructure, even if profits are assured for the future. In the majority of cases in which businesses have successfully integrated the SOA approach within their information systems, the infrastructure was already in place and the idea of processes based on business services already existed. The example of Air France (a French airline) is interesting because the restructuring of their information system by adopting the SOA approach is actually a modernization of the infrastructure by using business components that probably existed previously. The infrastructure used by Air France was implemented in the framework of the merger of Air France with the Dutch company KLM, and provided the new infrastructure (after the merger of the two companies) with some of its new business components.

The issue of what methodological approach should be used to facilitate exchanges between the IT specialists and the users of information systems comes to the fore the moment SOA is due to be launched within a company's information system. The method adopted is essential for the correct development of business services; it is also essential for increasing the number of times a particular business service can be reused; and, finally, it is essential in insuring the correct separation of business services from the ever-changing organization of the company. The adopted method must also be shared among the users of the system and IT specialists to get the most out of the exchanges that take place between both parties. It must also allow for the resolution of more technical problems, such as the separation of business factors from other technical factors, in other words, how can a business need be defined and how can it be translated into different current computing languages such as Java and COBOL, or into a non-specified language of the future, without having to rewrite everything? The adopted method is a vital tool that is used to help study and optimize the independence of business components as far as the lower technical levels are concerned (for example databases), and will place companies in a better position when dealing with suppliers as well as enabling them to better manage the costs of the information system.

The method must also be entirely open source, which enables companies to share resources with the largest possible number of other companies. The use of the same method by other companies, but in different technical contexts, favors its durability and independence in terms of software and infrastructure. It also allows for an easier mobilization of the competences acquired with the SOA approach. The open source Praxeme method (which will be discussed later in this book) responds to these strategic requirements. The profiles of the IT specialists as well as their training programs are to be planned, and the training of IT specialists can be a long process, depending on their experience. In the case of external IT specialists, internal staff must be involved in the project as early as possible to avoid the staff rejecting the project either by a lack of vision for the project or by not understanding the SOA approach.

The level of optimum maturity to be reached is the level at which a company functions around its business processes and services, for example: the infrastructure is in place and optimizes the work of the IT specialists; the creation of services is part of the normal everyday activity of the company in using an approach that facilitates exchanges between the users of the information systems and the IT specialists; the company's activities can be monitored and followed by everyone in the company in real time; and new processes can be created by reusing a large number of existing business services produced internally or by either partner companies or suppliers. The benefits a company can obtain are as follows: an increase in company efficiency thanks to the adaptability of processes and components used; a reduction in the time needed for implementation deadlines; a decrease in IT costs thanks to the reuse of components with a higher level of parametering; and the outsourcing of business rules through the use of flexible tools. Managers and customers benefit from a simplified work user interface thanks to the reuse of graphic components in the different processes, for example whether it be about customer services, product services, contracts or events, they are all presented in the same fashion in the screens of different processes. Learning how to use the systems is also greatly facilitated.

However, we should not ignore the time that is required to integrate such an approach. Time is needed to change the opinions of individuals and get them to share the same vision of the future. As soon as the majority of people share this vision, the organization of the teams needs to be changed and staff need to be trained in the new concepts, methodologies and technologies that will be used. This vision also needs to be shared with the contracting authorities of the companies and the various departments that will use the future information systems, and it is also necessary to get these groups to be actively seeking to use the technology that is on offer and available to them.

Chapter 3

SOA Maturity Levels

A RECAP OF IDEAS MENTIONED IN PREVIOUS CHAPTERS

– The structuring of information systems by silos leads to the systems becoming redundant and does not favor the reuse.

– The information system must change from the traditional silo approach and adopt the services approach, which favors an agile system.

– The SOA approach is a business initiative that takes several years to achieve and also takes human resource management into consideration, notably the retirement of a generation of IT specialists who have an understanding and widespread knowledge of the existing information systems in place.

NEW IDEAS PRESENTED IN THIS CHAPTER

– A service is highly reusable thanks to the management of variants.

– The levels of SOA maturity are: cosmetic SOA, overhaul SOA and extended SOA.

3.1. Towards the creation of a more agile information system

The SOA approach allows for the development of business processes thanks to the aggregation of highly reusable services. The services are created in such a way that they can easily adapt the way in which they function depending on the context in which they are being used. A simple redefining of the parameters of the business rules and master data that are used in the system is all that is needed to create a new variation of the initial function. For example, a given rate of reduction will have a different value depending on whether the purchasing service is used by a distributor or by a commercial agency. A new service for each sales channel that exists will not be created. For a particular service to function, the different data and business rules (which are necessary for each channel) must be taken into consideration. The following key principles must be respected if a company is to succeed in creating a flexible information system:

– The business services must be independent from one another; in computing terms, they must be loosely coupled together. Such services are created independently from their technology and their localization on the network. The fact that the different business services are loosely coupled together favors the rapid creation of new processes through the aggregation of reusable services. The new processes will be organized differently depending on the context in which they will be used.

– Communication between the different services is carried out through the use of messages in a standard programming language with the aim of increasing the integrity and strength of the information system. The integrity of the system is improved thanks to a business vocabulary that is shared in all the messages that are exchanged between the services. This is also known as a common language or unified language (for example, there is only one way to describe a customer). The strength of the system is improved because the contents of the exchanged messages can easily be validated in a non-intrusive manner, by rules which are placed outside the applications.

– The services are regrouped by abstraction level with the aim of separating different logics: for example, process logic and pure business logic, which is independent from the organization of the company, etc.

– The services must be reused by several different processes in different contexts. For this to be successful, the company must make a considerable effort in the generic design of the services, so that the way in which the services function can be easily redefined depending on the context in which they are being used.

– The services that are available must be documented and understood by everyone. To achieve this, a service directory must be used.

These principles cannot all be put into place at the same time. The current information system must be taken into consideration, and the IT specialists can then integrate these principles depending on the SOA maturity level of the system.

3.2. Cosmetic SOA

The organization of SOA for the progressive overhaul of an information system requires a renovation strategy for the restructuring of the system. This is time-consuming. It is not possible to start integrating SOA throughout the entire information system at once. As a first phase, SOA can be used on the periphery of the information system with a relatively low impact on the existing IS assets. The aim here is to take advantage of the information technology that is already in place, and to prepare this information technology to be progressively integrated within the renovated system, which will function around business services. It could be said that it is similar to the revamping of certain existing IT transactions (in service mode) which will be displayed in XML and which can be linked together depending on the needs of the company. This approach constitutes the first level of maturity of SOA, which is known as cosmetic SOA. At this stage, there is no overhaul or restructuring of the information system.

With cosmetic SOA there is a slight improvement in the flexibility of the information system thanks to the loose coupling that exists between the services, which can be reused in different processes. The ergonomics of the workstation is also improved if several heterogneous sources of data are incorporated together (in service mode) onto a unified UI. The components that display the existing information system communicate, not only with the different presentation layers in the system, but also with the other components of the system in XML. This slight integration of the SOA approach is also appropriate for the transition of software packages to service mode, and in particular for those packages that are unable to display services in native mode.

Cosmetic SOA generally results in the creation of services with capabilities that the users of the updated information systems do not expect. They are unexpected since the capability of a particular service is fixed by the existing system. It is therefore necessary to remain vigilant as far as the quality of services produced is concerned, and not to create any false impressions that might lead to the disappointment of any possible user of the system. In particular, the agile composition of new processes from services obtained through the revamping of a system is difficult to organize. In the majority of cases, these revamping services are not created for multiple compositions since they are too dependent on the existing information system. Cosmetic SOA does not modify the existing information system. The history of the system's information technology remains important and in SOA the quality of such a history is vital in the progressive overhaul of an information system.

The use of cosmetic SOA requires understanding of an infrastructure, which may prove to be important: such as communication between the systems with

EAI, the arrival of the new technological generation with XML (known as ESB), process engines (workflow, BPM), service directories, etc.

Each of these components requires an increase in the competences of the IT specialists as well as a stabilization phase. Their use in the framework of cosmetic SOA is an excellent way for the functional, development and production teams of a company to progressively implement these components within their projects. The strength of cosmetic SOA is the opportunity it affords to use all the components that are necessary for future overhaul and restructuring projects. Although the components will not be used to their full capacity, they will be used at a level that is sufficient for the running in of new modeling and IT procedures, confirming technological choices and refining production procedures. Since cosmetic SOA does not change the existing information system, it is possible to extend this approach to a wider area of the information system.

The amount of effort required for the effective use of cosmetic SOA calls for the mutualization of work methods and the different components of the technical infrastructure required. The use of cosmetic SOA must not hide the need for mutualizing the efforts that need to be made. The infrastructure that is used can only be completely reliable and profitable if it is shared with the all the teams working on such a progressive overhaul project within the company. The same applies to the methodological approach. Consequently, the chief information officer must provide the teams with the resources that are necessary for working on the issue of mutualization well in advance.

Some companies already have an existing information system that is very modular, and the granularity of their business components is judged as being sufficient. These are generally companies whose business does not require complex processes but rather the organization of elementary tasks. Companies such as these have almost succeeded in integrating cosmetic SOA within their information systems. Nevertheless, their technology is often of a previous generation to that brought about with the XML wave. Cosmetic SOA is therefore characterized by an overhaul project of their existing technology.

3.3. Extended SOA

If a company uses cosmetic SOA to its full potential so that it can capitalize on the infrastructure that this approach provides, then it can equip itself with several of the key factors that are necessary for it to continue with the evolution of its information system. It will then be possible for it to take into consideration procedures that favor the agility of the information system; in other words, procedures that form what is known as extended SOA. In practical terms, agility needs to be created in the following three areas of the information system:

– Data: the more the data (used by the different business services) can adapt quickly to the different contexts in which it is being used, the more flexible the information system becomes. To preserve a large part of the services' agility, companies must think of modeling the master data (in a generic and flexible manner) by taking into account the contexts in which the data will be used. The administration of this master data is carried out with the help of a business tool that enables functional teams to work on how the services function in different contexts, without the systematic intervention of information technology. This is the field of Master Data Management.

– Business rules: this is a question of extracting certain business rules from the services so that they can be localized within a business rules management system. The rules are implemented in almost natural language and modification of them does not require the intervention of an IT specialist. However, in reality it is best to involve an IT specialist to control the business rules so that creation of rules that could lead to a malfunctioning of the software is avoided. This type of solution increases the speed with which the business rules are modified and also improves the extent to which (as well as how) they are documented, thanks to the introduction and setting up of a complete business rules database. This type of solution also favors the reuse of business rules depending on the contexts in which they are being used; this includes managing the different versions of the business rules.

– Business processes: the process management level is often the level at which agility is most important. The software vendors strongly promote the idea of agility, which has also been promoted by the current craze surrounding BPM (Business Process Management). The agility of processes is important, but this agility alone is not enough for the evolution of the system to take place. If processes orchestrate business services that are rigid due to low flexibility and quality of data and rules, then the information system will remain rigid even when BPM is used.

It must be understood that functional agility is not a spontaneous value of SOA. It forces companies to make a real effort in getting their information systems to the correct SOA maturity level, which is known as extended SOA.

Extended SOA builds on cosmetic SOA, thanks to the contributions of Master Data Management, the Business Rules Management System and Business Process Management. Agility starts to improve and even more so if certain modifications to the existing information system are accepted, such as the outsourcing of business rules without starting the restructuring of the system itself. However, since the services come from a revamping of the existing system, the agility will largely remain dependent on the quality of the existing information system. To move ever closer to the creation of an information system with more agility, the progressive overhaul of the information system must be undertaken. This is known as overhaul SOA.

3.4. Overhaul SOA

Considering the complexity of information systems, their overhaul must be carried out in phases. Thanks to cosmetic SOA, which is widely used within a company, it is possible to interconnect the domain that is undergoing the overhaul to the rest of the information system. This is an important contribution that the SOA approach has to offer: the ability to rewrite systems in phases. It must be pointed out once again that cosmetic SOA should only be used (in a homogenous manner) with the idea of mutualization in mind. The more this idea of mutualization is adopted, the easier it will be for companies to deal with the alignment of the domain being restructured with the existing information system.

Overhaul SOA requires a complete methodological approach which covers the upstream models of expressing the business needs of a company through to the downstream models of creating the software.

The following chapters provide the key ideas that need to be taken into consideration to reduce the risks associated with SOA. A risk that is incurred during the overhaul phases of the information system is that of failing to create highly reusable components. In this case, companies use SOA to reproduce the equivalent of what currently exists. To make matters more difficult, the methodological and technical innovations that are brought about by using SOA increase the complexity level of the system, or at least this is the case during the adaptation phase. It is understood that the introduction of this complexity to the system must also provide some sort of advantage to the system, particularly when it comes to the creation of services that can be easily modified and reused depending on the needs of the company.

The creation of new services without a design phase and without an appropriate methodology runs the risk of creating an inflexible information system (as was the case in the past), with only a slight possibility of reusing the services. It is therefore necessary to find solutions that will make it possible to create flexible components that can easily adapt to the different contexts in which they are being used, and which can also be easily reorganized around new business processes. Consequently, the ability to change the behaviors of services with help from a functional parameterization (BRMS, MDM) and without implementing IT code is crucial. Doing that, the IS is really more in the hands of the functional owners of the system.

By contrast, developing SOA which does not allow for this level of agility would be like taking a step back and would lead to the production of fixed business services that are difficult to reuse during the evolution of consumption contexts: new versions, new channels, new subsidiaries, new partners, new market segments, etc. It is therefore necessary to combine overhaul SOA with extended SOA as soon as the project has started.

The opportunities that arise with the second wave of SOA, i.e. overhaul SOA combined with extended SOA, are much better than the opportunities that come along with cosmetic SOA:

– There is better alignment of the information system with company needs, notably with a more integrated, more ergonomic workstation. Such a workstation will not experience the breakdowns that take place during the transition from one system to another. Overhaul SOA makes it possible to find the best links between processes, which, originally, were not possible due to the existence of silo applications.

– The information system is more reactive to the evolution and is capable of creating new processes through the composition of highly reusable services. These services can be developed internally by the company and can be progressively purchased or hired on the market.

– There is an increase in the takeover of a part of the information system by the users of the system thanks to procedures that help set the parameters of the system. Such procedures have been brought about by the Business Rules Management System and Master Data Management.

– There is an improvement in the total cost of ownership of the information system due to the rationalization of the system's maintenance.

– Companies are managing the generational transition before some of the team members retire. Overhaul projects require the mobilization of mixed teams that are made up of more experienced (senior) members who have an understanding of the existing system and of staff management, and members with less experience (junior members) who contribute their understanding of modern technology.

These benefits can only be realized if a company is prepared to commit itself to a long-term project and if the teams can work with both cosmetic SOA and overhaul SOA at the same time. Overhaul SOA is incremental deploying across successive large business domains of a company. On the other hand, cosmetic SOA must be used rapidly on a large scale if it is to guarantee that the part of the information system that has been overhauled will be able to interconnect with the rest of the system.

3.5. The matrices of SOA maturity

The different levels of SOA maturity, i.e. cosmetic SOA, extended SOA and overhaul SOA, have helped us construct the following matrices, which show the possible associations between the different levels.

3.5.1. *The matrix showing the definitions of SOA*

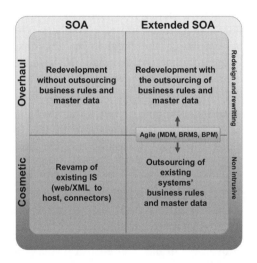

Figure 3.1. *The matrix of SOA maturity – definition*

3.5.2. *The matrix showing the quality criteria of SOA*

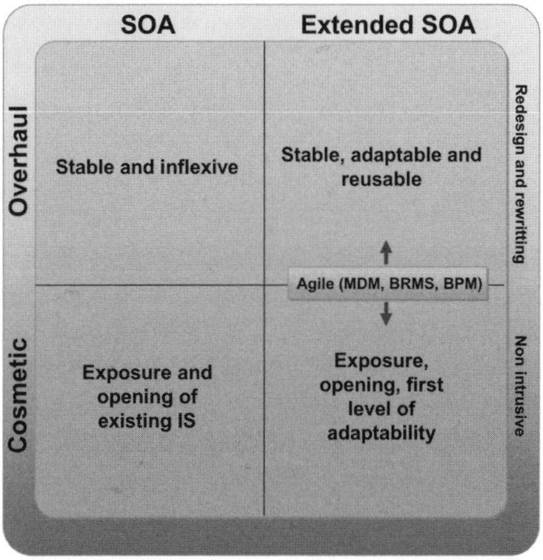

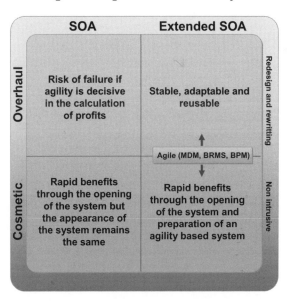

Figure 3.2. *The matrix of SOA maturity – quality requirements*

3.5.3. *The matrix showing the strengths and weaknesses of SOA*

Figure 3.3. *The matrix of SOA maturity – strengths and weaknesses*

Chapter 4

Economic and Social Aspects

A RECAP OF IDEAS MENTIONED IN PREVIOUS CHAPTERS

– SOA is an approach which is used for the progressive overhaul of an information system.

NEW IDEAS PRESENTED IN THIS CHAPTER

– the removal of obstacles that may slow down the progressive overhaul of an information system;

– making the senior and junior members of teams work together;

– asking the editors of SOA software to use new pricing methods.

This book could have been entitled *Where is Information Technology Going?* because following the path taken by the SOA approach requires an understanding of the expectations of everyone involved in the adoption and use of this type of architecture. This understanding therefore puts us in a better position in terms of judging the importance and the future of such an architecture.

4.1. Removal of obstacles that may slow down the progressive overhaul of an information system

An important criterion when it comes to deciding whether or not to invest in the progressive overhaul of an information system is the teams' ability to make the project succeed.

Today, in a world where businesses possess the financial means to give a new lease of life to their IS, the lack of ability to manage operational risks of SOA implementation at a large scale (overhaul and extended SOA) could slow down the SOA adoption. Consequently and unfortunately, companies begin to adopt this new information technology in small quantities following too heavy and long-term plans.

These plans are conditioned by a long preparation period for the integration of the information technology within the company, which in turn leads to the creation of teams that are no longer motivated to work, and this lack of motivation can also extend to managers. To overcome this situation, companies must use risk management and rely on proven manufacturing processes when it comes to renewing and updating their information system, which is the aim of SOA. It should also be pointed out that the working habits and nature of IT managers do not favor the idea of risk taking, which in turn does not allow for the undertaking of any in-depth renovation of a company's information system. IT departments have been able to produce first-generation systems capable of adding successive functional layers to the system without affecting the foundations of the system. They have also rationalized costs related to the creation and maintenance of the information systems.

However, things are currently changing. In a rapidly evolving business and technological world, the work that is expected from IT managers is more complicated than it ever was in the past. IT managers are faced with one factor that cannot be ignored: the aging of the existing IS and constant demand for the renewal and updating of that technology. They therefore need to come to terms with business projects that aim to overhaul and restructure the information system progressively. By showing concrete results and without affecting the everyday production of a company's information system, IT managers must be able to evaluate and deal with any risks linked to the modification of that system. In addition to this, they must try to avoid generating an information system that may be rejected by the users.

Over the years, the IT manager has become the manager of a company's well-structured and well-established information technology. Nowadays, IT managers must work with the general management of a company to establish the objectives linked to the progressive overhaul of the information system. They must then create and share this vision with the large majority of people working in the IT department and in the company as a whole.

4.2. The future of IT specialists

During the period between the 1970s and the 1990s, the IT specialist belonged to a quite homogenous profession with the codified competences of an analyst, analyst-programmer, production operator, database administrator, etc. Today things have changed and the IT specialist no longer belongs to one particular community. The codification of competences no longer exists due to the advent of modern technology and the increase in expertise brought about by the arrival of this modern technology. With the crisis that followed the burst of the Internet bubble and the worries linked to off-shoring, students no longer had faith in IT and decided to abandon such courses. At the same time IT teachers and professors were also faced with problems because what they were teaching had increasingly to take into consideration the evolution taking place in the profession. This was not a great time for students who were interested in IT and who wanted to be successful in the profession.

Today, however, the IT labor market is on the way up again, as can be seen by the shortage of well-trained IT specialists. This shortage generates a sort of instability among IT specialists, which may damage the proper execution of a project. It is necessary to create conditions that will lead to greater stability and this in turn leads to a certain level of professionalism within IT. Later in the book we discuss the fact that Enterprise System Topology (EST) makes it possible to clarify the competences of the IT specialist, which gives us a better understanding of what is involved in this job. This clarity and explanation of what is involved in the job of an IT specialist should be taken advantage of with the aim of offering career evolution plans and more codified training courses, in other words more fulfilling and more encouraging training courses. Such plans and courses will only strengthen the stability of teams, which is important for working on projects such as the progressive overhaul of information systems which demands a continuity of IT specialists.

4.3. Off-shoring

The rationalization of costs through the outsourcing of information technology to emerging countries cannot be the only factor behind the evolution of information technology, all the more so since it is the human factor which remains the key behind the success of the projects. The close work carried out between users and IT specialists is important regardless of the methodological approach and of the quality of the tools used. For IT off-shoring to make a significant profit, it is also necessary for a business to outsource, which is not possible due to strategic reasons. The outsourcing of certain activities of production such as call centers is not what we are talking about here; we are dealing only with the production of information systems and their maintenance.

Rather than outsourcing and risking a split between the business and IT teams, it is better to industrialize the working methods (which are already in place within the companies) of the users and of the IT specialists. This requires much more of an effort than outsourcing, but it will result in more long-term benefits. This industrialization is easy to achieve because it relies on the SOA approach, which combines several decades of the best practices in the production of information systems. The application of extended SOA, which increases the agility of information technology, will decrease the cost of ownership of the system. With the agility chain formed by the Business Rules Management System, Master Data Management, Business Process Management and Model Driven Architecture, there are no longer any economic reasons for off-shoring. By capitalizing on local teams, companies will be in a better position to reclaim their information system at a lower cost, which is one of the strategic objectives of SOA.

4.4. The generation mix

More often than not, functional and technical silos take over the organization of a company. This is a functional architecture which is relatively easy to understand because each silo is responsible for a particular zone of the information system. However, this type of architecture does not favor teamwork nor does it favor the mix of different ages and experience of IT specialists. The older, more experienced IT specialists, who created the existing information system, and the young graduates rarely work together. The more experienced IT specialists do not share their knowledge of the system with the new generation of IT specialists who, as a result, will have no real chance of taking the system into the future. The new generation of IT specialists does get to work on strategic projects. However, they are not strategic enough for this new generation to be able to adopt the correct methods of design, development and documentation that the more experienced IT specialists are used to dealing with. If this is the case, what can companies do when the older, more experienced IT specialists retire? They will be forced to act in haste with a maximum risk level to maintain the old complex systems and especially those systems reaching the end of their lifecycle. They will also be forced to work with young IT engineers, who will not have had the opportunity to gain hands-on experience in their job by working on important projects. This loss in knowledge can also be extended to the business users of the systems. Lack of ambition regarding the renovation of an information system and poorly managed integration of software packages within the systems decrease the business knowledge of the system's users. The system's users regard the information system as an IT tool, which creates a strategic problem as far as the quality of business know-how is concerned. Some of the users of information systems, who contributed to their creation in the 1980s and 1990s, have always had a larger vision and did not see these information systems as their only IT tool. These users will also be retiring over the next few years, and as a result this will reduce the optimal period for the progressive overhaul of the information system. The generation mix must be introduced or reinforced immediately, for IT specialists as well as for users of the information systems. For this to happen, a new context that allows for both groups to work together is required. Without this ambition, the undertaking of the SOA approach for the renovation of information systems will face problems when it comes to managing the project due to the fact that only experienced teams will possess the functional and methodological knowledge that is necessary for the project to succeed.

4.5. The role of software infrastructure editors

It is difficult to purchase an entire SOA software infrastructure, due to the fact that the use of different SOA functions comes about progressively over several years. It is therefore necessary for the editors of such software to create pricing methods that will enable companies to purchase these SOA solutions progressively. One example of an invoicing method would be to charge companies from 12 to 24 months after they have used the solutions, on the basis that the SOA functions have been successfully integrated within the companies' IT infrastructure. Moreover, performance for new operating systems such as Unix and Java are extremely difficult to evaluate and it is better to avoid a pricing method based on CPUs. Editors will have to offer prices that take into consideration the use of the software infrastructure, without having to introduce company licenses, which could be a step too far in terms of the overhaul of information systems. Editors will undoubtedly have to become more interested in the projects that their clients are working on.

Part II

The Principles of SOA

Chapter 5

The Properties of SOA

A RECAP OF IDEAS MENTIONED IN PREVIOUS CHAPTERS

– cosmetic SOA: presenting and displaying services after the renovation of the existing information system;

– overhaul SOA: rewriting of the existing information system in service mode;

– extended SOA: using solutions that favor the agility of the different services provided by the information system (business rules engine, Master Data Management, process execution engine).

NEW IDEAS PRESENTED IN THIS CHAPTER

– logical service;

– logical component;

– use cases (micro-processes), processes;

– loose coupling, communication by messages and design by contract;

– the version and the variant of a service.

In Chapters 2 and 3, the aims and objectives of SOA were introduced by distinguishing several levels of SOA maturity: cosmetic SOA, overhaul SOA and extended SOA. The following two objectives must be kept in mind:

– The SOA approach must allow for the rapid design and development of new business processes by simply linking reusable services together. This linking process does not require the use of a complex piece of development software. The process must be carried out with the help of high-level tools, which mask the underlying technical complexity that the services possess. The contribution that XML standards make to this process is extremely important because they allow for the creation of such services in a simple manner without having to worry about any subjacent programming languages or operating systems that could be heterogenous.

– To ensure that the previous objective can be achieved, the services must be highly reusable. Each service must be produced in such a way that it is possible to create new functional variants of the service without having to go through a phase of programming, which can increase production costs and delay the implementation of the services. These variants are created by a simple redefining of the data and the business rules. In this way the same service can function differently, depending on the business process in which it is being used and on the context in which the process is taking place: country, legislation, company, structure, organization, etc.

A greater in-depth study of SOA properties is required to understand the approaches that make it possible to achieve the objectives mentioned above. Although the properties of SOA can be very precise, it is still important to make an effort to understand them so that is possible to: find out what each level of SOA is capable of; organize a project team that is capable of working on projects in which the SOA approach has been adopted; and finally have a better understanding of the work procedures that are associated with SOA when a company decides to use the SOA approach in one of its projects. Before getting to the heart of the subject, time must be spent on carefully defining the services so that they possess traits that take them beyond the traditional characteristics of reuse and granularity. The definition of business services is important because it is from this definition that SOA is created.

For businesses the term "service" existed well before the arrival of SOA and there is no need to reinvent what already exists. For IT specialists this term needs to be explained in more detail because it represents different concepts. It is therefore necessary to define the service according to whether it is aimed at users of the systems or the IT specialists. These definitions of the term lead to the creation of different service categories and also include the concept of processes such as: service or enterprise business service (the service which is available to the users), presentation service (human–computer interaction), organizational service (includes an organizational process or use case), business service (includes issues which are independent of the enterprise business service) and primary service (used for technological implementation). The enterprise business service corresponds to a category of services for the IT specialist who needs to place this service within one of the different layers of the architecture: i.e. presentation (human–computer interaction), organization or business.

Figure 5.1 shows the links that exist between the categories of services which result from the definition of the term "service" for IT specialists, as well as showing the connectors that exist within each service.

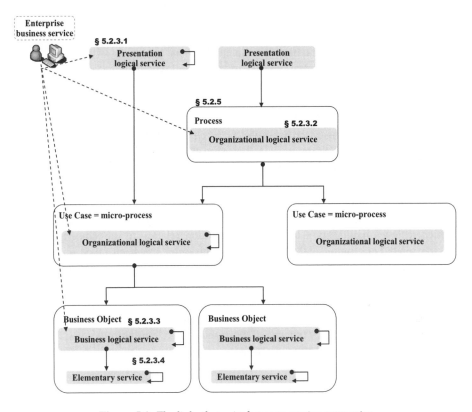

Figure 5.1. *The links that exist between service categories*

5.1. The definition of service for users

Users of information systems do not need to have an interest in the particulars of SOA, which, for IT specialists, remains a logical type of architecture for information systems. Nevertheless, the users are able to see the results of SOA thanks to the business services, since they actively use these services when using graphic interfaces. The users can also configure them thanks to parameterizing. In addition to this, it is also possible for the users to define service contracts and to follow their integration and use in the different states of management, etc. The user of the service is the key player in all this and it is worthwhile for a company to bear this in mind when defining its different services.

5.1.1. *The user of the service*

When we hear the word "user", we automatically think of the person who uses the information system on a day-to-day basis in his/her job. This user will primarily see the business service through a graphic interface. The user will find the same business service but it will be available in different processes, which will allow him/her to adapt the information system (more quickly than before) so that the system can work on a different business service in a different process.

Other types of users also need to be considered:

– the service administrator, who will be in charge of defining the parameters of the business service in terms of data (by using the Master Data Management tool) and in terms of business rules (by using the Business Rules Management System);

– the user who is the owner of a service. This type of user is responsible for the specification of the service, whether it is a service with a human–machine interface or not. An example is a service that is used for subscribing to stock-exchange orders which receives input data such as the information relating to the subscription and which sends back output data that confirms the order has been taken and entered within the information system. In this case there is no graphic interface, only a data exchange protocol which must be specified and which is the responsibility of the user who is the owner of the protocol;

– the user who needs to monitor how the available services are being utilized. The user may want to carry out statistical studies on the consumption of services, or verify billing procedures for the use of the services, etc.

5.1.2. *A business ambiguity*

We have to ask ourselves what the term "business service" actually means to users. The business service is seen as an operation that has an added value for a company in the sense that this operation would improve the efficiency and the performance of the company. How can the term "business service" actually be defined?

Business services are made up of two fundamentally different characteristics: a business side which is constant regardless of the company, country or organizational structure, and an organizational side which depends on the company's organization methods, on the legislation of the country, on the language of the country and on other extremely variable elements. Depending on the situation, the business service can be found at the heart of the company or at an organizational level, for example in the form of a procedure or a graphic component. The clarity of the term "business service" must be questioned. Depending on the situation, the term "business service" includes activities that take place within an industry (insurance, banking, transport, telecoms, etc), activities which take place at organizational level or even activities from the human–machine interface. It is quite difficult to understand that a business service can also refer to an organizational activity, a process or a screen.

IT specialists must make the information systems that they are working on as flexible as possible. This can be achieved by making sure that the software they are developing is able to adapt quickly to the continuous evolution of the organization of the information system. It is not necessary to redesign and redevelop the entire system each time the organization evolves. However, if the programs contain a mix of business, organizational and human–machine interface operations then it is impossible to meet the objective of flexibility. In order to ensure that information technology is flexible and aligns itself with the business, IT specialists need to make a clear distinction between activities that are at the heart of the company and those that concern organization and ergonomics. To distinguish between the different activities there are three logical layers: presentation, organization and business. This terminology may not be automatically recognized by users. The user, who is the owner of a service, may be interested in knowing this terminology with the aim of being able to judge the quality of the system and its capabilities when it comes to reusing the services.

We must be aware that the term "business service" does not have the same meaning for users as it does for IT specialists. For the user the term encompasses business, organization and human–machine interface all at the same time. For the IT specialist the term can be divided into other services, if necessary, so that each service can be placed in only one logical layer, i.e. presentation, organization or business.

5.1.3. *An example of a business service*

The commonest example of a service cited by editors is credit card payments. This simple example is not the only one that can be used to justify the implementation of an SOA approach. In an information system that has reached the level of overhaul SOA we will identify services which can be found deep within the information system. This then makes it possible to organize the ergonomics of workstations based on micro-processes in a different way than has been done in the past, and not only on the major non-intrusive processes within the existing information systems.

VOCABULARY NOTE: USE CASES AND PROCESSES

A use case is a set of micro-processes that manages the dialogue between a user and the system during the same time period and which takes place in the same location. To create a use case in SOA, the system must have reached the maturity level of overhaul SOA.

A process manages the dialogue between several users, generally during different periods of time. Processes can be created in SOA at the maturity level of cosmetic SOA.

Let us take an example which comes from the SMABTP project. It deals with a process for managing claims and works in the following way: after the declaration of an accident the processes of opening a claim, of evaluating a claim, of settlement for one or several insurance policies follow on from one another until the claim has been terminated and archived. If an expert has to estimate the risk, then the processes of assigning an expert and the analysis of the expert's report are also integrated within the claim process. The services that are made available to users, partners or customers are open-claim, settle-claim, assign-expert or terminate-claim.

With overhaul SOA, services can be reused and new services (which may not even be used) can appear. Everything depends on the quality of information technology that is used if new services are to be created. The service open-claim is itself made up of the services select-client, select-contract, enter-data-circumstances-claim, select-policy and evaluate-policy. In certain simple cases, the actions settle-claim and terminate-claim may be executed immediately after open-claim. Other use cases such as evaluate-claim or settle-claim reuse the same services as the open-claim use case, i.e. select-claim, select-client or select-contract, modify-circumstances-claim, evaluate-policy and settle-policy.

The reuse of services is maximized because the services can be selected in multiple use cases and processes. However, this example is only possible with overhaul SOA, which makes it possible to produce reusable business services within use cases and processes. If the aim is to reach this level of service reuse, it is not possible to use only cosmetic SOA when the existing information system does not have a sufficient level of quality.

5.2. The definition of service for IT specialists

5.2.1. *The granularity of service*

The term "business service" is also ambiguous for IT specialists. There are two approaches which make it possible to place the service within the architecture of an information system. The first approach considers the service as an element of the smallest grain that exists within the architecture of an information system, i.e. an operation. The second approach, however, places the service at a superior level, i.e. a logical component.

VOCABULARY NOTE: LOGICAL COMPONENT

In SOA, the logical architecture models the system in the form of logical components which group similar services together. For example, the logical component Client will display several services that are related to this business object. Accessing information related to the client is only possible by requesting the services of the logical component Client. In allocating the responsibilities of the logical components, as well as the precise rules of communication among them, the quality of the information system is improved because the allocation of such responsibilities and rules of communication favors loose coupling and the reuse of the services (see Part III, which is devoted to enterprise architecture).

Logical architecture manipulates the components and services that are used to organize the information system. The terms logical service and logical component are the principal metaphors of SOA, just like the terms zones and blocks are for the functional architecture of information systems.

As its name suggests, the service is the basic constituent of service-oriented architecture. In cosmetic SOA there is a restricted number of services because it is not possible to organize the interior of a service that is displayed to users in the form of other reusable services. However, in overhaul SOA it is possible to organize the interior of a service, and if the approach of object-oriented development is adopted then it is possible to have thousands of methods attached to these objects. Since SOA is based on elementary units which create services then it can be said that each method can be considered as a service, and it is therefore possible to have thousands of services. However, each service will have a different weighting and the logical architecture will arrange them into logical components according to certain criteria. The aim of arranging the services into logical components is to be able to distinguish between the business and the organization levels. Only a small number of these services will be recognized by users, however, a larger number of them will be reusable in the services that are made available to the users. If the approach based on logical components is not implemented, we will be faced with an object system that does not resemble the logical architecture in SOA. One of the objectives of SOA is to better urbanize the object developments by guaranteeing loosely coupled communications between components.

On the other hand, another IT group considers the services as already being a component that groups operations together. In this instance, the operations form the smallest constituent of the system, for example, a method which is executed in the object approach. This is the case for W3C, which uses XML Web service technology. It must be kept in mind that SOA does not depend on Web services. The use of Web services is not compulsory, even though the use of the XML language would be worthwhile in terms of interoperability. With Web services it is no longer a question of logical architecture but rather of software architecture, and for this reason it is not recommended to place a service at the same level as a Web service.

VOCABULARY NOTE: WEB SERVICES

Web services are standards that allow for the implementation and execution of services in XML. These standards include Web Service Description Language (WSDL) and Single Object Access Protocol (SOAP).

A Web service assembles one or several operations, which are then made available to consumers.

SOA does not depend on Web services. Web services remain a possible solution when it comes to the creation of SOA, not an obligation.

5.2.2. The separation of concerns

If the different processes relating to the business, the organization, the human–machine interface and the technology of an information system are poorly distributed within the architecture then inflexible, monolithic software which does not favor the reuse of services will be created. This well-known problem – known as the separation of concerns – can be resolved through the use of layered architecture. Each concern is dealt with individually and in a well-identified layer of the software. The separation of the business and the organization is an extremely important point as can be seen in [KRAFZIG, BANKE, SLAMA, 2006]: "The benefits of cleanly separating SOA services into services containing core business logic (with potentially long lifetime) and processes containing control logic (with a usually much shorter lifetime) are manifold."

Unfortunately, the approximate use of object-oriented design and its associated technology has led to a decline in the use of the separation of concerns. SOA forces us into renewing information systems in using the principle of object-oriented design because we have to favor the reuse of services and rationalize maintenance costs. How is it possible to renew a business service which deals with the calculation of financial risks if this service also deals with organization rules, and if such rules are able to evolve? How is it possible to change a development framework if this development framework is used directly within service programs? The separation of concerns is not easy when modeling new systems. During the modeling of business needs the principle of separation of concerns must be able to easily distinguish business rules from organizational rules. In the chapter that deals with enterprise architectures we will see that Enterprise System Topology (EST) anticipates the creation of a semantic modeling discipline (for business rules) and the creation of a pragmatic modeling discipline (for organization rules). IT specialists are able to develop services on two different levels thanks to the separation of business and organization rules, i.e. on business and organizational levels.

Separation of concerns leads us to defining service categories that will help IT specialists keep on top of layered architecture.

5.2.3. *The service categories*

The following logical service categories exist: presentation logical service, organizational logical service, business logical service and elementary logical service. IT specialists understand this terminology and having the different logical service categories makes it possible for them to place a service in the correct location within the logical architecture. The term "logic" is used in each category because it avoids any confusion with the term "business service", which is recognized by the user, although it can still create some slight confusion. These service categories should not be made available to users of the services, who understand and use the concept of enterprise business service as described at the beginning of this chapter. Depending on the situation, the enterprise business service can correspond to one of the service categories used by the IT specialists. However, this is not the case for the primary service category, which proves to be too technical for the functional teams.

For the IT specialist the way in which the services interact together is important in the production of high quality software: reuse of services, strength, reliability, improved maintenance. It is at this level that the rules of logical architecture come into force when it comes to rationalizing the exchanges between the different service categories. For example, an organizational service can organize a call to business services. However, the reverse situation is not possible. These principles will be discussed again in the section of the book that is devoted to enterprise architectures. For the user, these rules are unknown. The enterprise business services create functions that are offered by the information system, regardless of the logical architecture that is used to implement them.

5.2.3.1. *The presentation logical service*

The presentation logical service makes it possible to access the information system. It is often compared to a graphic service because it displays a human–machine interface. This service receives processes that make it possible to navigate between screens and processes. Being able to navigate between screens and processes allows for the implementation of organizational logical services.

5.2.3.2. *The organizational logical service*

The organizational logical service includes rules that are associated with organization. The rules can change rapidly depending on the strategies used by a company, and in particular strategies that deal with reorganization, management of subsidiaries, market segments, partners, acquisitions and mergers, etc. This category also includes capacity management, access rights, etc. This service also possesses a use case, i.e. the explanation of the interactions of a particular user with the system. Each of the user's interactions is carried out in a non-interruptible period of time (transaction). This interaction is also known by the term micro-process.

At a higher level, the organizational service can also possess a process which links several micro-processes together, i.e. the interactions among several users or even the interactions of one user but which occur over different periods of time (see Figure 5.2).

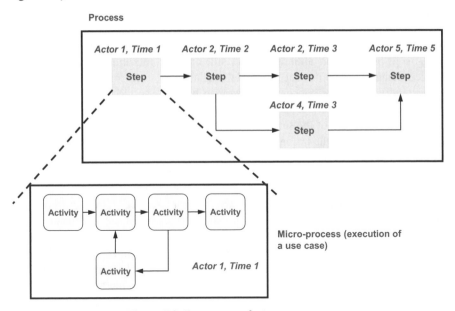

Figure 5.2. *Processes and micro-processes*

5.2.3.3. *The business logical service*

The business logical service includes the business rules. The business rules do not depend on the choices made at the organizational level. They evolve at a slower rate than the organizational services. The business rules form the stable basis of service inheritance, making it possible to select them as quickly as possible with the aim of creating new organizational services. These services are organized around business objects.

5.2.3.4. *The elementary logical service*

Unlike the other categories, the elementary logical service is not displayed through the use of a logical component interface. This means that this service does not possess a logical component. It is in this category that the services of create, read, update and delete are located. These services manage access to databases and allow for implementing private operations (not exposed via a service contract).

5.2.4. *Batch services*

To improve the adaptability of a system and to optimize production time slots it is best to use streamlined management, despite the fact that the adoption of such a management process will prove to be disadvantageous to the batch services. For the batch services, IT specialists try to reuse services even though performance constraints prevent this from happening. Services that are designed for transactional use work with unitary data (e.g. a client file), whereas batch services work with groups of data (e.g. all the client files for a region). The algorithms and strategies that are created to allow access to the databases are not always compatible between unitary mode and group mode.

EXAMPLE OF A BATCH IN SOA

An example of a batch service in SOA would be a company which uses monthly batch processing to spot customers who are likely to cancel their contract, and then come up with a more interesting commercial offer for each of these customers. In a proactive business approach the call center then contacts these customers with the aim of proposing these offers to them. However, whenever a customer contacts the call center to cancel their contract the customer service representative is unable to offer the customer such an attractive deal because the customer representative does not have the tool available for this: processes for calculating new offers are integrated in the batch chain and cannot be reused in the call center's software.

Thanks to SOA it is possible to redesign batch processing in the form of services, a certain number of which will be shared with the call center's software. Therefore, the customer service representative will have a real time tool which calculates more interesting offers for customers and which will be homogenous with the tool that is already used in the batches.

5.3. The properties of basic SOA

The architecture of an information system is said to be SOA if the architecture possesses the properties that will be mentioned in this section. In this section we will provide a checklist of the different properties that need to be met so that the architecture of an information system can be classified as SOA. These properties can easily be adapted depending on the different demands and requirements of the service categories in which they are to be used. Certain restrictions apply and these will be mentioned in the following sections.

5.3.1. *Loose coupling*

Loose coupling is the property of SOA which is quoted the most. It encompasses several principles, which are not necessarily all implemented at the same time:

– The consumer uses the service independently of the transport and execution technologies that are used by the supplier.

– The consumer uses the service without knowing the identity of the supplier. A piece of intermediary software ensures that the consumer is not aware of the supplier's existence.

– The consumer and the supplier exchange data that follows a particular standard format. The semantics and syntax of the standard format are identical for all of the services. For example, the structure of a postal address is identical for all of the services. In most industries the XML language is used to establish a pivot language, in other words an exchange base between companies, for example FPML (Financial product markup language) which is used in finance. However, it is not possible to use XML in all levels of communication between the services, but only in areas where the information system requires a high level of interoperability and a high level of exchange standards.

– A service is executed by following an asynchronous exchange model. In this case, rather than linking together the consumer's request with the supplier's response, the two elements are decoupled. As a result the consumer is able to continue doing what he/she was doing without having to wait for the supplier's response, which will come at a later point. Notifying the consumer can take one of the following forms: dealing with consumers on a daily basis, call-back or polling. In the case of event management, Event Driven Architecture (EDA) is used. EDA is compatible with SOA and extends the uses of SOA from the basic question-synchronous response format.

– A service does not directly prompt the use of another service, but uses a specialized function which deals with the orchestration of the services. This property forces the design and development of new services. If the system is constructed on the basis of services prompting the use of other services, then the services become difficult to reuse in different contexts. On the other hand, a service which is not linked to any other service can be used an infinite number of times in different contexts. However, in practice it is not possible to organize all of the communications that take place between the different services according to the orchestration mode. Constraints linked to the performance and clarity of the architecture mean that direct communications between certain services must be monitored, i.e. a propagation mode must be used, and in particular within the components of the services themselves.

– The previous property can be extended through the use of stateless management. A service does not remember what happened during its previous execution. A service must not keep or monitor resources each time it is used. The data which is used during any previous execution is kept in an orchestration function and sent in the form of parameters between services once the services have communicated with one another. This method improves the system's performance and in turn can easily increase the use of the system's services.

5.3.2. *Communication by messages*

In the object approach, instances that include both data and methods (treatments) are manipulated. Any incorrect design could lead to the exchange of objects that display methods to users that should remain private. If the design is correct and the software development is up to date then this risk will no longer exist. However, there will be no absolute quality of an information system. In SOA this risk will be removed by using communication by messages. Each message is embodied by data type (e.g. data type UML), which no longer contains any methods. This type of complex data (it is possible to have nested data types) forms the flows of information that the services use so that they can communicate with one another. These flows of information are largely designed to favor the reuse of the services and to guarantee the progressive nature of the architecture. The object approach can still be used, but within the reduced perimeters of the information system for the internal communications that take place inside each component.

Finally, the object is split into two constituents: a message (data type) and a reduced object, which only contains the code. This type of communication is coherent with the architecture that was mentioned previously in this chapter. By splitting the object into two constituents it forces the flow of data, which is necessary for the execution of a service, to pass parameters in each service category in which it is to be used.

During the exchange of information between homogenous and/or heterogenous application domains, i.e. through the use of ESB in XML, it is possible to automatically validate the data of which the messages are composed. For each message a set of XML instructions is required; this set of instructions will contain validation rules such as: compulsory data, format, cardinality, belonging to a list of values. This set of instructions is automatically generated from the process of logical data modeling. In the example in Figure 5.3, the validation rules would include the data relating to InfoCustomer.

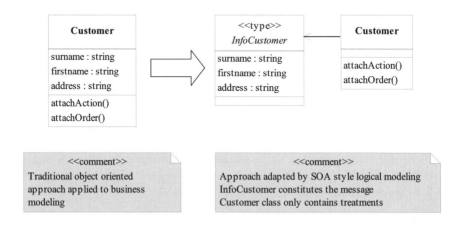

Figure 5.3. *The object abides by the rules of SOA*

5.3.3. *Design by contract*

5.3.3.1. *The principle of pre- and post-conditions*

Even if all the properties mentioned in the previous section are adhered to, this does not prevent the consumer and the supplier of a service from being structurally coupled to one another. If the supplier of a service experiences any problems then the use of the service by the consumer could damage the service during its execution. On the other hand, the supplier could be faced with run-time errors if the consumer uses a service in the wrong way. Since the quality of the service executed by the supplier and the consumer depends on the correct execution of the service, it can be considered that (in terms of exploitation) the coupling between the two parties is strong. It is therefore important to reduce the risk of problems from occurring at the level where interactions between the different parties who are exchanging information with one another take place. This is the aim of design by contract, created and defined by Bertrand Meyer in the middle of the 1980s with the help of pre- and post-conditions [MEYER, 1990]: "The pre-condition describes the properties which must be verified when the routine is called upon: the post-condition describes the properties that the routine guarantees in return." During this period, the term service was not used.

Consequently, the service will respect a strict architecture model, which is composed of its pre-conditions, its main body (the central algorithm) and its post-conditions. To guarantee the reliability of the service, the pre-conditions of the service are specified. The pre-conditions of the service which are specified include the rules that must be respected by the consumer at the moment when the service is launched. If these rules are not validated then the body of the service will not be executed. For example, the total amount for a stock exchange order is verified so that it does not exceed a maximum threshold after the current state of the market and the financial status of the customer are taken into account. On the other hand, the post-conditions are specified to guarantee that the result which is obtained after the execution of the service's central algorithm conforms to the possibilities which are expected by the consumer. If these rules are not validated then the service will return an error. For example, once the stock exchange order has been taken the customer's bank balance is verified so that the amount available in the balance is equal to the original balance minus the cost of the order and any associated charges.

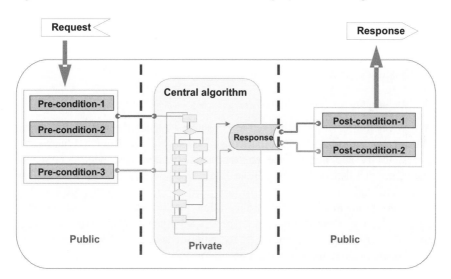

Figure 5.4. *The structure of a service with its pre- and post-conditions*

The pre- and post-conditions can be seen by consumers. They form the core of the service contract. Whenever they are used in different business contexts, such as a subsidiary, a partner, an access channel or a segment of the market, they form what is known as a service use contract. There are two different types of contract:

– The service contract contains the functional and technical clauses relating to the use of the service that are applied to each new consumer by default. The service contract does not have one specific rule for each consumer. The service contract is more of a framework contract (umbrella contract).

– The service use contract is specific to a particular execution context of a service such as an organization, geographical sector, access channel, segment of the market or consumer. In other words, the service use contract personalizes the clauses of the framework contract.

The concept of execution context is also mentioned in the definition of SOA, as stated by the standardization organization OASIS [OASIS, 2006]: "The execution context of a service interaction is the set of infrastructure elements, process entities, policy assertions and agreements that are identified as part of an instantiated service interaction, and thus forms a path between those with needs and those with capabilities."

The design model based on pre- and post-conditions can be applied to all services, not only those services which are made available to users. Companies should be aware of the sheer scale of this task. Once the algorithm has been drawn up it must be ensured that the rules that verify that it is possible to use the service are separated from the rules that verify that the end result is valid. Irrespective of the service category, this design approach must be adopted to increase the strength of the information system.

5.3.3.2. *Displaying the contract in XML*

Whenever the service is displayed to consumers outside the information system (client, partner, subsidiary) or to other consumers such as the front and back office, it is best to try and publish the contract in a standard and neutral computing language, i.e. one that is interoperable in XML. Web Service Description Language (WSDL) and XML respond in part to this need. WSDL and XML are unable to resolve every problem because they do not allow for the expression of pre- and post-conditions. They confine themselves to the syntactic aspect of the contract, i.e. the name of the service, its input message, its output message and identifying possible errors. To create a more complete description of the contract, it is best to use additional computing languages such as Schematron and WS-Policy, and to use business rules management systems.

It is best to use XML in contracts where interoperability is required. In other cases, the contract will be drawn up in a traditional computing language such as Java or COBOL associated with a Business Rules Management System for enabling the expression of pre- and post-conditions in a more flexible way, in particular for organizational logical service.

5.3.3.3. *The execution of the contract*

For the services that are exposed in XML, respecting the service contract is of more importance than respecting any of the other contracts that are applied to the internal services of an information system. For example, the supplier of a financial service must guarantee (depending on whether the conditions of the contract permit it or not) that a consumer who acts as a distributor is unable to use a version of the service that is two editions behind the most recent version. The exception to this is for the management of files that have information relating to the sale of products on the European market. It becomes apparent very quickly that there are a lot of complex rules in the contracts. It is a matter of carefully administering the rules and ensuring the automatic execution of the rules with a high level of reliability. An error during the administration of the rules controls could lead to the creation of an unknown quantity of contracts. IT production and the contracts must be aligned with one another. It is therefore necessary to set up a contract administration and an architecture that are able to automate the verification of the pre- and post-conditions. For this to be successful, it is not enough to have a written version of a service contract and then leave the information system to implement the pre- and post-conditions with no proper management system in place. It is best to use a business rules management system, which makes it possible to express and execute the pre- and post-conditions without any further software development. In this way it is possible to align IT production with the contracts.

Once the pre- and post-conditions are in place, it is then a question of determining who will execute them: the consumer or the supplier? Every mode of execution is possible. As an absolute minimum the supplier verifies the pre-conditions as soon as a request to use the service has been received, and also controls the post-conditions before uploading the response. The consumer can rerun the rules, since it is he/she who possesses the rules in the service contract. However, if the language that is used to write the rules is not standardized then the consumer will need to have the same business rules engine or programming language compiler as the supplier.

Suppliers may ask themselves why the consumers would be interested in testing the contract, since it is the consumers themselves who committed to the contract. It is therefore a question of confidence between both parties. For example, we have mentioned that in a bank the consumers (the leading distributors) test the pre- and post-conditions every night to monitor the supplier and to check that the supplier does not alter the contracts from one day to the next. The consumers try to detect any regressions that would not be identified by the supplier.

5.3.4. *The limits of the basic properties*

The properties that have been described in this section improve the quality of the information system thanks to the decoupling of services, the strength of communication by message and the formalization of contracts. However, these properties are insufficient when it comes to the flexible adaptation of business rules. The services remain traditional programs; of course they are more decoupled and can be better reused, but their algorithms remain too rigid in an implementation language such as Java. The reuse of the services is therefore average and SOA is not sufficiently agile.

In the next part we will describe the processes which make it possible to take SOA even closer to the notion of agility, which is the main objective when it comes to aligning the information system with the needs of the company.

5.4. The properties of agility

A recurring issue in computing is that of the construction of agile information systems, i.e. creating information systems that can quickly change the way in which they function by taking on board and adapting to new business needs. We have seen that over the past 20 years several projects have been carried out in particular areas with the aim of trying to reach this goal of creating an agile information system. We are aware of the object approach, which is used for making the processes reusable, and we are also aware of workflow engines, which are used for making the processes more flexible. Other approaches also exist within the business rules engine, such as the applications of client scoring and price setting. Companies have started to see the added value that business rules management systems bring to the evolution of their information system, yet they also see that there are limits when it comes to using such management systems. There are also specific developments which are required for parameter management, and this is particularly the case for companies that need to personalize their applications depending on certain criteria such as the language of a country, the legislation of a country or channels of distribution. [LAPASSAT, 2003a] states that defining the parameters of processes makes it possible to define the data values which are taken to be variables of program processing rules. The importance of reference systems stems from the possibility of being able to modify a business rule (and more precisely the values of its parameters) without having to modify a program's code.

Despite these different approaches, they have been unsuccessful in constructing an agile information system. There are many reasons for this:

– Companies have only worked on the agility of certain parts of the information system and very rarely on the information system as a whole; an example would be the organization of a workflow and the implementation of the object-oriented approach without the implementation of the business rules engine. This partial effort is not enough because the agility of an information system is a chain, with its power being the weakest link of the chain. If the process (configured in the workflow) is flexible, and if the rules that determine the process's progress through the chain are inflexible, then the overall information system will remain inflexible. Any modification to these rules would involve the use of an IT program. Companies would have to deal with the problems associated with using an IT program such as working to deadlines and making sure that there are people available who have knowledge of using the program.

– The technology that was used at that time was much less advanced in comparison to what is available nowadays. For example, parameter management did not correspond to a piece of structured software that was developed by software editors. The company had to construct its own application for parameter management, and had to deal with problems such as where the application would be used as well as problems associated with maintenance. More often than not this system for defining parameters did not exist or was located in several programs that were integrated within each project. Today, Master Data Management (MDM) solutions exist and these solutions are specialized in the management of master data and parameters. A company is now able to equip itself with one global solution for parameter management. This is undoubtedly a major advance in parameter management.

– To construct a successfully agile information system, it is necessary to have a design method that makes it possible to take advantage of the available technical constituents such as BPM and the business rules management system. Thanks to the SOA approach and the associated enterprise architecture there now exist proven processes which can be used in the construction of an agile information system (see Part III, which is devoted to the enterprise architecture).

Agility will become a reality if all the areas of an information system are worked on at the same time: master data, rules, processes and the use of adapted design method. If one of the areas of the information system is not worked on, then it will not be possible to create an agile information system. This is the principle of the Agility Chain Management System (ACMS).

As Figure 5.5 shows, there is an order of preference when it comes to organizing the technical constituents used in achieving the objective of agility. It is best to rationalize the management of the master data and the parameters in an MDM system; this will improve the quality of the data and the parameters and also means that there will be one central consultation and administration point. The Business Rules Management System (BRMS) is located at the second phase, just after the MDM phase, so that it can take advantage of the improved quality of the data and parameters, therefore allowing the BRMS to write rules with them. The same rule can easily adapt the way in which it functions depending on the context in which it is being used. For example, a rule will no longer test the threshold value of a particular transaction but will exploit a piece of the master data that can be found in a table. This piece of master data will provide a threshold value depending on the execution context such as: organization, file type, country, version, etc. The final phase of the agility chain is composed of Business Process Management (BPM), which is able to take advantage of the business rules engine and the parameter management application. The business rules engine increases the progress that occurs between each phase of the agility chain. Depending on the execution contexts, the parameter management application makes it possible to call the services through the use of different processes.

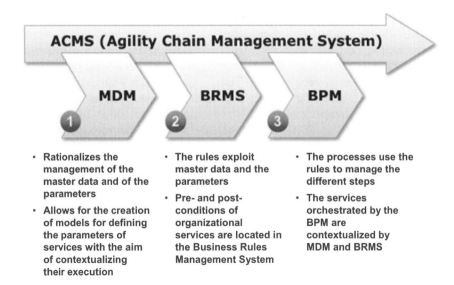

Figure 5.5. *The agility chain management system with MDM, BRMS and BPM*

5.4.1. *The difference between the version and the variant of a service*

The distinction between the terms "version" and "variant" must be understood if the processes that favor agility are to be fully comprehended. This distinction is the key to extended SOA. Whenever a service needs to be updated, two ways of managing the update are possible:

– Action must be taken in the service's program or in the data structure that the service manipulates. In this case a new version of the service is created and the involvement of an IT programmer is unavoidable. Since the software has been modified, an entire production cycle must be forecast and this can be a rather complex process.

– It is possible simply to redefine the parameter of a data element, a rule or a chain of services that are linked together. In this case, the ACMS tools (MDM, BRMS and BPM) are used without modifying the service's program. To configure the service in this way, a particular version of the software must be used and this leads to the creation of a variant of the service. Production is accelerated since the software has not been modified.

It is therefore necessary to manage several variants of the same service version. If the ACMS tools are secure and sufficiently ergonomic then it is possible for the accredited users to be able to create their own variants of a service without the involvement of IT programmers. If the software has not been modified then it is not necessary to follow a complete production cycle. Only the foundations of the parameters, rules and process configurations are involved in the production cycle. The duration for making any modification (which has been made to the information system) is reduced. This flexibility does not remove the software's testing mechanism, particularly non-regression testing.

As far as the reuse of the services is concerned, the following situation is not acceptable: a service that is reused in different contexts and which leads to the creation of a new version of the service. The increase in the number of versions of a service leads to complexities in the development and production cycles, and would thus be a failure in SOA. It should be understood that when a service is reused it is rarely reused in the same way in each of the different contexts in which it can be exploited. The service must therefore be made to evolve, and poor management of this can lead to an increase in the number of duplicate services available, which makes monitoring the capabilities of the services a complicated process. In the book *Enterprise SOA* [KRAFZIG, BANKE, SLAMA, 2006], the authors talk about the difficulties encountered in relation to the reuse of the services: "Unfortunately, it is not easy to achieve the goals of reuse. Large organizations have learned that reuse is not always efficient because it is particularly costly to administer, find and understand the components that should be reused, and sometimes this cost outweighs the benefits." To overcome these difficulties, it is important for companies to benefit from extra flexibility and this can be achieved thanks to the process of variant management. This concept of variants and variant management is being covered more and more by IT consultancy firms, as can be seen in SQLI's book on SOA. The book points out that "the concept of service variants highlights the importance, if not the obligation, of being able to define the parameters of how a service functions while the service is being created" [FOURNIER-MOREL, GROSJEAN, PLOUIN, ROGNON, 2006]. At Orchestra Networks the concept of service variants was introduced in 2004 in the publication, "The management of service variants in SOA architectures" [BONNET, 2004]. For certain evolutions of the service it has been noticed that the creation of a variant no longer responds to business needs; for example, if the model for defining the parameters of a service has not anticipated the modification of a particular data element. In this case the creation of a version has just begun.

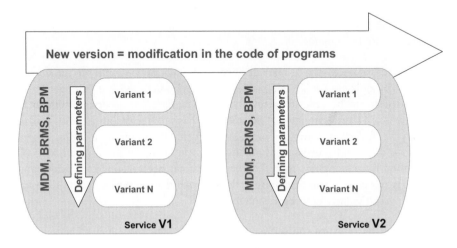

Figure 5.6. *Management by version and variant*

5.4.2. *Agility of the data*

The agility of the services is called into question if the data models are not extensive enough to be able to deal with the functional evolutions of the information system. This statement is not only valid for an SOA-style architecture, but applies to all types of architectures. Nevertheless, the best methods for designing databases will be mentioned in this section since they are, more often than not, forgotten about. We will then analyze how to deal with the partitioning of the databases, taking master data into consideration and modeling how the services' parameters are defined.

5.4.2.1. *A reminder of the best design practices*

For the data model to be extensive, the following design practices should be taken into consideration regardless of whether the architecture is of an SOA style or not:

– Carefully analyze the cardinalities that link objects together. If the aim is to improve the data model's capacity to continually evolve, then many to many (n, n) cardinalities are preferred. It is also best to create business rules to verify any problems and constraints that may arise.

– Do not freeze the value lists (code – label) in IT programs. It is best to use tables in databases. Trying to model these tables is not always an easy process, especially when taking into consideration the personalization filters associated with the context in which the data is being used.

– Use technical identifiers to express referential integrity constraints with the aim of being able to modify the business identifiers without affecting the entire data model.

– Forecast the creation of generic data structures that make it possible to add headings to certain tables in the database without modifying the data model.

5.4.2.2. *Partitioning the database*

Whenever we want to reuse a service, we also have to ask ourselves about the reuse of the data model on which the service functions. In SOA, the service level masks the data level. In other words, it is not possible to access a database without the use of a service. Ideally, it should be considered that each service is solely responsible for the update of part of the data and that there is no connection between the data and the different services; in other words, they are loosely coupled. With this theory in mind, it is possible to remove a service from a portion of the database to replace it with another service without affecting the existing information system. It is also possible to construct highly modular applications by following a plug and play mode.

Unfortunately, however, a service is too small a grain to be able to physically organize the database from the scope of each service. A system that is made up of several hundred services would have as many associated databases. With the current state of database system technology, this idea of freeing the database from the responsibility of each service is not possible. The idea of partitioning the database, by using the logical component network, which combines several services, should be raised. In the Praxeme method, which is described later in this book, the logic workshop component is used. The logic workshop component is equivalent to the category class in UML as described by Grady Booch [BOOCH, 1996]. Links between data from several categories of services are not permitted. The idea of creating a physical database based on the categories of services remains very ambitious, given the current state of the database systems. This approach would involve managing the transactions in a two-phase commit protocol for transactions that span several categories.

VOCABULARY NOTE: CATEGORY CLASS IN UML

In UML, a category class is a combination of classes that are based on the same business concept. The category is made up of approximately 20 classes at the semantic level. The category displays the services through an interface that prevents the use of the internal resources of the category. The loose coupling between the categories is maintained and the services are not linked together over several categories: no SQL joint statement between categories and no direct invocation of services belonging to different categories.

Over the past few years several works have covered the concept of categories with the aim of aiding the construction of reusable components. For example, [ROQUES and VALLÉE, 2002] stated that "a category is made up a logical grouping together of classes that possess a strong internal cohesion but which, externally, are loosely coupled".

5.4.2.3. *The master data*

Information systems often duplicate data which is shared by several applications. This data is known as master data. The process of synchronizing the updates of this data is complex and leads to inconsistencies in the data values. For example, data relating to credit rate which is duplicated in specific applications by channel of distribution (agency, call center, the Internet, etc.) must have a perfectly synchronized value across all the different channels of distribution. A simple development error could lead to the creation of different credit rates for the different channels of distribution. It is not enough to design and develop agile services if the master data (which is manipulated by these services) is subjected to a management process that leads to inconsistencies in data development. When using SOA it is necessary, first of all, to rationalize the management of the master data through the use of an MDM solution and by respecting the following points:

– a unified modeling of the master data. It is a question of a pivot language (common model) that is modeled in UML and then translated into XML Schema, which is a computing language that is a level above the specific data formats that are used in different applications. The unified modeling of the master data includes using the rules that make it possible to validate data updates, in relation to format and the referential integrity constraints, etc;

– creating a master data warehouse which physically stores the values of this data using the pivot language. This reference system contains the real information relating to the master data;

– setting up a business tool which will enable the functional and technical teams (depending on authorization rights) to be able to update and consult the master data. This tool replaces the old data-update solutions for the mainframe as well as for the Java, XML and database tools that are used by developers and production teams;

– modeling and implementation data integration processes between the applications and the warehouse. These processes are integrated by an Enterprise Service Bus (ESB) or Extract, Transform and Load (ETL) type of technical layer.

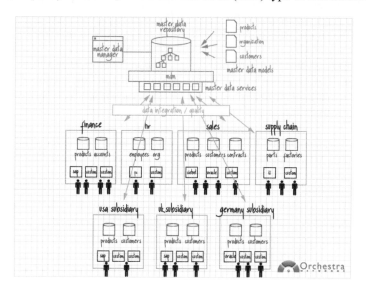

Figure 5.7. *The architecture of MDM (copyright Orchestra Networks)*

The warehouse and the associated management tool allow for data filling by context. For example, a marketing rate may be increased in value at head-office level; however, this value could be too high in contexts which take place further down the line, e.g. with a subsidiary, partner or market segment. The use of MDM is non-intrusive on the existing databases. The warehouse pushes master data values in these existing databases. In the case of an overhaul of the information system, the master data warehouse can replace the old master databases.

In this case the services interact directly with the warehouse. The master data is at the same time business related (products, customers, etc.), organization related (structures, authorizations, etc.), service level agreement related (response time, production opening times, etc.), ergonomic related (logos, colors, fonts, etc.), technical related (addresses of databases, logging information, etc.), etc. Consequently, the MDM solution is also used to manage all of the parameters that have been defined for the services.

5.4.2.4. *The model for defining parameters*

As soon as a service has been developed it is necessary to create a model that will define the parameters of the service, with the aim of making the service agile. The service algorithm benefits from parameters whose development depends on the context in which the algorithm is being used. This approach of designing services by parameters seems obvious. Unfortunately, it is not used often in practice. It requires generic modeling, which means having to anticipate future contexts in which the service would be used. The aim is to outsource (from the treatments) all the constants, variables and parameters that could be subjected to a different filling, depending on the contexts in which the service could be used.

In general, the designer only knows the first context in which the service will be used, i.e. the project on which the designer is working. The designer must be allowed to analyze the future contexts, which demands time and requires support for business and organizational analysis, which should come from all areas of the information system. To analyze the future contexts, a budget equivalent to 15% of the global budget is required. The return in investment is measured by the reduction in development and maintenance costs thanks to the reuse of services within the system. In terms of receiving support the help, which is to be provided from the information system as a whole, is boosted by the creation of a functional architectural team which works horizontally on projects.

The development of data by execution context is a key characteristic of extended SOA. It is important to work on only part of the functions of a service without systematically modifying the programs. As we have already seen, MDM tools allow for this type of management. In Figure 5.8, we can see contexts that describe geographic zones. Each development of the master data and of the parameters of a zone inherits the data from its parent zone. At the moment when a service is used, the service receives the execution context (in the example shown in Figure 5.8 this is the zone) in the form of a parameter. This enables the service to retrieve the correct master data and parameters and therefore use them to its advantage during its execution.

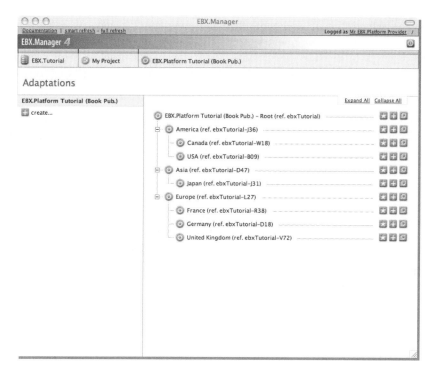

Figure 5.8. *Development by context (copyright Orchestra Networks)*

5.4.3. *Agility of the rules*

This property of extended SOA makes it possible to extract certain business rules from the programs with the aim of localizing these business rules within a business rules management system. The rules are written in an almost natural language, theoretically without the systematic intervention of an IT specialist. In practice, the use of information technology is necessary to make sure that the rules are properly integrated within the existing application system. This approach contributes to the increase in the agility of the services. In fact, an SOA approach whose services are systematically implemented in a traditional programming language such as Java or C+ does not lead to the creation of an agile information system. Any modification to the way in which a service functions requires work to be carried out within the programs, as well as a redeployment of the information system, etc.; in other words, complex work needs to be carried out.

With the outsourcing of the rules it has become possible to quickly modify the way in which the services function, and to create variants of the services without modifying the software. A designer who demonstrates a sound knowledge of rules language, which is more accessible than any programming language, is sufficient. The business rules management system offers more advanced rule administration functionalities to manage the versions, uses, documents, tests, etc. of a service. These functions are also discussed in the chapter devoted to the tools used in enterprise architecture.

The use of the rules is controlled by principles that are specific to logical architecture. For example, it is possible to place all of the rules of pre- and post-conditions into a business rules management system, and in particular rules which belong to organizational services and are able to evolve depending on the context in which they are being used. However, it is not possible to use the rules at all levels of the architecture, because it is impossible to substitute the rules for the algorithms that form the core of the execution of the system. For example, localizing a process of iteration in a business rules engine is not recommended. It is best to let the code of the services manage this sequence. The flow of data that is received by the rules must also be modeled in an extended manner. Within these flows of data it is also necessary to allow for more data than is necessary, so that it is possible to add new rules without having to modify the flow of data. It is also necessary for each flow of data to contain a context of information that will enable the rules system to choose from a set of rules to be executed, depending on multiple criteria such as the version, the technical environment, the effective date or the organization displaying the services. The services are decoupled from the rules system because the services do not know what sets of rules are going to be executed. Only the rules system (depending on the information context that it receives) will determine the set of rules that is to be executed.

The rules manipulate the data, of which the parameters of some of the data are linked to values that change depending on execution contexts. For example, the maximum value of an order may be different depending on whether the order is managed by head office or by an agency. The rule that verifies the total amount of the order manipulates a piece of master data, which is itself agile and is developed thanks to the use of MDM, which was mentioned in the previous section.

5.4.4. *Agility of the processes*

The idea of grouping services together with the aim of creating processes is an interesting, if not rather appealing, one. If the services are grouped together then users of the services will find themselves using the service-oriented approach. Nevertheless, it should be made clear that it takes much more than a graphical tool that groups services together to create agile processes. First of all, after the execution of one step of the process, it is necessary to work out the best route to reach the next step. In a real process there are often multiple routes and there are often many possible links between the different steps of the processes. It is therefore necessary to execute true business rules to determine how the process is advancing. If these rules are implemented in a programming language then any modifications made to the process require the systematic intervention of information technology. To favor agility, a business rules management system must be linked with BPM with the aim of outsourcing the calculation of the routes. The process itself is a service which manipulates data, and in particular the master data that it uses. If the parameters of this data cannot be easily defined then the intervention of an IT specialist is required to help with the updates of the process, as a result the agility of the process is reduced. To improve the agility of a process, an MDM solution must be used with BPM to define the parameters of the data that is manipulated by the process.

It is clear that the agility of a process depends on the agility of rules and data. We then arrive at the idea of globally configuring the processes, i.e. defining the parameters of services, rules (for the links that exist between the different steps of the processes) and the development of the master data. This global solution is powerful but remains rather complex to implement because of the fact that the technologies of BPM, BRMS and MDM have still not been integrated by software editors. This is the issue that ACMS raises, as described earlier in this chapter.

5.4.5. *Agility of the human–computer interface*

The screens are created from reusable graphical components. In order for the graphical components can be reused, each component must display data that comes from a unique business object. For example, rather than creating a graphical component which possesses a customer's data and that of the customer service representative, it is best to create two graphical components: one that deals with customer management and the other that deals with the management of the customer service representative. Users will not necessarily notice the existence of the two graphical components. The advantage of having two graphical components instead of one is that the components can be used in multiple screens. In the example of the customer and the customer service representative, the graphical component that deals with customer management can be integrated into other screens such as those dealing with managing payments, monitoring orders, etc. Using more than one graphical component provides significant functional support to the user since the ergonomics of the applications is rationalized; in other words, the user will always have the same graphical representation for the same concept.

The screen shown in Figure 5.9 is an illustration from the SMABTP project. This screen is created by using several graphical components. Each graphical component is responsible for presenting data that relates to one particular business object such as claim, contract, customer, claim-management, claim-circumstances, claim-specific data, lists of transferable insurance policies. It is possible to define the parameters of the graphical component, which makes it possible to adjust the way it looks (character fonts, colors, styles of buttons, etc.) and also to insure that the graphical component can easily adapt the way in which it functions, depending on the updates that are applied to it and on the way it is consulted by the users.

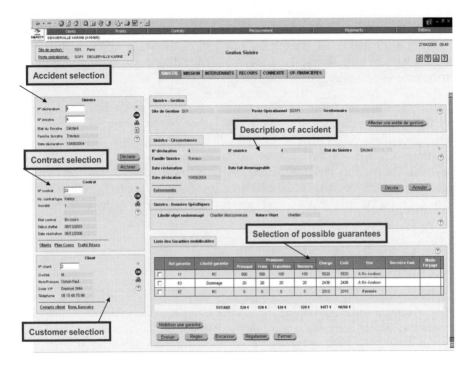

Figure 5.9. *Example of graphical components (portlet) – the SMABTP project*

Chapter 6

Orchestration (BPM and SOA)

A RECAP OF IDEAS MENTIONED IN PREVIOUS CHAPTERS

– Loose coupling: limits direct communication between services in favor of a function that is specialized in orchestration;

– Stateless architecture: the service does not have the capacity to store information relating to what happened during its previous execution;

– Enterprise business service: service that can be seen by users.

NEW IDEAS PRESENTED IN THIS CHAPTER

– Orchestration is a concept which can be found at many levels: processes, screens, micro-processes (use cases), business services, exchanges between domains, batch schedulers.

– Orchestration does not lead to the creation of a new service category.

– Several techniques and standards of orchestration exist.

– The idea of a composition of services being used by users with the aim of creating new processes is far from being a reality.

In Chapter 5, several service categories were mentioned, yet nothing was said about the concept of orchestration, which makes it possible to organize the communication that takes place between the different services.

Poor organization of this communication could severely damage the reuse of the services as well as increasing integration and maintenance costs. At the stage of cosmetic SOA this risk already exists but does not pose as a serious threat due to the fact that at this stage there are a limited number of services. With cosmetic SOA IT specialists only work with enterprise business services, simply because the different categories of services which are implemented later are available at the stage of overhaul SOA.

It is at the stage of overhaul SOA that the number of services will increase because IT specialists try to improve the reuse and agility of the information system within the enterprise business services. It is not necessary to re-create what already exists in today's information systems and what is also known as the "spaghetti system" effect. The lack of architecture in overhaul SOA could even lead to the creation of several networks of services because there would be more services than modules within the ancient information systems. This problem could be called the "risotto of services". The chances of the services coupling with one another are greater than would be the case in a modular approach. It is therefore necessary to orchestrate the services to organize the communication that occurs between them, and to ensure that there is a sufficient level of loose coupling between the services.

A service has to be reusable without being too closely connected to the other services that are associated with it. The service must be sufficiently autonomous. If a service code anticipates that there will be multiple communications made to other services then the reuse of a service requires that a large part of the information system must be used. It is similar to having a word processing package, which installs a large number of functions that users do not need whenever they want to use it. The more complex the communications that exist between the services, the more difficult it is to carry out maintenance and integration tests. The programmer will have problems in terms of monitoring the development and evolution of the communication. On the other hand, the concept of orchestration makes it possible to design and develop a logical architecture that is more ergonomic as far as the exchanges that take place between different services are concerned. If this architecture is accompanied by the use of suitable equipment, it will be possible for the programmer to use efficient debugging tools for debugging exchanges that occur between the services.

In this chapter we will see that orchestration is a concept that takes place on many levels, not only on the traditional BPM level. We will also see that orchestration must also be used in the lower layers of the system. The principles of orchestration are executed from the highest level of the information system (organizational processes) through to the lowest level (connections between the elementary services).

6.1. Multiple requirements in orchestration

6.1.1. *Orchestration and SOA maturity levels*

The use of director modules to manage other processes is not unknown. This is frequently the case in mainframe environments which are made up of transactional monitors. Orchestration is similar to the idea of the director module which links processes together from a formal description. This description can take the form of a model or of parameter defining tables. Why has orchestration come back to the fore today? New problems which are linked to cosmetic SOA and to overhaul SOA will be presented in this section respectively.

6.1.1.1. *Orchestration and cosmetic SOA*

The organization of cosmetic SOA does not require much effort as far as the orchestration of services is concerned. At this level it is only possible to link enterprise business services with one another and it is impossible to work inside these services. Even though orchestration does not play such an important role at the level of cosmetic SOA, it is still best to avoid implementing this idea of orchestration in a fixed manner. It is best to use a more powerful infrastructure. The use of a more powerful infrastructure means that it is possible to adapt the tools used in cosmetic SOA to the next level of SOA, i.e. overhaul SOA. It is therefore also possible to use a workflow, a BPM application or an orchestration which can be found in an ESB, etc. It is also possible to use an orchestrator as far as the screens of workstations are concerned because from the level of cosmetic SOA upwards, the aim is to construct reusable graphical components.

6.1.1.2. *Orchestration and overhaul SOA*

The transition to overhaul SOA means that an increased effort is required when it comes to the orchestration of services. At this level it is possible to work inside the enterprise business services with the aim of constructing new services that will be highly reusable in different contexts. These services are linked to categories; these categories make it possible to separate any problems that are associated with the organization and with the business. It is here that the process of orchestration comes into force in a different way than other approaches used in the past.

The main difference is the extended use of orchestration. It is no longer a question of managing connections that exist between the different process at the higher levels of the architecture, which was sufficient for modular approaches and also for cosmetic SOA. With overhaul SOA, the connections that exist between programs are in fact sequences of services. There are many more services than modules. Orchestration takes place in several levels of SOA, from managing the links that exist between the different screens, and the links that exist between the different organizational processes through to the lower levels of the architecture, which deal with the management of the sequences of elementary services. Orchestration therefore becomes a concept that can be used on all levels of an information system's architecture. The concept of orchestration can possess the same properties but may appear in different forms depending on the level of the architecture in question.

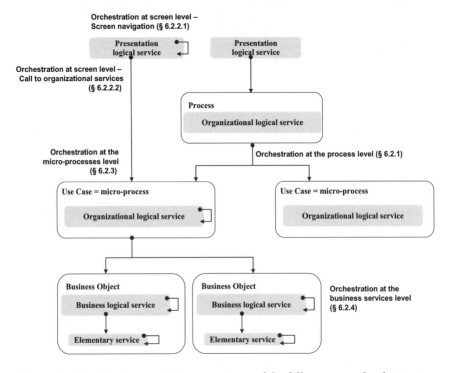

Figure 6.1. *The links that exist between services and the different types of orchestration*

Modern technology has tried to make software programs out of these orchestrations with the aim of making the work of developers much easier, for example the creation of Business Process Management (BPM) solutions, which are used for both workflow and the sequencing of services. To illustrate the fact that orchestration can be used on all levels of an information system's architecture, we only need to have a look at Figure 5.1, which shows the links that exist between different service categories. Figure 6.1 is a copy of Figure 5.1, but this time the orchestration that is suitable for each level of the information system's architecture has been added.

Orchestration does not lead to the creation of new service categories. Existing services will absorb the functions of orchestration. Each service will possess specific characteristics; these characteristics depend on the level at which the services are found within the architecture. For example, an organizational service which possesses an organizational process is able to benefit from workflows, while an organizational service which possesses a use case only needs a BPM application software because the workflow functions, such as the to do list, are not necessary. New service categories are not created.

A description of each of the levels of orchestration will be given later in this chapter.

6.1.2. *Functional requirements*

One of the objectives of SOA is the rapid creation of enterprise business services with the aim of producing new processes. To achieve this, it is necessary to possess flexible composition processes and it is also necessary to manage the variations of a service depending on the process in which the service occurs. For example, a product purchasing service accepts single orders when it is used by clients from small and medium sized companies. However, the same service will accept group orders if the service is used by clients from large companies. It is the same service and not a duplication of the software. However, the way in which the service functions are parameterized depends on the context in which the service is used. If software development is needed to take new service variants into consideration, then the rapid creation of new processes is no longer possible. It must be possible to configure each service through a simple redefinition of its parameters, which means that it is not necessary to carry out any software development.

If the composition of the services is managed in an inflexible manner, through using a traditional development tool, the agility of the services becomes insufficient. As a result, there is a risk that SOA will become inflexible since each new process that is created requires the systematic intervention of IT specialists. Written specifications of new processes can lead to maintenance problems because the documentation is not always up to date when the software is being modified.

Orchestration tools are introduced with the aim of improving the agility of the information system as well as improving the information system's alignment with functional needs. These tools force the formal modeling of the links that exist between services. In addition, the tools reduce the number of IT developments that take place within the information system; they also facilitate integration tests (debugging tools for debugging exchanges which occur between the services) and they improve the strength of the system's execution thanks to the use of specialized software engines.

Orchestration occurs at several levels within the architecture of an information system. It begins at the highest level, with the orchestration of organizational processes which can be seen by the users (workflow), as well as the orchestration of overhaul SOA through to the lowest level with the orchestration of elementary services which are only understood by the IT specialists. For the levels that can be seen by the users, the aim of SOA is to provide the users with an ergonomic service composition tool that is easy to use. This tool enables users to create new processes. These processes are then executed automatically by an orchestration engine. The use of this engine removes the stages of software development that were once carried out by IT specialists. This idea has been highlighted by the editors of BPM software.

However, in practice this rather appealing idea is not as easy to make a reality. The intervention of IT specialists is often necessary when it comes to helping the users model the processes. Despite the high quality of the BPM tool, it is still necessary to know how to model the processes. For example, the simple modeling of how a process normally functions is insufficient. It is necessary to be able to model the less predictable situations that may occur and may lead to the creation of errors, which makes designing the processes a more complicated task. Functional test cases must also be specified. Functional test cases make it possible to demonstrate the correct way in which a process functions when it is used both normally and in cases with errors. The design and development of tests also makes the work of the user more complicated and the use of IT is therefore necessary. Technical integration work cannot be avoided to control the proper execution of existing services within new processes. It is at this stage that the ability to define the parameters of a service proves to be important, with the aim of being able to adapt the way in which a service functions depending on the needs of each process. If the way in which a service functions is fixed within a software program that does not anticipate the agility of an information system, then any modification request made by a service (for the needs associated with new compositions) will require maintenance to be carried out on the software.

Other properties that BPM has to offer have also turned out to be important, even if they have not always been pointed out by editors:

– The formal representation of processes through the use of composition models increases the quality of communication that takes place between the users and the IT specialists.

– Models favor the exhaustive design and development of functional needs. They also reduce specification ambiguities which exist and which are shared by both the functional and IT teams. The ability to model and use suitable methodological procedures is essential for creating high-quality specifications (see the chapter devoted to enterprise architecture).

– Since the composition of services requires less specific developments, the user is able to execute the orchestration of such services more quickly than ever before. An iterative approach can therefore be considered with the aim of creating the target process in phases.

– The orchestration engine takes responsibility for the automatic execution of processes and provides value added functions such as debugging, logging, supervision (with the release of alerts in the case of an anomalous execution), metrology, simulation and the generic processing of errors. The integration work of the software benefits from these functions, which are often missing during any specific development. As a consequence, integration costs will decrease.

6.1.3. *Technical requirements*

6.1.3.1. *The links that exist between services*

Services are connected thanks to the use of business rules, which determine the routes that need be followed when it comes to sequencing the services. For example, different services will be used after the risk calculation of a particular file. The services that will be used depend on the client and on the risk level. So that orchestrations maintain a high level of agility, it is useful to implement these rules in a declarative manner within a business rules management system. Any implementation of the rules that relies only on the use of a traditional programming language such as Java or COBOL runs the risk of making the orchestration of the services inflexible. It is therefore necessary that the orchestration tool is able to communicate with a business rules engine. When the links between the services are being modeled it should then be possible to declare new rules in the most ergonomic way possible.

The rules are declared and then executed from data that forms what is known as an information context. This information context can be used throughout the duration of the orchestration's life: this is known as data context.

6.1.3.2. *Data context*

Among the many properties that exist within the SOA approach, we have only dealt with the execution of stateless services. The execution of stateless services favors the reuse of services since the services do not retain any data that is exchanged between any two executions of the service. The services only need to receive an input message, to execute the process (pre-conditions, body and post-conditions) and to send back an output message. However, the execution of a real system with links between services that work on the same information (for example a customer file) means that some sort of logic which compensates for the stateless architecture must be defined. This logic must be capable of retaining certain responses from services so that they can be recycled in the input messages of the services that will be used afterwards. This principle of conservation is dealt with by orchestrating the services and it corresponds to context management. The context brings together the flow of data that is to be retained for when the services are used.

The context has a lifespan that is limited to the execution of one orchestration, or on a larger scale this would extend to one user session in which several orchestrations are executed. The integrity of the saved data within the context must be ensured. This is particularly important in cases where several services, which are linked together, update the database within the same transaction. In the case of failure of one of the updates, the system must continue to provide the context in a coherent state: this is known as transaction management.

6.1.3.3. *Transaction management*

Remember that a transaction groups together actions whose creation corresponds to only one work unit: either all of the actions take place as normal, or the group of actions is cancelled. It is the concept of orchestration which possesses the data context and which possesses knowledge relating to the services that have been launched in a particular transaction. This means that the beginning of the transaction (begin), its validation (commit) or cancellation (rollback) can all be found in the service to which orchestration has been applied. Consequently, the sequenced services ignore the fact that the transaction, which is managed at a superior level (i.e. where orchestration is taking place), exists. The sequenced services can be reused in many different transactional contexts. In certain cases there will be some overlapping of transactions when the orchestrations (which are originally separate from one another) are being gathered together. In this case, the principle of master–slave transactions must be adopted.

To avoid problems linked with transactions that have been launched and that are open, all the data updates which take place on the persistent data supports (databases, files, etc.) must be carried out without any interruption. Starting a transaction on one screen and then letting the user continue the dialogue and validate the transaction on another screen is not recommended. In this case, the transaction which has been started on the first screen will remain open until the user validates the next screen, which is a tiring process, especially if a validation that is expected to take place does not happen (unstable state of the system).

The updates must be used to their maximum potential. This can be achieved by forcing the set of orders, which activate the persistence of the data, to be under the responsibility of the final service that is used within a transaction. This final service must have links with the other services that are used within the same transaction. This service receives an input message from the orchestration function. This input message contains the set of context data that is used to carry out controls and updates on the persistent data supports (it could be said that it is a sort of transactional flow). If all the controls and updates take place as normal, then the service will send back a positive result to the orchestration, which in turn will validate (or commit) the transaction. If this is not the case, then an exception is sent back to the orchestration, which will result in the transaction being cancelled (rolled back). This means that the updates will not be spread out over several services. It is better if the majority of services work with the data context and that the other, more specialized services (although fewer in number) are responsible for the updates that take place on the persistent data supports.

It is necessary to install software that manages data synchronization for longer transactions that interrupt the information system for a period of several days. The function of orchestration can also take responsibility for a part of this logic, for example by exploiting the objects that set off the transaction. Whenever the updates of one transaction concern several of the persistent data supports, it is possible to consider using distributed transaction management (two-phase commit) with standards such as X/Open XA, which are available in certain databases. However, the technical management of the XA standard remains a complicated process and functional distributed transaction management is often preferred.

6.1.4. *Enterprise architecture requirements*

SOA relies on the property of loose coupling. This property is important since it favors the reuse of services. It also conditions the way in which the services are linked together. Loose coupling prevents services that are located in the same level of the information system's architecture from using one another. On the other hand, strong coupling links the services together, which in turn reduces the capacity of being able to reuse the services autonomously. A service that is being reused is made up of all of the services that it relies on so that it can be reused.

A system that is highly coupled can quickly cause confusion as far as communication between the different services is concerned. This in turn makes it almost impossible to reuse the services and it also increases maintenance and integration costs: programmers are faced with a complete Web of services that they must work with ("spaghetti system" of services). This problem is also noticed throughout poor object-oriented developments. There are often a lot of objects and if they communicate with one another without any isolation rules (i.e. if they are highly coupled), a system with multiple interactions, a system which decreases readability, which weakens maintenance as well as reducing the reusability of services is created.

In SOA it is possible to correct this issue thanks to the concept of loose coupling. Since services which belong to the same level of an information system's architecture are unable to communicate with one another, sequencing these services becomes possible in a service that can be found at the next level up in the architecture. This service then takes on the role of orchestrator. For example, business services are loosely coupled because they are located on the same level of the information system's architecture, i.e. the business level. The services from the next level up in the architecture – in other words, the organizational services – take responsibility for the orchestration of the business services. Thanks to loose coupling the reuse of a particular business service does not mean that other business services that are linked to it will be reused.

Only keeping one communication mode for orchestration runs the risk of unnecessarily complicating the information system. In certain situations it is much simpler to let a service communicate directly with another service rather than having to use a third, intermediary service which takes on the role of orchestrator. If the perimeters of the services are well defined, it is possible for the services to communicate directly with one another. These perimeters form logical components whose cohesion is so strong that internal communication does not need to be raised in an orchestration function. However, communication between each of these components is forbidden, with the aim of favoring the use of an orchestration function that can be found on a level that is above the component in question.

6.2. The levels of orchestration

In the previous section we saw that orchestration includes multiple sequencing functions as well as the processes of context and transaction management. Orchestration can be seen by users when it is applied to the functional level of an information system's architecture. The concept of orchestration becomes rather technical when it comes to sequencing the services that are located deep within the information system. Orchestration is therefore a concept that can be applied to all levels of the information system's architecture, and it is not possible to use the concept of orchestration as a general purpose process. It is therefore necessary to decide on the best orchestration method to be used at each level of the information system's architecture.

6.2.1. *Orchestration at the process level*

The process manages the orchestration that takes place between several services. It is a question of linking several use cases together. Remember that a use case corresponds to a micro-process that specifies the interactions between the user of a system and the system. Each interaction has the same duration. Processes act above the level of micro-processes with the aim of linking the micro-processes together, as stated by the rules. For example, the execution of a micro-process that deals with the inputs of orders would let other users know that a micro-process that deals with manufacturing orders needs to be processed.

Known as BPM nowadays, this orchestration is managed by workflow solutions. To avoid any confusion between this BPM and the one that works on the other levels of the information system's architecture, it is identified by the term "Human-Oriented BPM". This BPM relies on "to do lists" for the different notifications that are sent between actors. Companies need to adopt advanced management functions such as the control of maximum deadlines for the processing of a task, the delegation of tasks and the management of availability calendars, etc. "Human-Oriented BPM" are capable of dealing with the sequencing of services over long periods, which arise during temporal breakdowns of the information system. These BPM therefore manage a persistent context of the set of processes that are executed as well as managing the data that is associated with these processes.

It would be interesting to add other functions to the concept of orchestration (which is located at the highest level of the architectural model) so that it could be used by users of the information system. It would be particularly interesting to add the function of metrology to the concept of orchestration to monitor a company's activities. Metrology is a function that was identified by the concept of Business Activity Monitoring (BAM). It would also be important to add the simulation function, which simulates the execution of a process with the aim of predicting how an organization will function based on parameters which act on the level of process requests, and based on the availability of other key factors within the information system.

When it comes to modeling the processes, organizational process design is used. This is achieved by using the Business Process Modeling Notation (BPMN) or UML in the form of an activity diagram. Competition between these two standard notations should disappear in the future because the Object Management Group (OMG), the provider of UML, has integrated BPMN within the services that it offers. This joining together is good news because BPMN only covers upstream modeling (the expression of needs) while UML deals with downstream software implementation. To rationalize project costs, it is better to use just one notation on all the phases of the software production cycle. It would be expensive to create a set of processes that are formalized in BPMN and then have to translate them into UML when it comes to moving on to the stages of logical design and software development.

On a technical note, several XML standards exist which can be used for managing the processes. Two are of particular interest: XPDL and BPEL4People. These XML languages are still relatively new. BPEL4People is a special case because it aims at extending the BPEL standard, which is more advanced but is limited to orchestrations which exist at the lower level in the information system's architecture (BPM applications). What makes these standards interesting is that processes can be executed from different orchestration engines. This mobility, based on XML, should also allow companies to display some of their processes outside their own information system in a non-intrusive manner for those users who use the companies' processes.

6.2.2. *Orchestration at screen level*

6.2.2.1. *Navigation*

After a screen has been validated, the display system must know what screen is to be presented to the user next. This information is transmitted to the display system through the use of a service, because the choice of the next screen to be presented to users depends on management rules that are located outside the layer that manages presentation. The principle of layered isolation insures that these rules, which are integrated in services, are reusable when they are used in different contexts on different screens. Navigation at this level is a simple process. It must remain basic and must not require any effort to be made in terms of modeling or in terms of using any specialized equipment. Choosing to use a specific program at this level is acceptable.

6.2.2.2. *Call to organizational services*

From just one action carried out by the user on the screen – for example, making a selection from a customer list – the screen layer has to use one or several organizational services which manage the requested use case (in this case the selection of a customer). At this stage we are no longer at the level of orchestration in a micro-process, but beyond this level where the screens meet the use case.

Depending on the result that is sent back by the organizational services, this orchestration could link other services together before giving control back to the superior level of the navigation, i.e. the screen display. For example, selecting a particular customer from the database might require certain parts of the screen, such as the summary report of a customer service representative who dealt with the customer in question, to be refreshed. This level of orchestration also manages the data context which exists throughout the duration of a user's work session with the aim of conserving information from one screen to another. Remember that one of the properties of SOA is the execution of stateless services. If the navigation between screens does not provide a tool for storing information, the user will have to re-enter all the data on each screen.

It is important to limit the concept of orchestration that has been mentioned in this section to the management of human–machine dialogue only. All of the organization's rules which are unchangeable vis-à-vis the choices made in relation to the sequencing of the screens are found in the level after orchestration, i.e. the management of micro-processes. This strict isolation which concerns problems linked to the ergonomics of the screens and to the management of the organization is important because it allows for the complete overhaul of the ergonomics of the screens without impacting the orchestration of the micro-processes. For example, it is possible to create orchestrations between different specialized screens through using different access channels (such as the Internet, a fixed workstation, mobile tools, etc.) by reusing the same orchestrations at the micro-process level.

As for modeling the screens, activity diagrams in UML are still used as well as finite state automatons. On a technical note, the XML BPEL standard is used. The XML BPEL language is automatically generated from the models that were mentioned at the beginning of this paragraph.

6.2.3. *Orchestration at the micro-process level (use cases)*

Each micro-process manages the sequencing of services, which makes it possible to execute only parts of the use case. At this level sequencing is independent of the choice of ergonomics. The services that are sequenced come from the services that are found at the organizational level. A model in the form of a finite state automaton is used. This model insures that the conditions, which activate the services, function in relation to the state of progress of the use case.

This modeling allows for the automatic generation of the automaton, which is written in XML BPEL or in a computer language such as Java. At this level it is possible to find BPM application technologies which (unlike workflows) do not need functions such as to do lists or group work management solutions (delegation of tasks, calendar management, etc.). Remember that the micro-process manages the interactions of only one user who uses the system: there is therefore no reason to be concerned about functions related to group work. Functions related to group work are dealt with at the next level up, i.e. the process level.

So that each organizational service can fulfill its potential, each of the organizational services communicates with the level located directly above it in the architectural model, i.e. the organizational services communicate with the business services. For this to happen, a more linear style of modeling is used in the form of an activity diagram or a sequence, rather than using a finite state automaton. The use of BPEL technology at this level is debatable. At this level the sequencing of the services looks more like a combination of different services. It is therefore possible to consider the use of a standard such as Service Component Architecture (SCA) which makes the BPEL standard more complete.

TECHNICAL NOTE: BPEL AND SCA

BPEL (*Business Process Execution Language*) is an XML schema language that makes it possible to define an orchestration of services. The use of XML offers interoperability but it can pose problems in relation to the execution of services if it is used at a level that is too deep within the information system.

SCA (*Service Component Architecture*) is a standard that does not force the use of XML. SCA makes it possible to define communication sequences that take place between the services. Since SCA is not dependent on XML the communication sequences can be executed in native mode in the programming language that is used; all this is possible without a decrease in the performance of the services.

BPEL and SCA complement one another: BPEL is used to manage the orchestrations which can be found at the highest level of the architecture with the maximum level of interoperability possible; SCA completes this orchestration by standardizing the collection of services at a more detailed level within the architecture.

6.2.4. *Orchestration at the business service level*

The business services are used by the organizational services and are also used by other business services, while respecting the rules of coupling that are specified by the logical architecture (see the chapter devoted to enterprise architecture). A simple modeling process is used; this process is similar to the one described for the organizational services, i.e. using an activity diagram or a sequence. The use of BPEL becomes incompatible with connections that exist between the services at this level.

6.2.5. *Orchestration between domains through the use of ESB*

Let us take an example to illustrate orchestration that exists between different domains. An information system is made up of three domains: customer, product and order. The order domain is dealt with in overhaul SOA with the use of the programming language Java. The order domain also organizes the set of orchestration levels that have been described in the earlier sections of this chapter. The other two domains are an old MVS system and another more recent AS400 that is equipped with a software package. Orchestration between the domains will manage the set of exchanges that takes place between the customer, product and order domains. In other words, it will manage exchanges that take place between three different platforms, notably Java, MVS and AS400. This orchestration is an integration of remote and heterogenous systems, and is located at the heart of the Enterprise Service Bus (ESB) platform. ESB is a software solution that specializes in exchange management. The concept of ESB will be dealt with in more detail in the chapter devoted to the interconnection of systems and the common language.

Orchestration between different domains offers advanced functions for controlling flows of data within the context of distributed systems. Orchestration ensures that exchanges between domains are not lost regardless of the remote locations of those participating in the exchanges. Modeling inter-domain orchestration is a complex process due to the fact that errors, which could occur during the long-distance exchanges, must be taken into consideration. Orchestration between domains groups together the functional and technical demands which the production teams have to work on. Modeling inter-domain orchestration involves the intervention of functional specialists and production teams. Studies also need to be carried out in this field to improve the modeling process.

On a technical note, the BPEL standard is used even more so in orchestration between different domains due to the fact that interactions between the different domains should be executed in XML with the aim of favoring interoperability. As is the case in other areas in which BPEL is used, the automatic generation of the XML schema language must be provided for. This can be achieved through the use of models such as activity diagrams or finite state automatons.

6.2.6. *The orchestration of batches*

Batch processing abides by the rules of SOA. In certain cases controlling the performances of the batches leads to a denormalization of SOA. In all cases the sequencing of batch processing comes back to the idea of managing an orchestration that is generally implemented by a tool that specializes in the organization of batches. This organizer accepts modifications that are made to the sequencing of the batches in relation to the needs of the production teams who will be using them. Depending on the resource systems which are available, it should be possible to carry out the following tasks: change the level of parallelism of certain processes; execute one process before another; stop the execution of a process if it means that it benefits another process; re-launch the execution of a process which has been placed on hold; as well as automatically recycling errors. It should be possible to carry out all of these tasks while maintaining the integrity of the information system. For example, it is possible to calculate the premiums of several thousand insurance files by organizing and processing the files by region, town, organization, etc. It is best to let production teams be responsible for the orchestration of the batches. This is because the production teams are capable of making the right decisions, as far as the correct orchestration of the batches is concerned, in relation to the resource systems that are available to them.

So that this flexibility is effective, it is necessary that the transaction management strategy that is used is not fixed within the service programs. It should be possible to adapt the transaction management strategy through a simple redefinition of its parameters. For example, the transaction is managed at either departmental or regional level for each file from a fixed number of files. It should be possible to organize and process the files from any location, and it is the work of the production teams to make sure that this is possible, without having to modify any software. If the software is modified the batch chains will become inflexible and it will no longer be possible to consider the way in which they function during the launch of transactional processing. None of the orders, i.e. begin, commit and rollback, will be part of the programs which favor parameter management, which is a management solution that does not interfere with the code of the services (see Chapter 10).

The dynamic adaptation of batch chains by the production teams requires the use of an orchestration engine which can be found within job scheduler. Today, the use of the XML BPEL standard to manage this type of process does not seem relevant. Production teams have been successfully using job scheduler for a long time now and for the moment there does not seem to be any reason which would justify moving towards the use of the XML standard.

When it comes to modeling batch orchestration, it is necessary to use a formal design of the batch processes, in accordance with processes that are also shared by the SOA approach. Diagram activities and UML finite automatons are used. This sharing of processes favors the integration of the development and design of batch processing within SOA.

6.3. The techniques of orchestration

In this section the different techniques that are used to implement orchestration will be presented. These different techniques include the BPM engine, the business rules engine as well as specific programming. In this section the batch scheduler will not be mentioned since it relies on specific equipment that is well known by the production teams.

6.3.1. *The BPM engine*

With BPM the sequencing of services respects a model that shows the pre-defined evolution of the services in the form of alternative services and iterations of services. This mode of functioning is also applied to both Human-Oriented BPM (workflows) and application BPM, the latter works on the sequencing of services without the intervention of users of the services.

BPM is a determinist approach which states that the sequences of services must be modeled. This modeling of the services is fixed and can have a somewhat negative effect on the information system if the orchestration itself has a significant number of variations: how is it possible to model several hundreds or thousands of possible links that exist between services? In these extreme cases BPM does not meet the demands of orchestration. It would be better to consider the use of a business rules engine (see section 6.3.2).

When BPM remains a possible solution, it means that the sequencing of services does not lead to the creation of a large number of service variants (there are undoubtedly fewer than 100 variants of the services). In this case, the agility of BPM can be increased thanks to the use of a business rules engine so that the sequences are not coded in a fixed manner in a programming language. Master Data Management (MDM) can also be added to the BPM with the aim of being able to work on the way in which orchestration functions at this level. For example, if it is possible to configure the version of the sequenced services depending on the context in which the orchestration is executed. The same definition of an orchestration will link different services together depending on whether the orchestration is being executed for a partner, a subsidiary or the company; in other words, different variants of services are applied to the same original orchestration.

Without these devices which improve agility there is the risk of having to model as many orchestrations as there are variants, or there is also the risk of having to integrate the variant tests within the orchestration model itself. In this case BPM does not work to its maximum potential in terms of agility. Every time a new variant of a service has to be taken into consideration BPM must be used; this task is carried out by IT specialists.

6.3.2. *The business rules engine*

With the business rules engine, determining the services that need to be sequenced does not depend on pre-defined algorithmic structures, but does, however, depend on rules that are executed at random within the business rules engine. It is therefore no longer necessary to model all the possible cases of the sequencing of services, as is the case with BPM. This is an important asset when there are a significant number of variations of the sequences. On the other hand, there is also the risk of no longer having a deterministic view of the sequences of services. Furthermore, if there are a large number of rule tests then it is difficult to guarantee that they are going to be used correctly. Some Business Rules Management Systems (BRMS) make it possible to organize a flow of execution between the different sets of rules. Once again BPM technology is used but this time it is integrated within the business rules engine itself.

To increase the level of agility it is possible to link MDM with a business rules engine with the aim of managing the parameters and the master data which are manipulated by the rules. The rules are not required to test the master values in a fixed manner. The rules need to manipulate the variables through the use of MDM.

The business rules engine generally functions on the basis of a stateless architecture, unlike BPM. Consequently, if the orchestration has to maintain a data context between several communications which have taken place between different services then using the business rules engine on its own is insufficient. The designer of the architecture will have to provide another mechanism that makes it possible to store the data context, such as http sessions or stateful objects.

6.3.3. Specific programming

If BPM and the business rules engine are not used, it is still possible to implement orchestration through the use of programming languages such as Java or C##. However, it is better to limit this manual programming to orchestrations that take place at the lower levels of the architectural model, i.e. orchestrations that concern the technical sequencing of the services. This method of implementing orchestration does not favor communication between users;

neither does it favor the use of an iterative cycle which helps to set up the orchestrations.

To ensure that the software is stronger and more agile it is best to use automatic code generators such as Java, C## or COBOL. These automatic code generators function based on the formal modeling of the orchestration, and in particular modeling in UML.

6.4. Towards the homogenization of orchestration

6.4.1. *Unified modeling*

We have seen that orchestration is a concept which can be found at many different levels within the architecture of the information system. All of these levels are linked to one another from the highest level (the level of organizational processes) to the most basic level (the technical sequencing of the services). To avoid any breakdown that might occur between the different levels, it is best to use the same notation for the entire set of orchestrations. The unification of models, from the upper level of the production cycle (such as the sequencing of screens, processes, etc.) to the lower level (the sequencing of business services), improves the rationalization of costs. This is because whenever the different models (in other words those used in orchestration) are unified, it is no longer necessary to modify the models when changing from one system of notation to another. This approach of unified modeling enforces the use of UML, since it is the only notation that is capable of working on all levels of an information system's architecture.

UML notation is often seen as being reserved for use only by IT specialists. If people believe that UML is only for the use of IT specialists, there is a risk that it will not be used in upstream modeling which is carried out by the functional teams. The fact that people believe this shows that there is a significant lack of know-how as far as modeling is concerned on behalf of both users and IT specialists. The IT specialists start to work on the technical side of the information system too quickly. The UML models that are created possess technical capabilities that prove useful as far as software is concerned, however, they are not considered as being useful for communicating with the functional teams. The UML notation that is used in upstream modeling changes depending on the technique of orchestration that is used in the architecture of the information system. This therefore makes it impossible for the functional teams to be able to read the notation. It is not the notation that is at issue, but rather the way in which it is used.

It is undoubtedly because of this that the Business Process Modeling Notation (BPMN) was developed to complement UML with the aim of providing a business representation of the processes. Since BPMN demands action on an exclusively functional level, IT specialists are unable to interfere with it in any way so that they can add their technical requirements to it. Users see BPMN as a better performing notation than UML for modeling processes. Once again this is believed to be true because of the poor use of UML by IT specialists.

There are, however, disadvantages to using a combined BPMN/UML notation. The transition from a diagram of a BPMN process to its representation as a UML activity diagram leads to additional translation costs as well as creating unnecessary complications in the modeling process. It is not possible to use finite state automatons in the modeling process if BPMN notation is used. It is also not possible to add business objects, which are manipulated by the process, to BPMN, which limits possibilities for modeling. UML, on the other hand, is able to offer all of this. With UML, if it is used correctly, it is possible to design process models at the functional level and then transform these models into other UML models which would be of use to the IT specialists. The continuity of the notation that is used preserves all the upstream work which has been carried out, as well as rationalizing production costs and model updates during maintenance phases which take place on the architecture of the information system.

Using the same notation also makes it possible to enhance the models by adding to them descriptions of the objects that are manipulated during the development of each individual stage of the process. All that needs to be done during the construction of an activity diagram is to take the necessary objects from within the UML class model. The link that exists between the process and the data is established immediately due to the fact that the notation being used is the same.

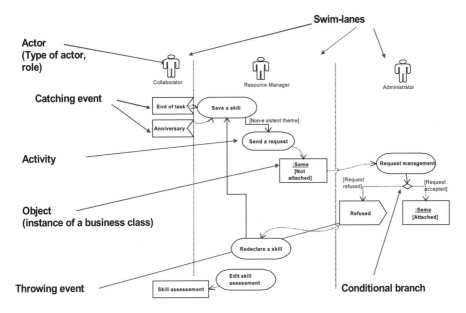

Figure 6.2. *UML modeling of an organizational process*

6.4.2. *Unified standard*

The techniques used in orchestration are not yet homogenous. Even if the XML BPEL standard is increasingly being used within orchestration, there is still progress to be made; for example, it cannot be used on all of levels of the information system's architecture. Let us take the example of a real overhaul SOA project that was composed of 1,500 services. It was noticed that among these 1,500 services, 400 were at screen level, 300 at organizational level, there were 700 business services and 100 inter-domain services, which were located within the ESB. In this system there are a lot of orchestration functions, indeed there are several hundred of them. These functions are divided into the four different technology groups that are used to implement orchestration: functions between screens (carried out by page sequencing technology), functions from screens to organizational services (carried out by BPEL technology), functions between organizational services as well as from the organizational services to business services (carried out by workflow and Java technology), functions between business services (carried out by Java technology), as well as the functions of inter-domain services (carried out by BPEL technology). Each of these different types of technology is accompanied by specific equipment that is used to help debug software. Whenever programmers carry out thorough tests on all levels of the information system's architecture they often have to deal with technological breakdowns, which unnecessarily complicate the work that they are doing. The production teams are also affected by these breakdowns since the monitoring of the different processes is only partly integrated within the architecture.

Even if there were a type of architecture that could be used to create all the orchestrations in Java (from simple UML models), it would be more than likely that the help tools that are used to facilitate the integration and administration of the orchestrations would be unable to do so. Once the Java code has been generated, only Java tools become available to work with and these tools do not focus enough on the debugging of orchestrations. Over the next few years IT specialists are still going to have to deal with multiple standards which are used in orchestration:

– Orchestration on a process level relies on the use of workflow technology that generally dates from the 1990s. Standardization, in the future, could rely on the use of the XML BPEL for People (BPEL4People) standard which involves the addition of a to do list to the BPEL standard. However, BPEL remains an unstable standard, and a few years still remain until the workflow functions will be taken into consideration.

– The XML BPEL standard can be found on many levels of the architecture, such as communication made to organizational services by the screens, the orchestration of micro-processes and inter-domain orchestration (ESB). The use of BPEL for orchestration at the business service level is too weak for XML to be of any relevance, particularly in terms of execution performance. Certain new and therefore unknown aspects of BPEL can create problems when it comes to the implementation of orchestrations. These problems include a lack of sub-process management in the initial version of the standard, an absence of standardization for integrating the orchestrations within business rules engines, and the instability of context management and transaction management standards that are used by BPEL.

– The orchestration of business services is, today, carried out within current programming languages such as Java, C## or COBOL. The new Service Component Architecture (SCA) standard should provide a solution to this issue for this particular level of orchestration.

As always, and to protect the information system from the evolutions that the standards will experience, the use of model-oriented design is required. The software will be automatically created from the models (activity diagrams and finite state automatons), either in the form of BPEL language or another programming language. In relation to the evolution of BPEL and the standards in general, it is possible to change the ways in which the software is created without having any effect on the models themselves.

6.5. The benefits of orchestration

6.5.1. *Advantages*

The concept of orchestration, as well as the tools used in orchestration, is proving vital since it is necessary to rationalize the communications that take place between the services. Without any formal orchestration, communications between services would remain fixed within the programs and this would decrease the chances of being able to reuse the services effectively. Orchestration is more than an opportunity; it is an obligatory part of SOA. Orchestration requires the use of model-oriented design, which makes it possible to formally specify the sequences of services found at different levels of the architecture. Modeling is required, even before the use of XML standards such as BPEL. Modeling is seen as an opportunity to renovate the information system. As soon as the models have been designed and people know how to use them, the costs for designing new compositions of services decrease because the models themselves are less ambiguous than any written specification.

The technical implementation of the orchestrations is more economical and more robust since the execution code of the orchestrations is automatically generated. For example, the code is generated in XML with the use of BPEL. The associated debugging tools also reduce integration costs. In terms of production, the monitoring of how processes function makes it possible to benefit from the following tools: the availability of different monitoring functions and an increase in alerts made by the system in the case of an anomalous execution. Production teams are therefore also interested in using orchestration.

6.5.2. *Disadvantages*

BPM type orchestration tools are still too technical to be used by everyone. If they are used, the assistance of IT specialists is required. To achieve a high level of functional agility, it is necessary to integrate BPM to the tools that belong to the business rules engine and to MDM. This type of integration is uncommon and the editors of BPM have work to carry out and information to provide on this subject. They have to carry out this work while respecting the standards that are in place. This will sometimes involve using the BPEL standard, which reduces interoperability.

The idea of a composition of services left in the hands of the users is not a reality within projects that are undertaken to progressively overhaul a company's information system. In practice, the following needs to take place: the rules for calculating routes must be specified, there must be a transition from functional and technical parameters to functional and technical services whose interfaces need to be modified, there must be error management, and test plans need to be written, etc. In other words, there is a lot of integration work involved and this work can quickly turn out to be rather complicated and uninteresting for the users.

Part III

The Need for an Enterprise Method

Chapter 7

The Discovery of Services
(Reference Framework and Urbanization)

A RECAP OF IDEAS MENTIONED IN PREVIOUS CHAPTERS

– Traditional urbanization is used in the information system in the form of functional domains. These functional domains do not reduce the redundancy of the information system, nor do they favor the reuse of operations.

– The business object approach is used in the information system in the form of non-redundant object domains in which reusable operations can be found.

NEW IDEAS PRESENTED IN THIS CHAPTER

– Reference frameworks.

– Expansive and progressive information systems.

– The wide range of competences that IT specialists possess.

– The benefits and limits of urbanization.

We are now going to deal with the question: how is it possible to locate the services? It is at this stage that the majority of SOA projects run into problems due to a considerable lack of methods.

Two different characteristics have been noticed:

– IT specialists design the services from traditional functional specifications. SOA therefore remains a process that is linked to software engineering and has nothing to do with the business. There is little chance of getting the functional teams involved in designing the services,

– The users specify the services they need in a similar way to how the traditional functional specifications would specify them. Only the vocabulary that is used changes: the term "function" is replaced by the term "service". This is what is happening at the moment, and SOA is reduced to a simple technical infrastructure.

To discover the correct services – in other words those that are relevant to a company – the company's needs must be modeled. This seems obvious. However, it is very often forgotten. Services are not created spontaneously. It does not make sense to deal with the issues of categories of services and the granularity of services if a company's needs have not been modeled. This modeling process has nothing to do with the SOA approach. However, this modeling process should guarantee the discovery of the correct services. Enterprise methodology is therefore required, which is not only limited to the development of the services.

This architecture should take into consideration the many different skills and expertise required to construct information systems based on the new requirements of flexibility and with the modern technology that is available nowadays. The definition of such architecture proves to be quite a challenge and we will see that existing approaches must be further developed to provide such a definition.

This chapter does not provide the solutions for designing services. These solutions will be explained in the chapter devoted to modeling with the Praxeme method. In this chapter we are going to introduce the different elements that need to be considered when it comes to defining a new method.

7.1. New needs for the information system

The motivation that leads to the definition of a new methodological approach is based around two key ideas. Firstly, there is the objective of making an information system agile. There are two properties to agility, namely, expansiveness and progressiveness, and it should be possible to address these two properties at the same time. Secondly, the different skills and competences that are required to resolve the issue of agility, and the ability to use the modern technology that is available, require companies to define a work organization framework.

7.1.1. *Expansiveness and progressiveness*

For a long time now the majority of companies have had to deal with demands that indicate that their information system should be expanded. These demands are a natural result of a company's economic growth. The information technology of a company normally expands when the company itself is expanding. This was also the case before companies started to grow rapidly due to the process of globalization. Thus it is only natural for companies that are experiencing a period of growth to find that their information system evolves at the same time.

Progressiveness is not an unknown concept either. For certain areas of the information system which evolve more than others, companies know how to use parameter management solutions, business rules solutions and workflow solutions, all of which improve the ability of the information system to adapt to new evolutions and new changes. A properly organized maintenance team makes it possible to improve the information system's ability to evolve. If the requirements of expansiveness and progressiveness are dealt with individually then it will not be possible to overcome them. It is possible to be expansive without making the existing processes evolve too much. Other users will be able to access the information system; a database by country will be created; new functionalities that do not affect existing functionalities will be created, etc. On the other hand, if we want an information system to evolve as a whole, it is necessary to define the precise area of the information system that we would like to evolve. For example, a business rules engine for pricing products would be set in place.

Today the situation has changed. Companies have pointed out that there are certain requirements which need to be dealt with to expand and to make certain areas of the information system evolve. They have also stated that these requirements cannot be identified during the design phase of the information system. It should be possible to expand the information system while maintaining a high level of flexibility. In the previous example, the pricing of products should not only be carried out on company offers but also on partner company products with the aim of offering the customer a package of offers. For this to happen the use of only one price setting device is not sufficient; it is best to have several price setting devices working together in service mode.

Will the traditional methods that are used in the construction of information systems be able to deal with these agile systems? We will show that the normal approaches need to be complemented with approaches such as the SOA process and many more.

7.1.2. *Mobilizing the many different competences*

Being able to control expansive and progressive information systems calls for the mobilization of the numerous technical and business skills that are required for working efficiently on any given information system. If the technical and business skills are not taken advantage of and are not controlled by homogenous work methods, then there is the risk of creating information systems that are rather confusing and complex. This is already the case for a large number of IT projects, and in particular for IT projects that are based on integrating up-to-date technology within the information system. We notice that many different people with different skills and competences are working on such projects. However, the exact functions carried out by the various people working on these projects are not very clear, such as: technical architects, functional architecture, EAI/ESB specialists, XML architects, software engineers, quality and method managers, BPM managers, Java architects, SOA architects, UML experts, MDA experts, Enterprise Architects.

With this in mind, the chief information officer sometimes finds it difficult to determine how to organize the responsibilities of the different people working on projects. This organization of responsibilities is even more difficult for the general management of companies to determine.

To see things more clearly, a company should use a framework that makes it possible to define the disciplines that are to be used. This framework will also make it possible to define the deliverables that need to be produced to create an information system successfully. The framework will also state the processes (procedures) that will make it possible to produce the deliverables homogenously. These deliverables are then verified by the people working on different aspects of the project before they are all grouped together. This leads us towards enterprise methodology.

7.2. Why are different methods seldom used within companies?

Whenever the term "method" is mentioned we often hear that it doesn't mean anything, that it is of no value, that it is too theoretical, too complex, etc. It seems that companies have already had significant experience of using different methods. Why would it be necessary to add more methods for companies to use? In reality, there is a lack of enterprise methodology available on the market for the following reasons:

– The existing methods deal with the management of projects (SDM/S, *Unified Process*, etc.), the rules of group work, and the general definition of the deliverables. However, they do not explain anything on the procedures that are necessary for creating the information systems. If each person working on a project is allowed to change the way things are done, there is a risk of creating a poor quality information system; there is also the risk of overspending as well as the risk of not being able to align software with the needs of the company.

– The best practices that TOGAF-type approaches have to offer (which will be dealt with later in this chapter) are not really methods. They describe principles, which can be interpreted in different ways by the different people who are involved in the projects. For example, the objective of loose coupling between components in SOA can be interpreted in many ways. For some, loose coupling can be seen as asynchronous communication, it can also be seen as an intermediary technical base, as an exchange of XML messages, and as the organization and development of a service orchestrator, etc. Such a wide range of interpretations slows down the transition to a homogenous and controlled project that can be completed in a short period of time.

– The division of work between the users and the IT teams remains important and leads to problems when it comes to bringing the information system into alignment with the needs of a company. We noticed too frequently that the IT department of a company was not interested in the users' modeling tools. The IT department believes that this task is not its responsibility. As a result, the expression of requirements is carried out with office tools, design tools and sometimes tools which can be found at a higher level in the company through the use of notations that cannot be exploited by the IT specialists, e.g. BPMN which is not compatible with UML. How is it therefore possible to be able to work efficiently in these conditions?

If there are any problems understanding why methods should be used, the following three questions should be considered:

– Does the company use a shared Computer Aided Software Engineering (CASE), which is shared between users and IT specialists, for modeling needs in upstream models? The only acceptable answer to this question is that the company uses UML both for business and IT requirements.

– Does the company have procedures which explain how to construct models during the different phases of the information system's production cycle? For example, how is it possible to describe scenarios of use cases which are written in UML? If the answer to this question is limited to a written description of the particular part of the use case in question, then this means that the procedures have not been properly defined. Companies should use a finite state automaton to formally design the dynamics of use cases. This example should grab the attention of companies. As far as use cases are concerned, the partial use of UML negates the importance of the modeling process. In a situation like this, UML does not describe all of the use cases' logic and therefore we rely on the use of a written specification, which does not allow for the proper alignment of the information system with company needs.

– Does the company have links that can be traced between the models and a list of requirements which list the business management rules? For example, as far as upstream modeling of needs is concerned, it must be possible to link a class operation with a business management rule that is expressed by the users of the system. If this type of link does not exist, it becomes difficult to justify the models.

If no action is taken to resolve these issues, it becomes increasingly difficult to use SOA. In the worst case scenario the use of SOA is even jeopardized:

– The improvement of the information system's agility will be slowed down since the modeling of all of the requirements will not be easily carried out by the information technology that is available.

– SOA and the modern technology that is available will be used in a way that is appropriate for each project, or even in a way that is appropriate for each individual working on a project. The absence of shared procedures makes it impossible to control SOA: there are integration problems, difficulties increasing the different versions of the individual layers of the architecture, problems linked to the cohabitation of services within the same execution environment, etc.

The intervention of general management is required to provide the solutions that are necessary for overcoming these problems. General management must also enforce a rationalization of the working methods of the information technology that is used. This involves a better definition of the relationship that exists between users and IT specialists and also includes the provision of better equipment to be used by both the users and the IT specialists.

The best management methods such as CMMI, COBIT and ITIL can only be understood and used if they are part of the working method of every collaborator working on a given project.

These management methods should not only be used in the rationalization of collective processes; they must be worked upon so that they can be used in the rationalization of individual processes and this is possible through promoting the use of procedures.

To be successful in doing so, general management must demand that the modeling tools be shared between the users and the IT specialists. This decision made by general management plays a vital role when it comes to managing an information system.

7.3. Reference frameworks

Several methods exist in the form of reference frameworks or even in the form of an Enterprise Application Framework (EAF). In the next part of the chapter both of these terms will be used. We are now going to have a look at the most popular reference frameworks, all of which originated in the English-speaking world: Zachman's framework, The Open Group Architecture Framework (TOGAF) and Peter Herzum's framework.

7.3.1. *Zachman's framework*

A lot of work that has been carried out in the area of enterprise methodology makes reference to the framework created by John Zachman in 1987. This framework is a matrix (Figure 7.1), which is the result of taking the product of the following two criteria:

– firstly, there is a series of questions that leads to the representation of different categories: the questions of who, what, where, when, why and how?;

– secondly, there is a list of different points of view: the points of view of the planner, proprietor, designer, creator and sub-contractor.

This framework makes it possible to list all the information that needs to be processed. However, the framework is an old model. It answers the questions of what and how in terms of data and functions. The information that is to be processed is located in a different place from the rules to which the information is applied. This separation of information and rules corresponds to the paradigm that existed in the IT world in the 1980s. This separation distorts both the representation of knowledge and the representation of the business. The object-oriented approach reduces the chances of this semantic breakdown from occurring. Zachman's framework does not take this semantic breakdown into consideration.

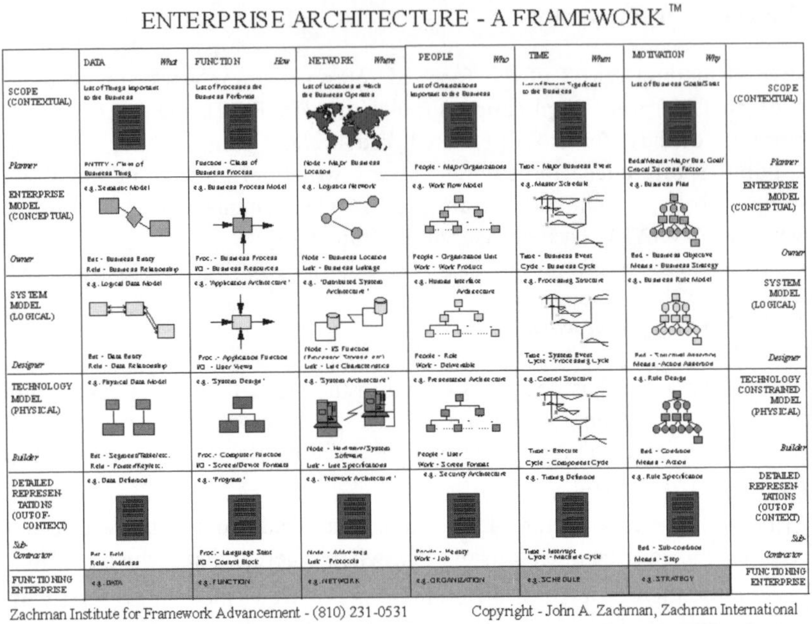

ENTERPRISE ARCHITECTURE - A FRAMEWORK™

Figure 7.1. *Zachman's framework (copyright John A. Zachman)*

By multiplying the six columns of the framework by its five rows the overall framework defines 30 models. We begin to understand the concerns linked to exhaustivity when it comes to listing the information and decisions that need to be dealt with in the activity chain. Nevertheless, we do not recommend that any project should create 30 models, especially when the structures between these 30 models have not been analyzed.

In conclusion, Zachman's framework remains a source of inspiration. However, it is impossible to implement the entirety of the framework.

7.3.2. *TOGAF*

The Open Group Architecture Framework (TOGAF) is the result of an investment made by the US Department of Defense and the Open Group. TOGAF was increasingly used by certain large multinational companies during the 1990s. For these companies, adopting the TOGAF approach brought with it the advantages of a recognized reference system, which is supported by a particular community of companies and is also open for discussion. TOGAF is a framework for enterprise methodology, i.e. it deals with everything related to the global image of the company. It identifies four types of architecture or four plans which describe the company:

– the business architecture describes the organization and the activity of the company in the form of functions and processes;

– the data architecture describes information, in the form of a logical data model;

– the application architecture evaluates the software;

– the technological architecture brings together all of the different technologies and infrastructures.

TOGAF is also made up of a process that describes the activities of the Architecture Development Model (ADM). The ADM does not deal with any transformations that occur within the company. TOGAF, as its name suggests, focuses on the work of the architects and this is what makes this reference system stand out from the others. TOGAF is also the starting point for companies that want to capitalize on the principles and patterns of architecture, architecture solutions, tools etc.

The 349 pages of TOGAF (version 8.1) certainly do not provide a complete framework that helps with the organization of the different disciplines and deliverables of a company. However, they do provide a wealth of recommendations and methods that should be adopted for architectural activities, which, up until recently, were unable to rely on a common reference system.

Other methods are available, which are similar to this enterprise methodology. These include: Command, Control, Computers, Communications, Intelligence, Surveillance, and Reconnaissance (C4ISR) from the US Department of Defense, Federal Enterprise Architecture Framework (FEAF) and the Reference Model for Open Distributed Processing (RM-ODP).

7.3.3. Peter Herzum's framework

In 2000 Peter Herzum and Oliver Sims created the concept of the business component factory, which is part of the component based software movement [HERZUM and SIMS, 2000]. They organized the production of information systems based on five dimensions:

– The first dimension describes three different types of component. The distributed component is the most basic level of component. It is a combination of classes which display services through the use of an interface. All the services can be used on a network. The business component is a combination of distributed components which form a business concept or a business process. Finally, there is the business component system (also known as a system-level component), which is a cooperation of different business components that respond to a particular functional issue.

– The second dimension defines four different points of view in relation to the architecture of the information system. The technical architecture groups together all the issues relating to the infrastructure of a particular execution, such as frameworks, etc. Application architecture deals with component design models. Project management architecture defines the organizational rules of a project. Finally, functional architecture groups together the different functional designs.

– The third dimension, development process, provides a detailed view of the development processes which are based around the components.

– The fourth dimension, distributed tiers, shows the projection of the components in the form of layers within the software.

– The fifth dimension, functional layers, introduces the notion of business component categories, and in particular the business process component.

This structure places the component at the center of the production process, which is the case with SOA. However, Herzum and Sims do not mention the processes that are used for the designing and development of both organizational and business needs. We have at our disposal an interesting reference framework, which is, however, limited to just the logical aspect of the information system. The upstream work that is carried out to express needs, as well as work related to software development, is still to be achieved.

7.3.4. *Important information to be taken from the reference frameworks*

The positive and negative aspects of the historical reference frameworks were mentioned in the previous section. The negative aspects are important since they force companies to create a new, more modern enterprise methodology, which is able to deal with all of the disciplines that are necessary for the successful creation of an information system. At this stage the following important information should be taken from the reference frameworks:

– Zachman's framework: the exhaustivity of the models should be borne in mind when reducing the representation levels with the aim of successfully creating a more operational approach.

– TOGAF: the best practices that take place within the architecture should be kept in mind. These practices will be reusable in the framework of a new enterprise methodology. However, the organization of the disciplines (which are too focused on the work that occurs within the architecture) needs to be redeveloped with the aim of including upstream modeling (business and organizational modeling) as well as including a logical architecture such as SOA.

– Herzum and Sims's framework: the importance of logical architecture that is based around components is what is key here. The architecture will be made smaller to comply with today's principles of SOA. The architecture will be monitored by upstream design processes, which are used to express company needs. The architecture will also be monitored by derivation processes, which are used for developing the services.

7.4. Essential tools

In addition to the advantages provided by the framework references, we can also benefit from notation standards that can be used with UML and MDA. A knowledge base, which was created in France and is known as the urbanization of information systems, is then added to these standards. All these different attributes, which are discussed in the next part of this chapter, allow us to unveil the foundations of the enterprise methodology that we have to offer.

7.4.1. *UML (Unified Modeling Language)*

An important event took place at the end of the 1990s: the standardization of UML.[1] For the first time ever, IT specialists now had access to a unique, unified and universal representation technique. We say "unique" because it is standardized, "unified" because all the different notations which were used in different architectures could be found in one notation standard, and "universal" due to its standardization and also due to the large amount of global support that it benefited from. By keeping this information in mind we can easily see why UML was so quickly accepted on an international level.[2]

The fact that UML was so quickly accepted internationally means that the process of standardization has removed certain preconceptions that used to exist within IT departments. At the beginning of the 1990s it was necessary to argue with chief information officers to try to convince them of the importance of object-oriented logic. Once this was achieved, it was then necessary to choose between 30 different architectures available on the market. For over 10 years now, chief information officers have been happier to accept the use of object-oriented logic. If

---

1. The first standardized version of UML dates from 1997. The organization in charge of the standardization is the Object Management Group (OMG).

2. The work was originally financed by a company known as Rational, which should be admired for its strategic perceptiveness.

the chief information officer is slightly worried about the quality of the software, he or she will support the modeling process and what it has to offer. There is no longer the worry of how the needs of a company will be modeled: they are modeled in UML. The chief information officer adopts and also enforces the adoption of the object-oriented approach. This does not mean that the different people working on IT projects will know everything there is to know about object-oriented logic. However, we find ourselves in a good position since all the theoretical problems and debates have already been dealt with.

However, there are certain limitations to UML, including the following:

– UML should not be treated as a methodology. This mistake led to the failure of numerous projects back in the 1990s. In fact, UML does not respond to practical issues such as: which model should be used? When should the model be used? Why should the model be used? What is a good model?

– UML is only a toolkit, a set of diagrams. UML is sometimes used without people knowing what exactly it is they are doing. There are many ways of interpreting and using each diagram. Furthermore, the diagram is not a representation of the final model, far from it.

– UML is somewhat oversimplified and is referred to as a software program. This is due to its origins and also to the increasing decline, as time goes on, in the number of people who are able to model company needs. The power of expression of UML is largely underexploited, and the areas in which proprietary and specialized notations remain in force are often forgotten.

The enterprise methodology that we have to offer is able to provide solutions to the limitations of UML. Our enterprise methodology designs modeling processes which can be applied to the different aspects of the enterprise system, and the method also equips each aspect of the enterprise system with UML. It also uses UML for the upstream modeling of company needs by using the same tool that is also used by the IT specialists.

7.4.2. MDA (Model Driven Architecture)

OMG released another standard, which is less well known but just as fundamental as UML. This standard is known as Model Driven Architecture (MDA). MDA promotes the use of an architecture which is managed by models and which relaunches an idea that was already around when software engineering first appeared. This idea is made up of two parts: firstly, it is necessary to create a model before developing any IT solution. Secondly, not just one but rather several models are required. Some of these models do not depend on the use of information technology. MDA refers to these models as platform independent models (PIM), other types of models are linked to these PIMs and these models are known as platform specific models (PSM). The PIMs are particularly important since they contain information relating to the business know-how of a company, without having to depend on the use of information technology. [BLANC, 2005] states that "the most significant advantage that MDA provides is the durability of business specifications. The aim of MDA is to make sure that the PIMs have a lifespan of more than 10 years". PIMs contribute to the idea of resilient information systems, which separate business needs from any technological problems that may occur in the future. These technological problems can change over time, and the users of the information systems will not be affected by the consequences of these changes.

MDA also restores the notion of the separation of concerns, which is a key element used in organizing communication between people from different cultures who are involved in IT projects. The original benefit of MDA was the way it helped the transition process from one model to another.[3]

MDA provides the framework which is used to create models and which also works on the ways in which these models can be exploited. MDA is a masterpiece as far as the industrialization of software is concerned. In the long term, MDA will have a larger impact than UML, even if it only seems to be used by the enterprise architect community for the time being.

As is often the case with various standards, MDA defines the format but does not mention anything about its content. In MDA the models are not defined, and the different types of the models (either PIM or PSM) are not identified. The enterprise methodology that we have to offer must conform to the MDA standard and will extend and improve the MDA standard by identifying the necessary models. The resulting methodology will either state the rules of derivation or the transition rules which apply from one model to another.

7.4.3. *Urbanization of the information system*

Faced with the increasing complexity of information systems, the process of IT urbanization is used to create a large map of the systems. At first, the existing information systems are mapped out and then this is followed by mapping out the more specific target information systems. Notation is used to help carry out this mapping process. Generally speaking, the process of urbanizing information systems adopts the idea of urban planning, as a metaphor. The information system is therefore compared to a town, and just like a town it is divided into zones, districts and blocks. Rules are also set for the development of the information system's

---

3. The mechanisms of derivation rely on the use of UML, which will be dealt with in Chapter 10.

structure and to regulate the traffic within the information system; once again this is similar to rules that are set for towns within the context of urban planning. In 1998 Jacques Sassoon published a groundbreaking book on the urbanization of information systems. Some of the findings in this book have been researched in more detail and have subsequently been published. The term urban planner is used by the IT departments of large companies in France to describe the people who are responsible for the urbanization of the information system. The urban planners of the information system have a long-term global vision of the urbanization of the information system, whereas the functional architects possess local and precise knowledge as far as the information system is concerned.

With traditional urbanization, however, there are several problems when it comes to the representation of the information system:

– Urbanization uses the process of functional cutting, which reflects the state of the existing information systems. The use of functional cutting leads to a high level of redundancy of the information systems. Data is often duplicated within the existing information systems and is too often duplicated within the urbanized information systems. Data reference systems are also located within the urbanized information system. The data reference system makes it possible to place the product catalog in just one area of the information system. However, the functions that use the product catalog are located in an area that is parallel to the product catalog. The aim here is to try not to isolate the functions which deal exclusively with other product catalogs. The object approach is simply ignored.

– A consequence of the previous point is the absence of any modeling of the business objects. In other words, there is no modeling of large blocks of information. It would be useful to organize certain functions around these large blocks of information, and in particular functions which do not depend on the organization of the information system and which can be referred to as business services. This type of concept started to appear in the urbanization meta-model, which was originally described in UML in Grady Booch's Category Class [BOOCH, 1996] and then reproduced by Pierre Bonnet in 2003 in his SOA reference framework [BONNET, 2003]. Category classes respond to the issue of being able to organize the information system around large homogenous blocks of data and not only around functions. Although this concept has certain advantages, it is still not able to bring the process of urbanization into alignment with the enterprise methodology, a point which will be discussed at the end of the chapter.

– A lack of structure in Business Process Management (BPM) has also been noticed. BPM works on the dynamics of the information system (with the help of the urbanization map), which at the moment remains too static.

Urbanization is a powerful communication tool that can be used for the functional reading of an information system. This functional reading can be easily understood by general management, the users of the information system and also the IT specialists. This functional reading also enables IT departments to make strategic choices when it comes to how the information system should be structured. However, it is not able to respond to the requirements of the enterprise methodology that we are looking for. The company SQLI has carried out even more research into the urbanization of information systems. [FOURNIER-MOREL, GROSJEAN, PLOUIN, ROGNON, 2006] state that urban planners run the risk of producing a significant number of abstract documents which are not used when it comes to urbanizing the information systems. We believe that more work needs to be carried out in the urbanization of information systems with the aim of responding to the following issues:

– How is it possible to model business objects in a non-redundant manner? How is it also possible to position the reusable and flexible business services around these business objects?

– How is it possible to link dynamic modeling (which is based around BPM) with the representation of the business objects?

– How is it possible to translate the different components of urbanization (zones, blocks, etc.) into non-redundant and reusable logical and software components that conform to the properties of SOA (see Chapter 5).

We insist on the continuity that exists between the process of urbanization and SOA. There is no split between the two. Some people believe that SOA only applies when the urbanization maps of the existing information systems are re-examined in more depth. This is not the case for cosmetic SOA, which is only slightly intrusive on the information systems that are in place. It is possible to improve the agility of the information system by using extended SOA, thanks to the Business Rules Management System and Master Data Management. Cosmetic SOA follows the path that has been marked out by the urbanization process. Cosmetic SOA does not provide an in-depth correction of the duplications of the functions within the information system. However, it does improve the quality of the information system. Whenever overhaul SOA is used, urbanization becomes an essential tool that is used to decide which zones would provide a better level of productivity when an information system is being overhauled. Remember that overhaul SOA is the most powerful level of SOA and is also the most intrusive into the existing information system. Without the process of urbanization it becomes more difficult to define what will happen during the progressive overhaul of an information system.

Chapter 8

The Praxeme Enterprise Method

A RECAP OF IDEAS MENTIONED IN PREVIOUS CHAPTERS
– The service is the smallest unit of the logical architecture, in other words of SOA. In SOA terminology the service is known as a logical service.

NEW IDEAS PRESENTED IN THIS CHAPTER
– The Praxeme enterprise method.
– Enterprise system topology is divided into eight aspects.
– The discovery of services is carried out by applying derivation rules to the upstream models used for expressing the business knowledge of a company (semantic aspect) and for describing its organization and activity (pragmatic aspect).

In the previous chapter the positive and negative aspects of the most influential reference frameworks were presented, and particular reference was made to how they could be integrated within the new concept of agile systems. We also showed that it is vital to accept standards such as UML and MDA, as well as listing the ways in which the process of urbanization can improve the management of SOA projects.

It is now necessary to bring all these different elements together with the aim of creating a modern and operational enterprise method that can be used to organize the different disciplines, as well as defining the deliverables and the transformation processes of a company. This enterprise method is known as the Praxeme enterprise method.

8.1. Praxeme: the initiative behind a public method

The majority of companies and organizations are faced with the same difficulties when it comes to the design, development and management of information systems. Rather than trying to overcome these difficulties in any random order and with the use of limited tools, several different companies and organizations got together with the aim of creating an enterprise method available to the general public. These companies include SAGEM, SMABTP, the French Army and the French National Family Funding Office. Other organizations involved in the creation of this public method include consultancy firms, Orchestra Networks and Softeam as well as other large organizations such as Logica and Sun Microsystems.

Praxeme is the result of the joint investment made by all these companies and organizations. It is an enterprise method which can be used to provide solutions to issues that arise in any department within a company, from a company's strategy through to its software development. Praxeme describes the procedures which could be considered to help design and develop companies, and describes the processes which are necessary for the design and development of information systems. Praxeme also describes the procedures that are involved in the semantic modeling process (business reference model) as well as describing the procedures that are involved in SOA, etc.

The people involved in designing and developing methods believe that the most important quality of a method is that it should be a shared method. This is why the Praxeme method is a shared method. The not-for-profit organization, the Praxeme Institute, is the authorized depository for the collection of material and is the coordinator of all the work that takes place in relation to the Praxeme method. The Praxeme Institute is also responsible for keeping Praxeme an open source method. The website of the Institute has published all the elements that are included within the Praxeme method.[1]

8.2. The Praxeme method

Methodology is divided into three main dimensions: product, process and procedure.

---

1. http://www.praxeme.org.

8.2.1. *Product*

The product is the object which is to be manufactured or transformed. Depending on the level of abstraction that is in force, the product could be a company process, a business object or a logic model that is constructed on a structure that is made of components[2] and services, etc.

In this dimension of methodology the Praxeme method views the enterprise system as a set of eight aspects. These different aspects make up what is known as Enterprise System Topology. For example, the pragmatic aspect of topology contains the set of products that are used to define an organization (organizational charts, models which provide information about the organization, use cases, organizational processes, authorizations, organization rules, etc.). The semantic aspect of topology, however, contains the set of products that are used to capture the business knowledge (business domain maps, models which provide information about the business, lifecycle of business objects, business rules, etc.). The Praxeme method states the rules of derivation that exist between products. For example, the Praxeme method outlines how the elements and how the pragmatic model can benefit from the semantic model.

The eight aspects of enterprise system topology – semantic, pragmatic, geographical, logical, technical, software, physical and hardware – will be presented later in this chapter.

8.2.2. *Process*[3]

A process responds to the question: how is it possible to organize the work that is involved in creating an information system? A process contains a definition of roles, phasing, organization rules and lists of activities. A process is in fact the aspect of a method that deals with how an IT project should be managed. In reality, there are other well-known and proven methods that exist in the market, such as UP, RUP and SDM/S, and the Praxeme method can be articulated with these methods.

For example, the specification of a system's needs (a phase in the SDM/S method) provides access to the complete semantic model, as Praxeme defines it. The

---

2. In the Praxeme meta-model the term "logical constituent" is preferred to the term "logical component". This is to avoid any confusion that may arise with the software vocabulary that is used. In this book the term "logical component" is used; this is the term that is more commonly used today.

3. The term "process" is used here to describe the construction of a company's information system.

deliverable which ends the inception phase in the Unified Process removes the important decision points which are spread out over the different aspects of enterprise system topology. The later phases of the UP method work on the different models that exist within the different aspects of enterprise system topology.

In a waterfall lifecycle, a particular phase can only deal with one aspect of enterprise system topology at a time. However, when it comes to iterative cycles, several different aspects of enterprise system topology can be dealt with at the same time. In any case, the process must deal with all the decisions that need to be made on all aspects of enterprise system topology.

With this mechanism in mind, Praxeme is used in combination with other methods. Such combinations are quite common and quite easy to create with methods that are focused on the production processes of an information system. The Praxeme method provides solutions to the other two dimensions that constitute the general field of methodology: product and procedures.

8.2.3. *Procedures*

Procedures and methods provide solutions to the following questions and many more: how can we work on an information system on an individual level? How can we construct a good model? How can we find the services in an SOA approach? How can we break new ground as far as business processes are concerned? This category of methodology is about the operation modes that are necessary for homogenizing the quality of work that is carried out as well as guaranteeing productivity.

8.2.4. *Combining the three dimensions*

In order to provide solutions to the issues that arise from the projects and to provide as much detail as possible on the work that needs to be carried out on the projects, it is necessary to include these three different dimensions of methodology within an enterprise method. These three categories are very seldom combined within the same method. Furthermore, for the past 15 years or so the different methods that are available have had a tendency to focus on the process category (UP, TOGAF, ITIL, CMMI, ISO 9000, ISO 12207, etc.).

The process dimension of methodology is the dimension that can be seen by the manager, in other words the person who makes the decision of investment. This fact in itself leads to the creation of a sort of favoritism within projects: the manager pays more attention to this organizational and group dimension than to the more technical dimensions of product and procedures. The dimensions of product and procedures should be a part of everyday projects. These everyday projects have real needs that can only be addressed by the product and procedures dimension of methodology. However, in some cases it is not possible to highlight these needs and they are therefore ignored.

Having distinguished between the three different dimensions that exist within the field of methodology, it becomes much easier to combine different contributions from various methods or repositories. As far as the Praxeme method is concerned, the product dimension (based on the different aspects of enterprise system topology) is a requirement. The procedures dimension is much more flexible and the Praxeme method can incorporate several alternative procedures. Different elements, stemming from the dimensions of procedures and processes, can be easily added to the methodologies that are used to create a production process. This production process can then be used to construct information systems.

8.3. Enterprise system topology according to the Praxeme method

Enterprise System Topology is the basis of the Praxeme method. A lot of the procedures that the Praxeme method has to offer are based on the eight aspects of Enterprise System Topology. The topology identifies eight aspects that exist within a company. These eight aspects contain varying pieces of information about a company such as: the fundamentals of the company, its business activities, its tools and all the decisions that it needs to make. These aspects are then modeled (primarily in UML) and provide information on the whole of the enterprise system, or at least on the parts of the system that can be formalized.

8.3.1. *Upstream models*

The first aspect of enterprise system topology that needs to be considered is the semantic aspect. What does the company do? What physical or abstract objects does it create or transform? What are the fundamentals of its business activity? These questions seem rather easy to answer. However, the process of semantic modeling is not so common, nor is it easy to comprehend. Many business object models are only poor renderings of conceptual data models. What is worse, the majority of the different sets of methods that are available ignore this level of abstraction. The best way to describe a company, more often than not, is in terms of processes. This method of describing a company conveys the different work habits of the company; it also conveys the organizational rules as well as showing the preconceptions that exist within a company in relation to how things should be done. The semantic aspect can be found in an upper level of abstraction above these kinds of things. It is necessary to isolate the semantic aspect. The level of abstraction that is required by the process of semantic modeling is largely rewarded:

– On the one hand this semantic model acts as a huge source of inspiration. Semantic modeling is not only about obtaining the maximum amount of knowledge possible about the business activity of a company; semantic modeling questions this activity, pushes it towards genericity and removes any preconceptions which may have existed in the business practices.

– On the other hand this model is a convergence tool. The semantic model is aimed at being an all-purpose model. The designers of the semantic model remove elements from the models that would see them only being used in one specific context, for example models that are only used within a particular department or within a particular organization. From now on the semantic model can be shared between several organizations. As far as the development of SOA is concerned, this fact is extremely important since it is through using the semantic model that it is possible to discover the most reusable services.

The next question to be answered is who does what? The answer is in terms of people, business activity and processes. The processes give a global representation of a company's business activity. As far as the business activity of a company is concerned, UML provides the use-case diagram and the activity diagram. The use case corresponds to people working individually. All these representations describe the pragmatic aspect of the company. The term "pragmatic" counterbalances the term "semantic". The semantic aspect describes what needs to be done, whereas the pragmatic aspect describes how things should be done.

Finally, the question of where must be answered. It introduces us to the geographical aspect of topology. The geographical model is, strictly speaking, not very complicated: it shows the physical distribution of sites such as headquarters, regional departments and agencies. The geographical aspect is interested in the possibility of linking these sites with one another, and is also interested in structuring these sites into physical networks. As far as linking the different sites with one another is concerned, the geographical model pays close attention to people working from home, to mobile solutions and to continuous communications which enable people on all the different sites to communicate with one another. The geographical model is an important source of input for the architects who design IT infrastructures. It is also of interest to strategists. The localization of business activities, as well as how to physically organize them, are among the important strategic decisions that need to be made.

8.3.2. *Logical (SOA), technical and software architecture models*

The logical aspect plays a fundamental role in the SOA approach. The logical aspect acts as an intermediary between the upstream and downstream aspects, and as an intermediary between the business and its information technology. The logical aspect tries to be independent of any of the technological decisions that are applied to the information system. The logical aspect describes the information system in non-technical terms. The logical architecture establishes the decisions that need to be made as far as the structure of the information system is concerned. One of the first decisions in the matter of logical architecture is the type or style of architecture that should be used. In other words, it states the type of basic building block that should be used, and also the way in which the different elements (which make up the architecture) should be arranged. In this book only one style of logical architecture is studied, and that is SOA. SOA is different from another style of architecture which, today, is used in the majority of information systems, i.e. functional architecture whose basic unit is the function.

If we begin to structure the information system in logical terms, this means that we are confident that currently available IT is able to make one part of an information system communicate with another part of the same system. It means that we also have faith in IT to be able to transform the logical constituents into software components. Before investing heavily in an SOA project it is necessary to undertake the process of logical/technical negotiation, which has been provided for by the field of methodology. The logical/technical negotiation process consists in a communication exchange between the logic architect and the technical architect. The method that is used provides the list of themes that are to be dealt with. The technical architect works on the framework and on the technical devices that are necessary for transforming the logical model into software. The software aspect takes place after the logical and the technical aspects. It is best to model the software aspect before producing the software itself. The software model receives the latest details relating to the production of the software before the code has been generated. The software model also prefigures the software configuration management.

8.3.3. *Hardware and physical architecture models*

Enterprise system topology isolates hardware as an aspect in order to describe the machines and IT networks that exist within a company. If any technical decision is made it is made in relation to the company's hardware. In terms of dynamics, all cases are possible: what tends to happen in the majority of cases is that the pre-existing hardware architecture forces certain technological choices to be made. If we consider the process dimension from the methodology mentioned earlier in this chapter, it will not change the topology of the enterprise system. Topology is a fixed way of arranging documentation. The technical specifications of the architecture refer to hardware and networks within a company. If we apply enterprise system topology to the architecture, the description of the hardware architecture does not make any reference to the technological choices that are to be made. This means that the description of the hardware architecture will not change, regardless of any technological changes that might be made to the architecture.

The final aspect of enterprise system topology to be considered is the physical aspect. The physical aspect is the result of projecting the software architecture onto the hardware architecture. This involves placing software components (executables, databases, resources, etc.) onto the nodes of the hardware architecture.

8.3.4. *Enterprise system topology*

The eight aspects of enterprise system topology make it possible to arrange, in order, all the information relating to the information system as well as all the decisions that are made in relation to the information system. In Figure 8.1 it should not be possible to see any processes or any procedures, remember that we are dealing with the product dimension.

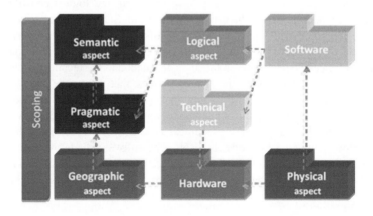

Figure 8.1. *Enterprise system topology – Praxeme*

Figure 8.1, which shows Praxeme's enterprise system topology, can be compared to Zachman's reference framework, which was described in Chapter 7. The 30 models that are part of Zachman's reference framework have been concentrated into the eight aspects which together form Praxeme's Enterprise System Topology. Praxeme's enterprise system topology can also be compared to the four plans that were created by urban planners, or the four plans of the Enterprise Architecture (according to TOGAF for instance).

The reader of this book might well ask themselves why these specific aspects, and why are there eight of them? The Praxeme Institute provides a theoretical explanation, which goes into more detail on how Figure 8.1 was constructed. This explanation can be seen on the Praxeme website.[4] What is more important is that several projects have adopted the Praxeme method, which has proved to be an extremely efficient tool. This highlights the fact there was a need in the market for something like the Praxeme method. The Praxeme method has one major advantage: it points out the different competences that are necessary for the successful completion of a project. This method makes it possible to re-examine the different disciplines within a project, to clarify responsibilities, to identify and to locate the people who are involved in working in such a project as well as identifying the languages of these people. For example, the modeling of processes requires the people involved in this job to have a certain level of competence as well as a background in the sociology of organization. Another example is that topology defines the areas in which the logic architect and the urban planner can work.

It is not enough to list the different aspects of enterprise system topology; they need to be structured. The different people working on the projects need to know what a certain representation element or information element is, or what they refer to. They also need to know how these elements can be transformed at different phases of the activity chain. This concern, which is linked to the structuring of the different aspects of enterprise system topology, characterizes the industrialization of software. These elements can be formally written by using the MDA standard. More information on this will be given in the chapter devoted to modeling with the Praxeme method. In that chapter the rules of derivation are also introduced.

8.3.5. *Pre-modeling*

Before starting to model the upstream aspects of topology (semantic, pragmatic and geographical) the different people working on the information system need to produce a written specification of requirements. At this stage, the written specification is in the form of general functional specifications, which are replaced by more detailed functional specifications at a later date. These documents form the terms and conditions for the upstream aspects of topology. Within these documents there are also specifications that state what the layout and design of the computer screens should be. These specifications can also be used for the software aspect of enterprise system topology. Pre-modeling gathers

---

4. http://www.praxeme.org.

together all the different aims and objectives, as well as the different requirements and vocabularies.

8.4. What the Praxeme method means for SOA

In this part of the chapter the Praxeme method will not be discussed in its entirety.[5] What will be discussed, however, are the principles of the methodology that many different procedures rely on, and this will be achieved by highlighting the effects that the Praxeme method has on SOA.

8.4.1. *How can we find the correct services?*

It must not be forgotten that SOA is placed within the logical aspect of the Praxeme method. This fact does not reduce the responsibility of the technical architects who work on a project to which SOA has been applied. The technical architects work to ensure that the SOA architecture is reliable. The advances in modern technology have meant that modern information technology has replaced some of the work carried out by technical architects. It is also possible to create an SOA architecture by using traditional information technology. The main characteristic of SOA is the way in which it structures information systems: it relies on the use of the logical aspect. Once the technical architect has stated the conditions that are necessary for making SOA a reliable architecture, the projects find themselves having to deal with the issue of how it is possible to find the correct services that can be integrated within the architecture. The technical architect is unable to provide a solution to this issue. It is not a question of the technology that is used. This issue can be avoided if the information system is properly designed and structured. If this issue does arise it cannot be resolved through the use of vague terms and expressions, therefore more precise information is required. For example, it is not enough to say that certain categories of services exist; a detailed list of the exact categories that exist is required. To resolve the issue, assistance should be given when it comes to making decisions that relate to how the information system should be structured. In other words, the decisions that are made should improve the quality of the information system and should have a long-term influence on the information system as a whole. This solution is part of the logical design process.

---

5. Any reader who wants more information on the Praxeme method should read the General Guide on the Praxeme method (reference PxM-02) as well as the Guide to the logical aspect (PxM-40). Both documents are available on the website of the Praxeme Institute: http://www.praxeme.org.

The Praxeme method also defines what a service is. Too much time is wasted in companies trying to define what a service is. One of the major advantages of a public method is that it is possible to end debates by setting a fixed reference terminology. As far as the Praxeme method is concerned, the service is the primary element of the software system. From outside the software system nothing exists under the level of the service: this, however, excludes the direct manipulation of data. A consequence is that the application becomes a secondary notion. The concept of application is becoming less and less prominent in the way software systems are structured.

The Praxeme method also contributes to SOA by providing a solution to the issue of how it is possible to find the services. It even provides a solution to the more fundamental issue of what makes a good service. Since the Praxeme method deals with all aspects of a company, it is able to create processes that assist with the designing of services. These services can be designed from a simple business representation. Enterprise system topology shows that two of its aspects are located above the logical aspect; these include the semantic aspect (business fundamentals) and the pragmatic aspect (the organization and the activity of a company). The Praxeme method provides precise derivation rules which, when applied to the semantic and pragmatic models, lead to the creation of the logical model. The logical model is made up of two parts: the service level and the data level. The service level tends to overlook and mask the data level. The logical data model is derived from class models, and this is primarily the case as far as the semantic model is concerned. However, the pragmatic model can also contain some organizational object models. The next chapter deals with derivation rules and the procedures involved in logical design.

The multi-aspect approach of the Praxeme method can be used on the entirety of the activity chain, from the expression of business needs right through to the creation of information technology.

8.4.2. *The link between urbanization, the object-oriented approach and SOA*

The Praxeme method also clarifies the principles that should be adopted when it comes to structuring information systems. It defines a link between the urbanization of information systems, the object-oriented approach and how all of this can be integrated within SOA. The Praxeme method makes it possible to have better control over the complexity of information systems. Information systems normally experience problems that relate to their expansion and evolution. This link is generated as follows:

– The idea of the functional domain that is used in the urbanization process remains. However, the Praxeme method confines it to the pragmatic aspect as defined in the Enterprise System Topology. By applying the rules of derivation, the functional domain becomes a logical component that is part of the logical architecture. However, these logical components do not cover the whole of the logical architecture. These logical components can only be found at the periphery of the logical architecture. The services which are also found at the periphery of the logical architecture orchestrate the internal services which are found at the heart of the information system.

– As far as the internal part of the system is concerned, the Praxeme method relies on a key concept that is used for structuring the information systems, the object domain (business objects). This concept is an unnatural concept for the urban planner since the urban planner works with functions. This concept is more natural for the object-oriented designer. The semantic model can be broken down into object domains; in other words, it can be broken down into smaller portions which incorporate the main business objects. This concept can be found in the UML Category Class, which was defined by Grady Booch [BOOCH, 1996]. This notion of breaking down the semantic model is very different from the breaking down of functions. The logical architecture graph takes over these object domains in the form of other components and places them at the heart of the information system. These components form the main part of the services which can be reused the most, i.e. those services which ensure the business fundamentals.

The urban planner who works on information systems, the logical architect and the logical designer all work within the same substantive context and deal with the same logical aspect. The Praxeme method changes the metaphor that is associated with urbanization and makes it the same as the metaphor that is associated with SOA. The Praxeme method also standardizes the views from each of the different businesses that are involved in designing an information system.

This convergence of SOA and the urbanization of information systems appears whenever their aims and objectives are re-examined in more detail. These two approaches have the same objective and that is to make an information system evolve into as efficient a structure as possible. The two approaches have or should have the same views: they are both long-term approaches which take into consideration both the size of the information system as well as the company itself. This posture is natural and constitutes the starting point for IT city planning (urbanization as Jacques Sasoon originally described it). It is less prominent in SOA, however, due to the fact that the SOA approach was originally a technical approach. Remember that, whenever SOA projects are mentioned, the letter A stands for architecture and that the SOA approach is about creating an architecture. In other words, the whole of the system must be taken into consideration. It is impossible to have a service architecture if the whole of the information system is not considered.

If we compare the representations of information systems that are produced by traditional urban planners and logic architects, it has been noticed that the urbanization maps only show us with an overall structure and zoning regulations. The addition of reference systems and data repositories show that urbanization does not use the principle of encapsulation. This means that the process of urbanization leads to the redundancy of the information system as well as leading to a high level of coupling within the system.

The logic architect who uses SOA can create zoning regulations and urbanization maps, through the use of a logical architecture graph. At first, this representation seems to be the same as that established by an urban planner. Nevertheless, the work carried out by the logic architect is very different; the logic architect uses a more rigorous notation that enables him/her to study both the statics and the dynamics of the information system at the same time. Whenever the logic architect divides the information system into large components, he/she then starts to work on the dependencies that arise from the division of the information system. The logic architect also works on the communication and exchanges that occur between the different components of the information system once it has been split up into the larger components. If the logical architect divides the system at one point rather than another, it means that he/she knows exactly where to divide the information system so that the maximum optimization can be achieved. The logical architecture graph is only the first of many diagrams that show the logical model. The logical designer is also able to use the logical architecture graph to carry out his/her work right up to the phase where a detailed specification of the logical services must be given. There is a sense of continuity right the way through the activity chain, and the software programmer makes use of the logical model in any way: the software programmer transforms the logical model into a piece of software.

What else does the urban planner do that the logic architect is unable to do? The answer to this question is that he/she takes on the role of intermediary between the business and the information technology that is in place within a company. The urban planner is the only person able to gather together information relating to the strategies that are used by a company, the only person involved in trying to resolve general business concerns, the only person who can anticipate how these general business issues might evolve and the only person who knows what impact these business concerns will have on the information system. The logic architect is unable to take on this role of intermediary since he/she is too busy working on the software system itself. If the logic architect did take on the role of intermediary, he/she would become too involved in making formal decisions, or making decisions that do not relate to the business. The job of the logic architect is to work more on the information system than on the business.

8.5. Advantages of the Praxeme method

8.5.1. *A method that unites different approaches and integrates SOA*

With enterprise system topology, the Praxeme method is equipped with a general framework that organizes the different aspects of a company and its information systems. The conceptual framework of the Praxeme method enables it to carefully structure the different competences that are needed to successfully create an information system. With the Praxeme method it is possible for different people to communicate with each other once again, e.g. people from different cultures, working on different aspects of the enterprise. This generalist framework also takes into consideration methods whose origins can be traced back to another method; in other words, there is a sort of heritage that exists. For example:

– The process of semantic modeling in Praxeme and the transformation of the semantic model into a logical data model use the rules of the entity-relationship approach.

– Topology can be compared to the Zachman framework. Topology uses a simpler, more operational framework by reducing the number of models to a more manageable number, and also by fixing the relations between the different categories that are in place. The data and functions, which are separated in the Zachman framework, are reunited in the Praxeme method through the use of the object-oriented approach. The transition from one level of concern is essential for the creation of the activity chain, and this too can be addressed by the Praxeme method. The Praxeme method sets out the rules of derivation that need to be adhered to in order to create an effective activity chain.

– TOGAF and the other methods from this generation are full of useful recommendations that can be used to create an effective activity chain. However, their recommendations cannot be applied to the activity chain as a whole. They are aimed at the specialists and architects. The recommendations do not clearly clarify the boundaries that exist between functional architecture and technical architecture. The Praxeme method adds a further level of abstraction to the four types of architecture that exist in theory; this superior level of abstraction is known as the semantic aspect. The re-adaptation of the business fundamentals takes place in the semantic aspect. The semantic aspect is the area in which the logical architect can trace the origins of the most stable components, as well as the origins of the most reusable services that can be found in the information system.

– Peter Herzum's framework explains how to structure the information system. A general narrow-mindedness (companies concentrated too much on the logical and/or the software aspect) prevented him from being able to trace the origins of services. This meant that this approach remains a functional one.

– The urbanization of information systems is, today, as relevant as it ever has been in the past. The Praxeme method adds two new concepts that should be taken into account when it comes to the urbanization of the information system. Firstly, the object domain (which comes from the semantic model) needs to be integrated within the logical architecture. Secondly, it is necessary to use a logical architecture graph, which analyzes the real dependencies that exist between the different components of the information system. The use of a logical architecture graph is much better than using a traditional urbanization map.

– Bertrand Meyer's design by contract method distinguishes the pre- and post-conditions of services. The use of state diagrams in the semantic and pragmatic aspects of Enterprise System Topology follows this inspiring work.

– The standards of OMG, UML and MDA can be used on the entirety of the production chain, as well as being used in the derivation of the different aspects that make up enterprise system topology. Right up until the logical model, IT specialists work on Platform Independent Models (PIMs). The models that come from the software aspect are those that contain the technical guidelines. According to the MDA standard, they are called the Platform Specific Models (PSMs). They can be partly produced by means of UML profiles.

– The Business Rules Management System is also integrated into the production chain. We distinguish between business rules and organization rules. The former are inescapable, as they are determined by environment, regulations and so on. The latter, relating to decisions of the enterprise, can be changed. The organization rules (pragmatic aspect of enterprise system topology) are the rules that will be created within the Business Rules Management System. The majority of the business rules (semantic aspect of enterprise system topology) are created in a more traditional manner, in so much as they are not subjected to change. The link that exists between the Business Rules Management System and SOA can be found in the pre- and post-conditions of the organizational services. Coupling between the services and the business rules engine: the services do not know which rules are going to be used, only the business rules engine is aware of what rules are going to be used (for more information go to the chapter on the tools used in enterprise methodology).

– Master Data Management (MDM) is also integrated into the production chain. Modeling the data in both the semantic and pragmatic aspects of enterprise system takes into account the needs associated with the rationalization of the repositories, as well as the requirements associated with defining parameters.

– There is also the technological advantage of using service orchestration engines such as Business Process Management (BPM), workflow BPM and application BPM. Modeling processes and use cases within the pragmatic aspect of enterprise system prepares the use of BPM. The lifecycle of the business objects within the semantic aspect of enterprise system topology requires the implementation of application BPM.

The different technological advantages associated with MDM, BRMS and BPM all lead to the creation of the Agility Chain Management System (ACMS). The ACMS was described in the chapter dealing with the properties of SOA.

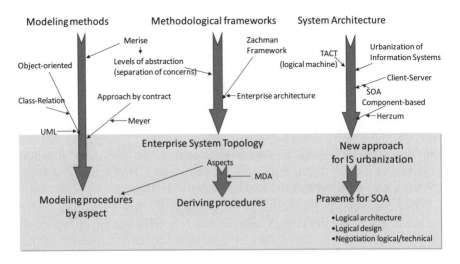

Figure 8.2. *How the Praxeme methodology has been inspired by other methodologies*

8.5.2. *Risks associated with the Praxeme method*

Everyone agrees that a methodology is required to manage a successful SOA project. However, it is not enough to use a specialized methodology only dedicated to SOA. If the first phase of a method already provides information on services and on how the services can be identified, this means that the upstream aspects have not been integrated within the method. A lot of SOA projects that have been too focused on the technical aspect of the information system tend to forget about the representation of business needs, which is necessary for the successful management of an SOA project. Other SOA projects do include these business needs, but they are represented by expressions that do not provide an accurate representation of the business. This is often the case with use cases, the description of which conveys preconceived ideas about the solution. When this happens it becomes very difficult to detect the services that can be reused. The Praxeme method avoids this obstacle by promoting the use of semantic modeling. Semantic modeling is the only business approach that is capable of cutting itself off from the hazards that are linked to the organization and to the different work situations of the organization. In order for an SOA project to be successful it is necessary to express the different business fundamentals. By expressing the different business fundamentals we have access to the source of the most interesting services that exist within an information system.

For IT departments there is the temptation of creating an in-house methodology. This temptation increases as the size of the company increases. However, there are several risks associated with the use of an in-house methodology:

– Regardless of the size of the IT department, it is seldom possible for it to be able to come up with a budget that is large enough to consider all the aspects that are required for the creation of an effective method. The in-house method will be a reflection of the concerns that a company is currently facing as well as of the people who are working on the method. There is the obvious risk of creating an incomplete method, and if this turns out to be the case then it is impossible to overcome this issue once the method has been used in different projects.

– Designing a successful methodology is a process that involves much more experience and much more thought. To create a successful method it is necessary for an IT department to have dealt with many different issues in the past. It is also necessary for the IT department to have a firm understanding of the history of software engineering, as well as the exchanges that have taken place among peers on an international level. The profile of the methodologist is different from those of method engineers and method managers.

– Even if the two previous issues are resolved, there is still the fact that the in-house method is a proprietary method, which means that is not made available to or used by a large community. Any IT department that lets company partners, or anyone else for that matter, use their in-house method also forces these users to pay an additional acquisition cost. This acquisition cost is seen as an additional cost that needs to be taken into consideration when working on the projects. This cost not only includes the acknowledgement of the in-house method but also includes the resolution of any interpretation conflicts that may arise during a project.

Another risk is the notion of the proprietary method which is developed and sold by service providers. The cost of the proprietary method is less than the total investment that an IT department puts into its in-house method. However, the negative aspects of the proprietary method must be highlighted and they are as follows: the proprietary method is an incomplete method. The proprietary method is adopted too quickly to put an end to any doubts a company might have as far as its information system is concerned. It is not possible to guarantee the durability of the method and it is also not possible to ensure that the method will evolve in the future. Finally, a proprietary method rarely benefits from research within the academic world.

Chapter 9

Modeling with Praxeme

A RECAP OF IDEAS MENTIONED IN PREVIOUS CHAPTERS

– According to Praxeme, Enterprise System Topology (EST) is organized in eight aspects. The semantic, pragmatic and geographic aspects structure the representation of the enterprise and its business. The logical aspect shelters the SOA style of architecture. The technical aspect describes the technical architecture in detail and ensures that the logical architecture is implemented. The software model takes on the form of logical models to add directives to them. These directives allow the code to be managed. Physical and material aspects lead to the deployment of the software solution.

NEW IDEAS TO BE INTRODUCED IN THIS CHAPTER

– semantic modeling;

– pragmatic modeling;

– logical modeling based on SOA;

– logical modeling of batch computing;

– logical/technical negotiation;

– modeling of a solution.

9.1. The modeling of requirements

If it is well done, the modeling of requirements allows for the appropriate services to be found automatically. This applies to the services that are situated at the heart of the business (due to semantic modeling), as well as those that are linked to organization (due to pragmatic modeling). The modeling of the core business knowledge and the organization are not to be mixed. If this is not respected, the concept of reusable services cannot be maintained. For information systems there always needs to be a guarantee that the organization can develop further without applications having to be rewritten. Due to methodological confusion in the past few years, the requirement of not mixing is no longer valid:

– The discipline of BPM (*Business Process Management*) starts the construction of an information system directly based on processes without worrying about modeling of data and the business basics. It therefore determines the second stage in the process.

– IT urbanization does not distinguish the level of organization from the conceptual level of the business knowledge. These two levels are absorbed and diluted in the functional domain of traditional urbanization.

– Last but not least, the object-oriented approach with its intention of representing the system's reality based on a tree of unified classes also leads to diluting the business knowledge and the organization.

All these disciplines are necessary, but their isolated use provokes derivatives in the construction of systems that cannot be renewed with SOA. We aim at aligning the information system with business expectations. We also wish to increase reuse of services. Both motivations lead us to eliminate the causes of variation from a stable core.

In the Praxeme method these disciplines are united and then situated at the correct place through semantic and pragmatic modeling. These disciplines perform at an even higher level when used in synergy.

9.2. Semantic modeling

9.2.1. *The basic principles*

Semantic models express the foundations of the business knowledge. They have to describe it without anything else: no organizational choice, no mention of how-to-do. The first difficulty is to separate what is essential from what is contingent and linked to the local organization of practices, habits of working and choice of tools. Semantic modeling requires that a real effort is made on the level of abstraction. This is the most delicate part in the chain of activities. The semantic model plays an essential part in ensuring the system's quality. The SOA approach emphasizes the importance of a good semantic model. On the basis of this semantic model, the most reusable and sharable services can be defined.

What cannot be classed as a semantic model? A semantic model is not a model that represents a process or an activity. A semantic model can be defined as upstream. Neither the parties involved, organizational structures, nor habits of working are part of a semantic model. "Business objects" are linked to semantic models. However, many so-called "business models" are only bad conceptual data models. They only capture a tiny and truncated part of the business knowledge. Their structure needs to be handled with care because the stability of the model cannot be guaranteed until operations and rules are firmly rooted in it.

What is a semantic model? A semantic model represents the objects and concepts that the company handles, due to its activity. Inside the Praxeme methodology, the semantic modeling technique adopts an object-oriented approach and makes use of this logic in great depth. Objects and concepts are represented as classes. The model expresses the entire semantic that has been attached to the objects or concepts, i.e. information, actions and transformations. Considering only the information side generates a data model. However, this is still insufficient. Information is subject to certain limits and used as input for calculations. Classes are linked via inheritance and association links.

This technique benefits from UML's capacity to express associative classes, qualified associations, derived properties, etc. The semantic modeler has to master these possibilities of expression otherwise he/she might provide a false expression of the business knowledge. The modeler does not deal with Java classes, attributes or operations to be programmed. A semantic model expresses information, actions and transactions and many other features that are linked to a concept or an object. The UML attribute translates a piece of information. The UML operation translates an action. Transformations will be expressed by a combination of operations and transitions. This technique applies the UML standard notation but after the UML meta-model has been filtered by the Praxeme meta-model.

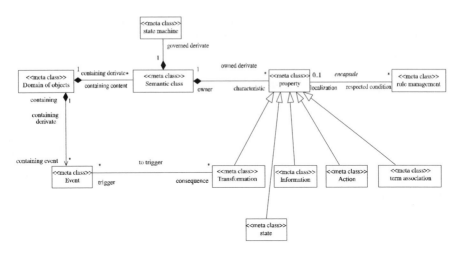

Figure 9.1. *Extract from the Praxeme meta-model for semantic modeling*

Resorting to the states machines is a major criterion which distinguishes semantic models. Important objects transform themselves and move from one state to the next. This movement from one state to another happens according to precise rules. The lifecycle of objects is a source of complexity in traditional IT. The modeler currently deals with simple means to express the lifecycle of an object. In UML the states machine is represented by one or many states diagrams. This modeling technique guarantees the object's behavior. The states machine is an important tool when it comes to ensuring the quality of systems. It also plays an important role when services are being carried out.

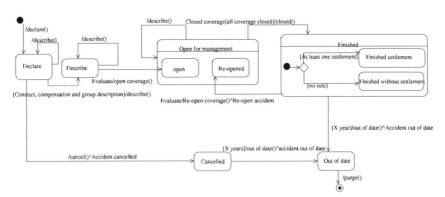

Figure 9.2. *States machine of semantic classes – SMABTP project*

What is a good semantic model? The quality of the model matters to the people in charge. They need to know at what point the model can be moved on to the next activity without any risk. The work in this field carried out by the French researchers Moulin, Tardieu, Teboul, etc. was picked up again by the American Peter Chen in his book *The Entity-Relationship Model* (*ACM, Transaction on Database Systems*, 1976). This book provides answers in the field of conceptual data models. The answers, i.e. normal forms, still apply.

The first form, for example, states that all attributes of the class have to receive one single value at every moment of their lifecycle. We might criticize this by saying that this type of requirement leads to a certain type of purism. On the other hand, this requirement ensures a clear perception of the business reality and "purifies" the concepts. The same applies to other normal forms. At least in theory, these concepts are justified by relational algebra, i.e. by the behavior of relational DBMS. Moreover, these rules help the semantic modeler and function as guides that carefully reveal the concepts.

As the object model is more expressive than the conceptual data model, it is necessary to complement the normal forms with other forms that consider new trends such as mastering genericity, exploiting polymorphism or functioning of states machines. Further details will not be provided in this chapter, but bear in mind that semantic modeling, as a form of art, needs to be carried out in the right way.

9.2.2. How to obtain a semantic model

Before establishing the first diagrams, the semantic modeler applies traditional procedures of collecting and analyzing. These are interviews with business experts, examination of texts describing the rules and the analysis of existing models (particularly data models).

A situation in which the model is used as a basis for discussions on the business knowledge has to be avoided at all costs. Indeed, the major difficulty in the management of projects lies in the confusion of form and content within the expression of the knowledge. The modeler is not necessarily familiar with the domain, at least not as familiar as the business expert. The expert might also be confused because of the form the model takes as well as the required level of abstraction and genericity. A third party will sometimes create the link between the two. Introducing an intermediary is not always the best solution as this representative often has an IT background and therefore does not understand the business reality in detail. They might forget about being a representative and influence the situation due to personal preferences or preconceived ideas. The representation they deliver might therefore be heavily influenced by IT.

9.2.3. *How to validate a semantic model*

The question of how to validate a semantic model also has to deal with the difficulty described above. To do so, the overall validation process needs to separate the validation of the content from the verification of the form. To make good use of the models, some basic requirements need to be met:

– Establish several simple diagrams (only a few elements) that correspond to the intent of communication (expressed in the title).

– Add comments to the diagrams (comments should also be added to the elements of modeling).

– Illustrate subtleties of models. This can be done with the help of objects diagrams that "unfold" the model.

– Reconstruct natural language on the basis of the model (e.g. create full sentences that reproduce the associations and their cardinalities).

– Establish the traceability of models and requirements.

In practice, this advice does not have much of an effect if it is being applied in an environment where there is no cooperation between IT and the user.

9.2.4. *Semantic models and property rights – who owns a semantic model?*

The semantic model expresses the basics of the business knowledge. Therefore, its natural owners are the "users", the real actors of the system. They are responsible for consolidating the model and promoting it through many different channels such as IT development, knowledge management, transformation process and training. This idea is based on the balance between mastering the content and understanding the form.

In our experience, when it comes to fully completing a project like this, one factor is more important than any other, namely, the involvement of a sponsor. The involvement of the sponsor has a great impact on how convincing the semantic model is. The sponsor should create a balance between those who advocate a traditional approach ("data-oriented") and those who would like to elaborate rigorous and exhaustive semantic expression.

A sponsor needs to intervene in order for the object-oriented logic to spread. Object logic leads to more genericity, the innovation of hidden concepts, and creates new structures which often change normal perceptions.

9.2.5. *The structure of a semantic model*

When the semantic model starts to expand, reaching hundreds of classes, the modelers have to structure the model. Structuring it will create a better overview of the model. The pitfall would be to introduce functional domains. A functional domain nearly always represents segmentation linked to the organization. This functional approach is closely linked to traditions in IT and the characteristics of these traditions are often forgotten about. The functional domain reveals its character by its denomination and variations in its verbal form, e.g. inventory, monitoring operations, human resource management.

The Praxeme methodology preserves the notion of the functional domain but it localizes this notion within the pragmatic aspect, which will be covered in the following part of this chapter. The pragmatic aspect includes everything that is linked to the organization.

The semantic model, with a superior level of abstraction, has to be kept separate from all forms of contamination caused by organizational decisions. This is why semantic models cannot be decomposed according to functional domains. It is necessary to resort to another idea that respects the object logic and does not include any previous organizational assumptions. This idea is the "object domain". When decomposing the semantic model, the criteria used to do so have to be kept in mind at all times. The action of decomposing will have a strong impact on the activities throughout the lifecycle of the system.

The semantic model can naturally be broken down into object domains, i.e. a domain of knowledge that is linked to one main object (either real or business object). There is a sort of violence in the functional way of breaking down a system. On the contrary, the semantic modeling approach lets the objects arrange themselves along the lines of their natural links.

This point is of great importance as the object domains will play an important role in the logical architecture, especially in the SOA style. The system's features could be changed due to object domains. The advent of this new way of structuring helps us to escape the functionalist approach.

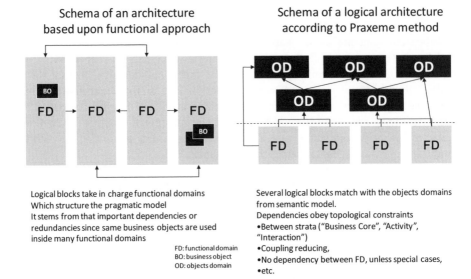

Schema of an architecture based upon functional approach

Schema of a logical architecture according to Praxeme method

Logical blocks take in charge functional domains
Which structure the pragmatic model
It stems from that important dependencies or
redundancies since same business objects are used
inside many functional domains

FD: functional domain
BO: business object
OD: objects domain

Several logical blocks match with the objects domains
from semantic model.
Dependencies obey topological constraints
•Between strata ("Business Core", "Activity",
"Interaction")
•Coupling reducing,
•No dependency between FD, unless special cases,
•etc.

Figure 9.3. *Functional architecture and Praxeme*

To conclude this section on semantic modeling, it is also important to mention that this approach deals with the basics of the business knowledge. This is why this approach leads on to generic models. If a model is liberated from all local variations linked to organization, there is no reason for it to differ from one company to another. At least this is the case if both companies are working in the same sector. In the insurance sector, for example, a network of alliances and partnerships is predominant. There is, therefore, a strong interest in an insurance reference model that is adopted by many companies. If different parties in a group or a network are connected, the semantic model favors convergence. This level of convergence could not be reached when using other aspects, processes or different forms of IT.

Zones of semantic models can be relevant for different economic sectors. A good example might be a "repository of persons" shared between the public and private sectors. All parties involved would refer to such a reference model. Based on the importance of semantic models it becomes possible to produce banalized components. Semantic modeling aims at mutualization and is the first step towards standardized components. Modeling relies on generic solutions and open source since companies share meaning rather than software or data.

9.3. Pragmatic modeling

9.3.1. *The basic principles*

The Enterprise System Topology (EST) locates the "pragmatic aspect" behind the semantic aspect. The semantic model is exclusively interested in the business objects and concepts. The pragmatic model introduces action to these objects as well as actors and organization. Pragmatic modeling is a procedure that recycles the functional approach. Depending on their education and culture, the modelers might perceive a company as a set of activities. The state of the art in the field of methodology reinforces this natural trend. On the one hand, this aspect is commonly used as the first level of representation. On the other hand, it promotes the idea of the process being a major category in the representation of the enterprise and its business. This aspect is closely linked to action and can be found in the architectural plans of TOGAF and in meta-model of IS urbanization. In the latter, the "business object" can be found but it is not very important in comparison to the process.

To represent organizational processes, the modeler has the choice of several forms of notation. Some are standardized, such as BPMN, and others are proprietary. Of course, standards make it possible for representations to be shared between several parties and for the linking of tools in the transformation chain. After all, the symbols that are being used are not very important; it is the categories of representation that count. The Praxeme methodological framework is compatible with the usage of several forms of notation. However:

– The UML standard is favored. The creators of UML have not introduced this modeling language to model processes. However, UML contains everything that is needed to do so. Using the UML standard to model a process offers two advantages to a company. First of all, there is a financial advantage, as the same tool can be used twice in the transformation chain. Furthermore, there is an operational advantage as linking together models of different kinds makes it possible to apply an MDA (model driven architecture) approach.

– The possibilities of expression that UML offers for the modeling of processes are largely sufficient. These possibilities rely on the diagram of activities and create an innovative approach towards the process, which will be explained later on in this text. In comparison, specialized forms of notation might appear complicated and suffer from one major fault: they do not exchange information with other models, especially not semantic models. Furthermore, they do not provide any answers to difficult questions in the modeling of processes, such as common activities, two activities being carried out simultaneously but at a different rhythm (such as common activities like production and management), etc.

Praxeme suggests a procedure of modeling a process that stimulates organizational innovation. First of all, analysis and design need to be distinguished. The term "design" is commonly restricted to software development. According to the dictionary, "analyzing" means studying a phenomenon. To design implies coming up with a solution. These two terms are relevant to all aspects of the enterprise. In semantics, analysis identifies business concepts. Due to genericity and abstraction, the semantic modeler also makes decisions when elaborating a more efficient structure, enlarging a concept, transforming the knowledge. This is design, in the field of the semantic aspect.

When it comes to processes, the majority of efforts in modeling are limited to describing existing practices. This analytical approach is reinforced by the taboos that exist in the field of organizational science. Designing a process is part of designing a form of organization. One cannot exist without the other. Whether this type of project can be carried out successfully depends on the willingness of the organization to introduce reforms, how receptive the stakeholders are and the competences of the organizer or modeler, as well as their capacity to distance themselves from current practices. It is not enough to know how to represent processes. The organizer and the process designer need to know a bit about the sociology of organizations and have a background in management theory. In most cases, this work is carried out by software engineers who lack this knowledge. The reason certainly lies in the fact that IT is one of the last fields where modeling skills survive. Organizational inventions are currently decreasing. On one hand, they are limited by directors who hinder organizational innovation. On the other hand, the process modeling has been limited to laborious and pernickety descriptions of procedures.

Furthermore, the functionalist culture hinders the capacity for innovation. The modeler sees the process as an activity and breaks it down into subactivities until the necessary level has been reached. Strangely enough, the methods of modeling often impose a fixed number of levels in the process of decomposing. This rule is entirely artificial. It does not reflect any constraint in the real world. The traditional approach to processes suffers from another fault. This approach reproduces the compartmentalization that it encounters. Compartmentalization is reinforced by the identification of the same, often intra-functional, processes. The modeler therefore reinforces the organization and distribution of roles and, as a result, the enterprise misses an opportunity of improvement.

9.3.2. *A new procedure for designing processes*

The procedure of designing a process suggested by Praxeme alters the traditional approach entirely. Instead of separating actors and actions, it carries out the following steps (see Figure 9.4):

#1. Identifying the main object in the heart of the process. This object is already present in the semantic model.

#2. Establishing the lifecycle of this object. The main objects are semantically rich and nearly always equipped with a states machine.

#3. Turning the states diagram upside down to obtain an activity diagram that in someway represents the "conceptual" process. This "conceptual" process is still free from organizational hypothesis.

#4. Distributing the actions according to the type of actors.

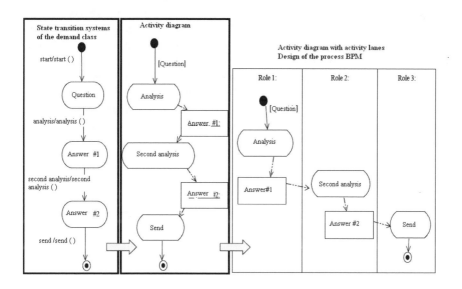

Figure 9.4. *Moving from a diagram of states to a diagram of UML activities*

In this approach the actor and the organization are discovered at the end of the procedure. This way, the designer gains the freedom to create new distributions. The designer does not carry out the observation of practices but observes the basics, i.e. semantically free from all contingencies. This approach positions the designer of the process, as well as the organizer, between what is essential and what is superficial. What is essential can be found in the core knowledge that the semantic model emits and transmits.

9.3.3. *Usage view*

The models of processes and organization belong to the "organization view", i.e. the global representation of a pragmatic aspect (previous section). The same aspect also shows itself through a local view. The local view is the view of operators that are directly involved in the systems. Their point of view is expressed in the usage view. Praxeme recommends expressing this point of view based on use-cases. A use-case describes a situation of work, i.e. an elementary interaction between the actor and the system. The procedure of modeling is based on this precise definition. This precision is necessary to avoid issues that have arisen in several projects. The notion of the use-case is applied at many different levels when it comes to creating links between those levels.

The project manager has to be warned about one issue. The first version of the use-case description is a version used for analysis. It describes current practices and is influenced by assumptions rooted within the IT tool. This first version is always badly structured and subject to many redundancies. Before taking this model into the next phase, it is important to restructure it and produce a new version. The second version cuts out the redundancies. This effort is necessary to prepare the version for SOA's activities. Indeed, the rules of derivation are applied to this model and allow for its logical structuring and reduction of some services. If the rules are applied to a badly structured pragmatic model, they take the redundancies with them and introduce them into the logical architecture, and later on into the software. This should be avoided at all costs!

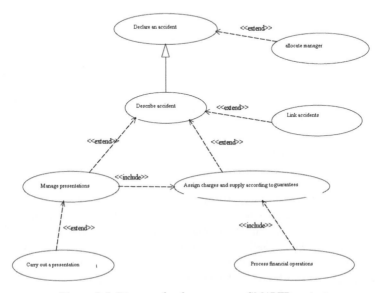

Figure 9.5. *Diagram for the use-case – SMABTP project*

The use-case "declaring an accident" consists of several activities (see Figure 9.6). Business activity means carrying out an update which will change the state of the system. In the example, these are "cancel an accident", "declare", "enter the circumstances of the accident" and "allocate to management."

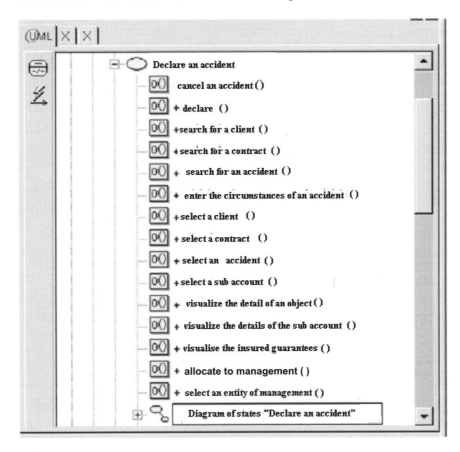

Figure 9.6. *The "declaring an accident" use-case – SMABTP project*

The scenarios of linking activities and business activity for the use-case are modeled in the form of a states machine which can be observed in Figure 9.6 entitled "declaring an accident."

Instead of specifying the scenarios describing the use-case in an informal way, it makes more sense to use UML. UML allows for the states machine to be directly linked to a use-case. Figure 9.7 has been obtained for modeling "declaring an accident".

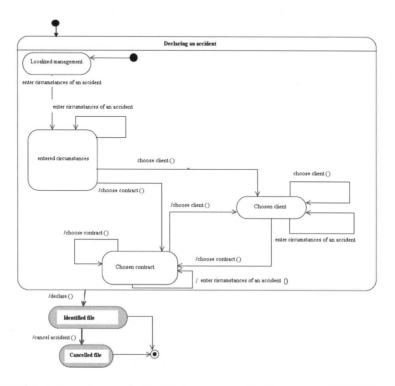

Figure 9.7. *A states diagram for the "declaring an accident" use-case – SMABTP project*

9.4. Pre-modeling

According to Praxeme, the eight aspects of topology in Enterprise System Topology (EST) are all likely to undergo formal modeling carried out with a UML notation. However, before starting a UML modeling it is useful, and nearly always necessary, to ask the users to express their needs in a more textual form. This type of file is known as General Functional Specifications (GFS) or Detailed Functional Specifications (DFS). These specifications serve as a very useful basis for the formal semantic and pragmatic modeling. So as not to alter the specification of pre-modeling, as well as the semantic and pragmatic models, the following precautions must be taken:

– On the basis of GFS and DFS it makes sense to feed a formal nomenclature of the identified business rules. It is important that these rules are distinguished according to whether they concern the business basics or the organizational how-to-do. Here, the modeling tool should include or interface with a tool for requirements management. Future UML models of semantic and pragmatic aspects could create links that would ensure the traceability of the requirements expressed in GFS and DFS.

– The screen models are produced at the same time as GFS and DFS. The descriptions associated with the linking of screens and the trigger of actions should also be modeled in UML. At this stage, a purely textual description would be very long and difficult, as well as incomplete.

– A repository of terms would be required from the very beginning of the project. This repository gives a precise overview of the vocabulary and definitions that would allow for communication between users and software engineers.

9.5. Logical modeling

Service-oriented architecture is situated on the level of a system's logical modeling. This type of architecture is obtained by a derivation of semantic and pragmatic models. Like all other aspects of the Enterprise System, it retains the standard UML notation. The aim is to structure the system in the form of logical components that are similar to services and work on the level of the identified issues. Here the "business services" (derived from the semantic model) and "organization services" (derived from pragmatic model) are distinguished. Precise rules of communication between logical components allow for loose coupling, separating " Business Core" and "Activity" strata, flow of normalized data, etc. to be favored.

The rules of logical architecture in SOA are numerous. They absorb best practices from several disciplines. These include contract-based design, the design of languages for specialized data, algorithms, object approach for this type of architecture, etc. This chapter provides an overview of logic modeling. All rules are summarized in the Praxeme corpus, which can be accessed freely.

9.5.1. *SOA's style of logical architecture*

Every style of logical architecture is characterized by a specific terminology based on a metaphor and even more so on the criterion of decomposition and solutions that ensure communication throughout the system. The traditional style is marked by the functionalist approach. Functional architecture is logical architecture whose criterion is the breaking down of the system into functions. This functionalist perception dominates our culture. Therefore, it comes as no surprise that the majority of existing systems are marked by this style. Designers who do not question whether they are using the right approach will automatically choose a functional style.

SOA is a style that is defined by the elementary unit of the service and by the type of communication, i.e. the call for service. The logical model of this style requires a generalized device to ensure the communication between all points of the system via call for service. All points can be related to each other while respecting topological limits. Other styles are also possible. Some are already applicable today, while others will only work in combination with future technologies. EDA (*Event Driven Architecture*), for example, is a good candidate and might be mixed with service-based architecture. EDA reduces coupling within the system, as communication is no longer based only on call for services but also on the transmission of events. In the call for services scenario, the client needs to know who their provider is. In EDA the transmitter does not need to know who will process the event. Coupling is therefore reduced. For IT architecture an object-oriented style is also possible. In the current state of technologies, this style is already being used at the level of applications, but does not work very well on the level of systems. An object-oriented model, which has been created based on cooperation between objects, encourages the propagation of calls. At a higher level, this propagation puts the functioning of the system at risk. Logical architecture makes it possible to mix several styles with results just as beautiful as an art form! Mixing SOA and EDA has several advantages but makes the designer's task much more difficult. Indeed, mixing styles provides several different solutions for the same problem. Unless the method establishes precise directives, the designer needs to ask questions with the risk of obtaining different answers from different designers.

9.5.2. *Service-oriented architecture as logical architecture*

Service-oriented architecture is situated in the logical aspect. The logical model describes, in non-technical terms, the company's information system. The object is in fact the IT system. It is vital to provide a representation of the system, so that the parties will understand the main decisions. Such a representation cannot bear technological details.

To ensure that the information system is understood by the actors, the logical model uses metaphors. The metaphor "urbanization" has been used in France for about 15 years. The system is compared to a city and decomposed into different zones, areas, districts, etc., with the aim of this metaphor being sustainable development. The older TACT method introduced the idea of the machine as a logical component. SOA is based on the metaphor of services. The system is seen as a collection of components that function as service providers. The key point of this metaphor is that internal details and necessary resources for the provider disappear. The client (consumer of a service) needs to know only the result it expects.

Furthermore, a logical model is independent of technological choices and lasts longer than technical architecture. Logical modeling is the basis for long term vision and knowledge on the information system. This stability is a key factor. Indeed, urbanization is implemented over the long term. A stable description in the long term is a necessary condition for continuous work on the system carried out over 5, 10 or 15 years.

FOCUS ON VOCABULARY: LOGICAL SERVICE

In the Praxeme technique of logical modeling, the logical service is represented in the form of a UML operation.[1] This position disagrees with usage which is inspired by Web services. Web services describe "services" as a component that offers several operations.

According to the Enterprise System Topology (EST), techniques such as Web services are situated in the software aspect.

In the perspective of overhaul SOA, thousands of services cover the entire IT system. The logical modeler groups these services together, according to their origin: either semantic aspect or pragmatic aspect. Creating these links leads to the concept of logical aggregates.

FOCUS ON VOCABULARY: SERVICE INTERFACE

The interface of services is the only means of communication with a logical component. It contains services that are openly shown on the component and private services that cannot be seen on the outside of the component.

9.5.3. *Types of logical components*

Every concept of upstream modeling (semantic or pragmatic) derives from SOA's logical architecture in the form of a logical component that offers services. Praxeme is based on the metaphor of a factory to name different levels of logical aggregates. Figure 9.8 shows derivations. The functional domain "Claims management" inside the pragmatic aspect transforms itself into an "organization

---

1. This operation is a "stereotype" (as defined in the UML standard). The mechanism of a stereotype allows for the UML's syntax to be enriched. Stereotyping an operation means imposing certain rules.

workshop" in the logical aspect (aoAccidentManagement). The use-case "managing an accident" is transformed in a logical machine "moDeclareAccident". Every use-case is picked up again by a logical model in the form of a "logical machine". This exemplifies the derivation rules Praxeme proposes in order to build an SOA.

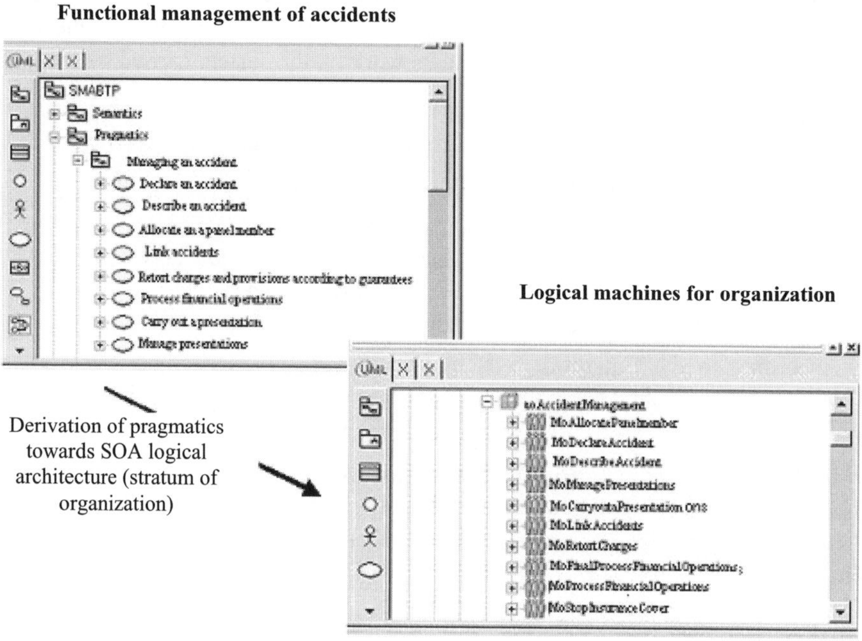

Functional management of accidents

Derivation of pragmatics towards SOA logical architecture (stratum of organization)

Logical machines for organization

Figure 9.8. *Logical machines for organization – SMABTP project*

Every logical machine contains services that allow for activities to be carried out and business activity from the original use-case. Figure 9.9, for example, shows the services presented by the "MoDeclareAccident" component which is a logical machine for organization. The "InfoDeclareAccident" type of data describes the flow of information by "MoDeclareAccident" in order for the task to be carried out.

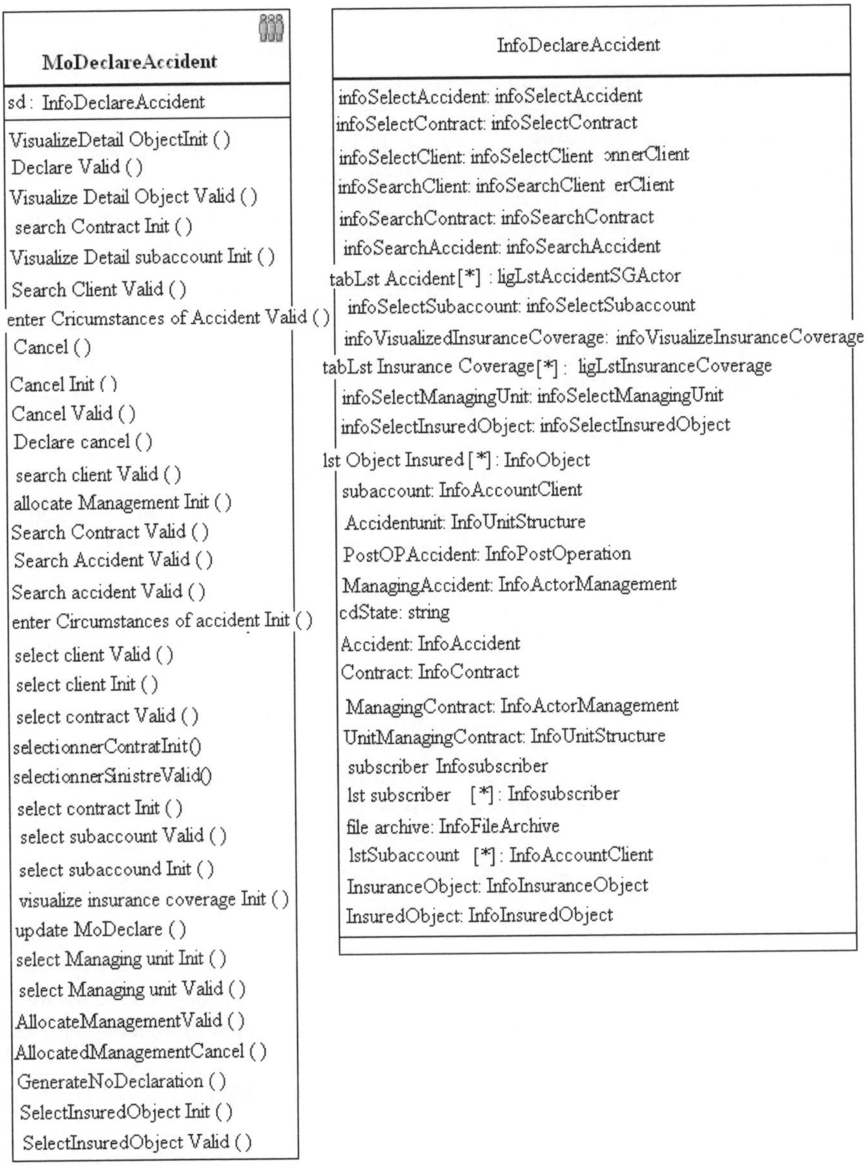

MoDeclareAccident
sd : InfoDeclareAccident
VisualizeDetail ObjectInit ( ) Declare Valid ( ) Visualize Detail Object Valid ( ) search Contract Init ( ) Visualize Detail subaccount Init ( ) Search Client Valid ( ) enter Cricumstances of Accident Valid ( ) Cancel ( ) Cancel Init ( ) Cancel Valid ( ) Declare cancel ( ) search client Valid ( ) allocate Management Init ( ) Search Contract Valid ( ) Search Accident Valid ( ) Search accident Valid ( ) enter Circumstances of accident Init ( ) select client Valid ( ) select client Init ( ) select contract Valid ( ) selectionnerContratInit() selectionnerSinistreValid() select contract Init ( ) select subaccount Valid ( ) select subacound Init ( ) visualize insurance coverage Init ( ) update MoDeclare ( ) select Managing unit Init ( ) select Managing unit Valid ( ) AllocateManagementValid ( ) AllocatedManagementCancel ( ) GenerateNoDeclaration ( ) SelectInsuredObject Init ( ) SelectInsuredObject Valid ( )

InfoDeclareAccident
infoSelectAccident: infoSelectAccident infoSelectContract: infoSelectContract infoSelectClient: infoSelectClient onnerClient infoSearchClient: infoSearchClient erClient infoSearchContract: infoSearchContract infoSearchAccident: infoSearchAccident tabLst Accident[*] : ligLstAccidentSGActor infoSelectSubaccount: infoSelectSubaccount infoVisualizedInsuranceCoverage: infoVisualizeInsuranceCoverage tabLst Insurance Coverage[*] : ligLstInsuranceCoverage infoSelectManagingUnit: infoSelectManagingUnit infoSelectInsuredObject: infoSelectInsuredObject lst Object Insured [*] : InfoObject subaccount: InfoAccountClient Accidentunit: InfoUnitStructure PostOPAccident: InfoPostOperation ManagingAccident: InfoActorManagement cdState: string Accident: InfoAccident Contract: InfoContract ManagingContract: InfoActorManagement UnitManagingContract: InfoUnitStructure subscriber Infosubscriber lst subscriber   [*] : Infosubscriber file archive: InfoFileArchive lstSubaccount   [*] : InfoAccountClient InsuranceObject: InfoInsuranceObject InsuredObject: InfoInsuredObject

Figure 9.9. *The "MoDeclareAccident" logical machine – SMABTP project*

Logical architecture is obtained by a derivation of upstream models. This is the reason why these models need to cut out all redundancies. Otherwise, the redundancies will be reproduced in the service-oriented architecture.

Beyond these few examples, the types of logical components allow for the construction of an entirely service-oriented architecture:

– Stratum: imposes a structure that maintains the separation between semantics and pragmatics (the strata are "Business Core", "Activity", "Interaction").

– Logical Business Factory (LBF): corresponds to an object domain from the semantic aspect.

– Logical Activity Factory (LAF): groups together logical aggregates which take charge of pragmatic specifications.

– Logical Activity Machine (LAM): results from the derivation of a use-case.

– Logical Business Machine (LBM): derives from a semantic class.

– Logical Activity Workshop (LAW): creates a group of LAMs linked to cohesive set of activities. The number of LAMs in a workshop is generally reduced (fewer than five) and does not impose the implementation of a service interface. Every LAM exposes its services that can be accessed from outside ("Interaction" stratum). Each LAW derives from a functional domain found in the pragmatic aspect.

– Logical Business Workshop (LBW): creates a group of LBM linked to the same business object. This is a category class concept explained by Grady Booch in UML [BOOCH, 1996]. An LBW usually includes around 15 LBMs and contains an interface that offers services to other components in the system. An LBW never directly shows its services. LBW is the only mechanism that takes on the role of an interface and provides access to data in respect of usage. This data might be restricted to each LBW. Loose coupling between workshops is favored when it comes to accessing data.

Communication between logical components respects strict rules that favor loose coupling. Machines are part of logical workshops that are united in logical factories.

Figure 9.10 shows the vocabulary used above. There are only three levels of aggregation, from the machine to the factory.

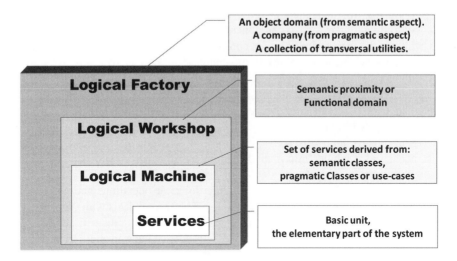

Figure 9.10. *Different types of logical components*

The stumbling block of SOA is the question of how to find the services. A method must be found for SOA to be able to provide not only the aims but the details of the design techniques. By applying the Praxeme method for SOA rather than inventing everything, the designer discovers the services. He/she obtains the services through derivation. Let us take a look at the position of the logical aspect in Enterprise System Topology (see Figure 9.11). The logical aspect depends on the semantic aspect as well as the pragmatic aspect. The arrows in the image emphasize these interconnections.

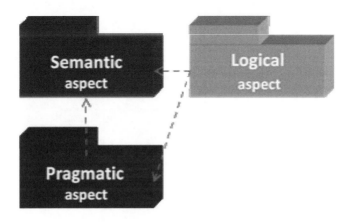

Figure 9.11. *Position of the logical aspect in topology*

Every arrow (or dependency) sums up the rules of derivation that enable the designer to obtain their logical components from the basis of an upstream model. In this way, the logical designer is not confronted with a blank page and obliged to produce the service specifications from scratch. This way of working also ensures that the services are not too orientated towards IT. Due to a lack of method, designers reduce services to mere "accessors" which are void of semantics and limited to CRUD (create, remove, update, delete). These are largely insufficient when dealing with an object throughout its entire lifecycle. An example of derivation rules is applied to semantic classes. A semantic class gives an overview of semantics as a whole (information, action, transformation) and is attached to a concept or a set of objects. Its derivation towards a logical model produces two "logical machines". The first logical machine looks at operations and corrects the services by considering the general limitations. The second deals with "set services" such as the creation of a new instance, search functions, statistical services and asynchronic services used for batch processing. The "Guide to the logical aspect" (available on the Praxeme website) describes the rules of derivation precisely.

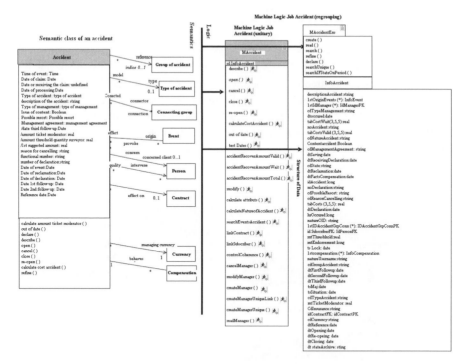

Figure 9.12. *The derivation of a semantic class – SMABTP project*

Figure 9.13 shows another example. This example represents the derivation of object domains found inside the semantic aspect. These are produced in "logical business factories", the largest aggregates among the logical constituents.

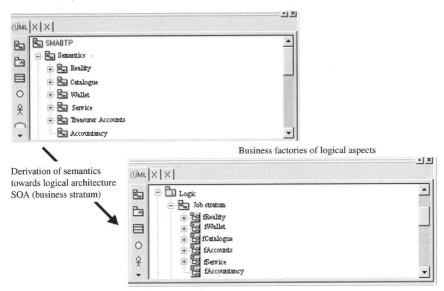

Figure 9.13. *The derivation of object domains – SMABTP project*

9.5.4. *The strata of logical architecture*

As shown above, logical conception is based on two sources. These are the semantic and pragmatic models. Pragmatic models express a choice of different forms of organization and the company's ways of working. Semantic models isolate the key factor of common knowledge that is shared by a sector of activity. Logical architecture needs to maintain this separation in the description of the company. The challenge is considerable and includes the quality of the system, its agility, its interoperability and its capability to work over a distance. This is why Praxeme provides a structure that logical architecture can use. As a first step, logical architecture stratifies the system. All systems contain the following three strata:[2]

---

2. The term "stratum" was chosen to avoid confusion with layers, as this term is used in technical architecture.

– The "Business Core" stratum is the system's nucleus. It was created by a semantic model and contains the essential information on the company. This is the only place where job objects can be found.

– The "Activity" (or "Organization") stratum surrounds the nucleus and protects it. Its content derives from a pragmatic model. Organizational specifications can be found in this stratum.

– The "Interaction" (or "Presentation") stratum is the system's input/output device. It allows for interactions between the system and its environment. This interface allows for the exchange between humans and the machine, as well as between different systems. The logical model of this stratum tells of exchanges and interactions, regardless of technical choices.

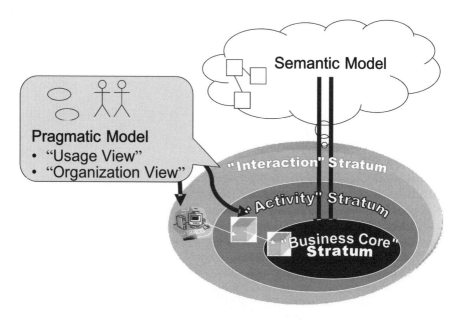

Figure 9.14. *Strata and their origins*

The principle of stratification restructures the IT system, at least in the field of its logical aspect. Stratification goes hand in hand with the following topological limits:

– polarization of communication. Calls move from the outside to the inside. The components of the organization stratum can call upon the components of the "Business Core" stratum. The opposite is, however, impossible;

– reduction of horizontal dependencies. The components of the "Activity" stratum cannot call upon each other (except with special dispensations).

These rules of architecture help to reduce coupling and to master the system.

9.5.5. *Pivot language*

Logical architecture is not only limited to elaborating and structuring logical components, it also contains a dynamic dimension. Without this dimension there would not be much interest in logical architecture. While decomposing the system, it needs to consider communication between logical components. The aim is in fact to improve communication for a better functioning of the entire system. This type of exchange is described as a form of flow that goes hand in hand with services. The signature of services leads the flow. There is an entering flow, which ensures the functioning of the services, as well as a flow that exits and communicates the results. The procedure describes these flows as complex types in UML. They derive from upstream models according to the rule defined by the method. The following principle is used. A class contains attributes that represent information on a business object created on the basis of manipulated concepts. This data structure is reproduced from within the logical model. Precise rules impose alterations and assembling. These complex types appear in the signature of logical services such as the parameters or the result. The set of descriptions is the pivot language. The essentials of this language come from a semantic model and can therefore be shared to a large extent.

This principle of organizing exchanges around the flow of standardized data (at least for the IS perimeter) is very different from a form of organization that is based on the passage of data, issued bit by bit according to the needs of the exchange. The pivot language, for example, defines that the "client" data structure can contain 50 pieces of data that are systematically being exchanged. The other approach consists in transporting only a sub-group of these 50 pieces of data. The sub-group is defined according to the needs of every exchange. The use of data flow is more efficient for the services' evolutionary process. When modifying a service, a supplementary data element therefore might need to be exchanged. When using the system of flow there is a high probability that this piece of information has already been transferred via the flow. If this is not the case, the flow can be increased without changing the services' signature (the same type of complex attributes is still being exchanged). The transmission of parameters in the form of flow does not decrease the legibility of the services' interface. The service contract states all information exchanged in the flow of data. The consumer deals with of all manipulated data, not only the name of the respective flow.

The consumption of resources in the system could be rather worrying, as the level of performance might decrease due to the use of amounts of data flow. In practice, the correct use of technical architecture ensures high performance. In particular, the XML flow-based exchange is less rapid than native calls, but has to be reserved for services that are either situated on the borders of IT system and/or exposed to the outside of the company. At this point XML's interoperability becomes interesting. The services and flow represent an average of 20% of all data to be processed. The other 80% is inside the information system and has to communicate in the native technology of platforms, e.g. Java. In this case, the number of variables interacting with services does not have an impact on performance. Due to the mechanisms of the Praxeme method, it is possible to dynamically reduce the content of the flow. This reduction can be carried out if a piece of software should only be partially exposed. MDM allows for the configuration of these parameters.

9.5.6. *Service algorithm specification*

An exhaustive logical modeling is favored by a formal language used for service algorithms, i.e. a pseudo-language also known as pseudo-code. One basic condition is that the data to be manipulated by algorithms is identified in the formal terms of a pivot language, i.e. under a precise form of notation. The cost of an accident is, for example, established with the notation "InfoAccident.costInitial". This procedure helps the software developer as he/she does not need to investigate the flow of data and the variables that are used in the software. Pseudo-language will be covered in the chapter dealing with the tools of the Praxeme method.

For the algorithms of organizational services, pseudo-language is reduced because the organizational rules are implemented in the rules engine. Algorithms of organizational services are therefore limited to iterative structures that cannot be implemented in the rules engine. These structures are used in the preparation of the flow that sends data to the rules engine as well as for the invocation of the engine when generating an answer.

9.5.7. *Specification of the services' pre- and post-conditions*

States machines are also used in the logical aspect. They help to determine the pre- and the post-conditions of services. These models have been obtained by a derivation of states machines from semantic and pragmatic aspects. Their representation works as shown in Figure 9.15 (according to UML syntax the transition reads "event [condition]/action").

Figure 9.15. *The representation of pre- and post-conditions*

In UML the transition between two states is expressed with the help of a syntax "event trigger (condition of onset)/action". The procedure of logical modeling makes a restricted use of the possibilities of expression of the UML's states diagram. The event trigger is the name as the service. The condition of onset represents the service's pre-condition. The action takes place when the service is being carried out. The post-condition is represented in the form of a state condition that is linked to the "finish line state." In Figure 9.16 the following information can be obtained: pre-conditions service1 = state 1 + pre-conditions01; post-conditions service1 = post-conditions01 under the condition of state + state 2. In a real example similar to this one, which represents "Claim" logical business machine, there is a variety of ways in which pre- and post-conditions can be expressed.

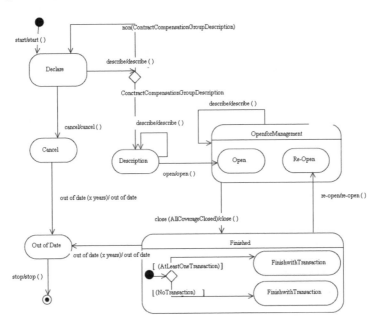

Figure 9.16. *Pre- and post-conditions accident states machine – SMABTP project*

9.5.8. *Logical architecture of data*

So far logical modeling and the architecture of services have been presented. These are, however, only a part of logical models. Logical models can be seen as two juxtaposed layers. The "layer of services" is put on top of and hides the "layer of data". From the outside (i.e. from another system, logical workshop or user interface) only the services can be seen. However, for these services to function they rely on hidden sources, i.e. data support.[3]

Logical modeling also has to produce a Logical Data Model (LDM). To obtain this model, the designer uses the rules of derivation based on a semantic model as well as on models of classes that derive from a pragmatic model. These rules of derivation for computer system engineering have been adapted to deal with the new, object-oriented approach.[4] To produce an LDM the designer cannot simply apply the rules of derivation, they have to choose between possible options. First of all, the designer needs to establish data architecture. To do so determinants have to be decided upon. SOA aims at the construction of autonomous constituents. In Praxeme's terminology, the logical workshop is a good candidate for becoming a deployment unit, in the physical aspect. These units will be covered later on when dealing with the physical aspect.

Ideally, the system's architect can take this unit and replace a hub of physical architecture with another one. In this case, all the unit's resources are also moved from one position to another. This is the description of a component which is compatible with SOA. This definition leads to the following conclusion. For an easier movement and deployment of logical blocs, the database needs to be included inside the same perimeter as the blocs themselves. Designers use the architecture of services as well as the architecture of data. Of course, a radical SOA architecture would lead to an insufficient exploitation of relational DBMS. Indeed, it would prevent most of the jointures between tables which are under the control of different logical workshops.

---

3. Physical resources are not mentioned here as the logical aspect is being examined. Physical resources are treated when looking at other aspects of the system's topology. These are the material aspect (infrastructures) and the physical aspect (localization of a program's components in physical machines).

4. Previous research is, of course, taken into account. Qualified associations, associative classes and state transition systems, etc. also have to be considered. This subject is covered in the Praxeme repository (reference PxM-41).

To illustrate this suggestion, the following set of rules should be applied according to aims of the architecture in question:

– Every table is under the exclusive control of two machines. One is the "elementary" machine, while the other is the "set" machine which is in charge of the collection operations.

– Tables that belong to different workshops cannot be linked unless there is an express permission.

– If it is possible to produce a new data architecture, the designer will attempt to adjust it to the architecture of services, i.e. the database has to correspond to a logical aggregate (a logical workshop or a logical factory).

– Choosing a logical aggregate (workshop or factory) that reduces the limits of the database depends directly on the degree of freedom that we look for at the moment of deployment.

9.5.9. *Logical architecture of data repositories*

Data repositories concern the business information (client repositories, configuration of offers, catalog of products, structure of the organization, etc.) as well as encoders (tables of codes and labels) and functional parameters and techniques. Logical modeling of these repositories has to take the requirements of all systems into consideration, no matter whether SOA is being used or not:

– Managing versions on the level of a data model (structure of reference data) as well as on the basis of values. Associated administrative functions need to be accessible. There is, for example, the differential analysis and comparison between different versions, the fusion of different versions, going back to a previous version, etc.

– Managing the contexts. The same piece of reference data must be capable of being of a different value, depending on its context of consumption. The "rate of credit" reference data takes on a different value according to its context of distribution per headquarters, subsidiaries, segments of the market, partners, etc. To factorize these values the context takes the form of a tree of values.

– Managing the process of submitting modifications of reference data and parameters for approval.

– Managing authorizations to provide access to administrators (managers of reference data) to applications that consume and update the reference data. The right to access a certain area is granted in groups of data, elementary data, tables, etc.

– Creating a history of data. Every reference data update is saved in the history.

– Total traceability. All modifications of reference data are traced back in an audit file. This function is important in the context of rules that impose a detailed trace of certain types of data.

These functions require specialized tools that are used for the management of references and parameters, i.e. an MDM solution. MDM absorbs all types of reference enterprise information (client repository, configuring a product, product catalog, etc.) as well as on functional and technical aspects (tables of labeled codes, parameters). The human-machine interface for the administration of data can also be managed automatically. The administration of data includes the distribution of values according to context, managing different versions, queries, etc.

9.5.10. *Logical architecture and user interface*

For interactive systems, a user interface is integrated into the stratum "Interaction." The logical modeling of user interface cannot be neglected, as its running might require a complex workflow system to manage the respective screens and services. The following issues of modeling need to be kept in mind:

– static components: portlets,[5] pages, etc. in the form of classes with embedded classes;

– possible actions on static components in the form of signals;

– workflow orchestration of the services in the "Activity" stratum with the help of an activity diagram;

– structures of data presented in portlets in the form of classes. These structures serve the user interface and allow for loose coupling with manipulated flow on the level of organizational services;

– lifecycle of the data's context. The lifecycle is determined by states machines that model the clean-up actions and update the context of data according to the current state of events that enter through the user interface.

Figure 9.17 shows an example of invoking services from an organizational machine MoDistributeCharges. This process of invocation is carried out with the help of a window which shows possible types of compensation.

---

5. Part of the display that is reusable.

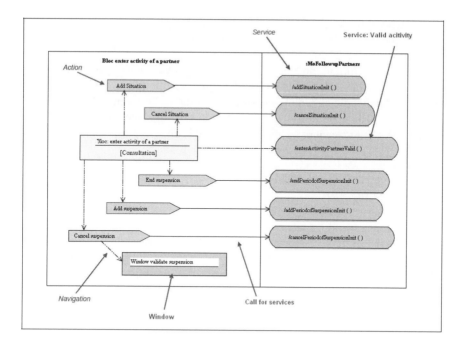

Figure 9.17. *An activity diagram showing interaction between user
interface and services – SMABTP project*

9.5.11. *Designing a logic for tests*

Logical modeling of services goes hand in hand with the design of tests and the associated sets of data. This concept should be anticipated on the level of aspects for upstream semantics and pragmatics. In practice, it is rare that projects experience the necessary upstream investment for tests. At best, the design of tests comes into play during logical modeling. If the design of the test fails, the team of designers has no means to test their products.

As the modeling of services is based on a formal notation, the same level of formality should be used in the tests. On the basis of this modeling, a technical device should be created which would automatically generate a test for the respective services. This automatic generation of a test would be based on a database of all tests and their logical components.

If the test is designed successfully, the team of designers will obtain the test tools that enable them to check whether the program has been developed correctly. Without these tools, the designers have to write the tests themselves or hire logical designers who will take over this task. Working with logical designers requires a form of organization that is adapted to this type of cooperation.

The success of formal modeling of a test also depends on the quality of the tools that the designers have at their disposal. Managing the lifecycle of the tests of sets of data is particularly crucial. Unless the structure of data is being modified in an UML tool UML, the data capture tool for tests has to take the automatic functioning of data structures into account. This is rather difficult given the current level of technology. This aspect will be covered in Chapter 10.

9.5.12. *Considering ERP*

ERP solutions could be integrated into the architecture of services. The easiest procedure, if their size and structure allow for it, is to assimilate these solutions as logical aggregates. A logical aggregate is, for example, a logical factory, e.g. an accountancy module. A logical workshop provides services for a GIS.[6] Even in complex cases, the ERP solution is projected over several factories and needs to be considered as a resource hidden below the layer of services.

9.5.13. *Considering existent assets*

Combining a target with an existing system works in the same way. Considering an existing system should not hinder the design of the target as it has been expressed in the logical architecture graph. Existing applications appear in the software model as resources for the services.

9.5.14. *Federation of systems*

Praxeme's method for SOA considers the federation of systems. Every organization in the company network is represented in the form of a logical factory in the "Activity" stratum.

The logical factories of this stratum are not linked in any way. They share the common resources in the "Business Core" stratum (see Figure 9.18). That is the secret when connecting many systems and still handling the complexity.

---

6. Geographic information system (GIS).

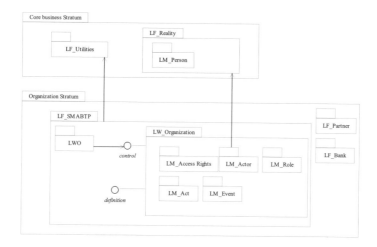

Figure 9.18. *A federation of systems*

9.5.15. *Roles of logical modeling*

When managing SOA projects and an overhaul of systems, the person in charge looks out for mobilization and management of competences. The methodology and the cartographic overview of those competences provide the criteria of excellence. From a logical aspect, the construction of an entire system requires three disciplines, which are in competition with one another. These are IS urbanization, logical architecture and logical design. The next section shows how these three disciplines are linked to technical expertise.

The enterprise architect develops the "big picture" from what has been observed in the company, possible evolutions of the business and strategic objectives. The enterprise architect's role is to create a link between the "business actors" and IT.

The logical architect adds details and dimensions to this map and makes an evaluation on the basis of the logical architecture graph. This graph shows the main decisions about the structure of the system. It has been linked with precise decisions on how to implement the logical model, devices and rules of logical design.

The dossier on logical architecture discusses the target of urbanization by considering both statics and dynamics. This dossier preserves and justifies the decisions of logical architecture. When looking at the results, logical architecture appears in the form of several diagrams with comments that explain the choice of structure.

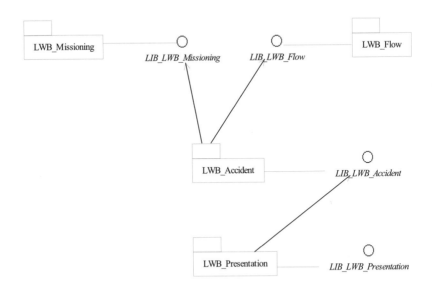

Figure 9.19. *Example of an architecture graph (extract) – SMABTP project*

This global vision has been elaborated by a logical architect on the basis of the urbanist's indications. This vision is progressively developed in more detail by the logical designer. Logical designers intervene to respond to a specific need. Their work often takes the form of a project. Their project only ends when the formal specification of services is completed.

The use of a pseudo-language guarantees exactness. The best solution for ensuring continuity between three disciplines is to generalize a standardized notation and adopt the same tools. The UML standard is therefore convenient for this type of usage. A UML profile can transport the vocabulary of the logical aspect and, last but not least, the method into the modeling tool (see Chapter 10).

9.6. Logical modeling of batch computing

As is the case for interactive forms of processing, the logical design of batch processing is based on the following two main aspects:

– The semantic aspect is used for the modeling of data. The batch programs use this type of data. The descriptions for the map and the volume of information also need to be provided. These precisions are necessary to evaluate the consumption of the system's resources when executing batch programs. Consolidated information and important calculations also receive a semantic definition. This definition is prior to, and independent of, the decision to process in the form of a batch.

– The pragmatic aspect is used for modeling use-cases that allow for the implementation of batch type activities. Among the users of these cases there are often teams working in the field of production or exploitation that are responsible for processing batches.

The logical design of batch programs respects the same principles as those used in interactive processing. The same types of components are manipulated. These components are logical machines, workshops, etc.

Some adjustments have to be made. References describing these adjustments are created and stored by the method. These will not be described in detail but can be looked up online on the site dealing with methodology.[7]

9.7. Technical modeling

9.7.1. *Required competences*

On the technical side, the cartography of Praxeme's competences reveals three profiles. These are the technical architect, the technical expert and the technical designer:

– The technical architect does not necessarily have a profound knowledge of all technologies. His/her main strength is communication. The technical architect is responsible for organizing and merging the work carried out by technical experts. Technical experts and sometimes even technical architects do not have enough experience in the field of information systems to deal with miracle solutions and compare several scenarios. The technical architect ensures coherence.

– The technical expert has detailed knowledge and specializes in one technique. He/she has a complete knowledge of this technique. The technical expert has an in-depth knowledge in comparison with the architect, but lacks the architect's broad overview. It is a risk for a chief information officer to believe that an expert could do the architect's job. The expert is not impartial and might make a pre-established choice. Other scenarios would then no longer be taken into consideration.

---

7. http://www.praxeme.org.

– The technical designer intervenes to elaborate on technical devices. His/her work is led by a technical architect and assistance is provided by technical experts.

9.7.2. *Technical/logical negotiation*

Praxeme's methodology insists that technical/logical negotiation is of utmost importance.

The logical aspect is independent of technical choices. However, this independence needs to be put into perspective. The people involved in projects share the same fear of creating a logical model that is useless if a program is unable to translate it.

It is vital to establish that the logical model is convertible at an early stage in the project. This needs to be done before investing means of logical modeling. The logical and technical architects meet at this point and carry out a logical/technical negotiation.

The content of this kind of negotiation can be subdivided into the following two parts:

– Firstly, the two parties verify that a form of exchange can be established between logical modeling and technical possibilities. A logical constituent such as a workshop could become an EJB or a COBOL module when looking at the technical side of things.

– Secondly, they examine the list of topics that are likely to be sharable, such as the processing of transactions, resorting to states machines, managing volume of the flow, history, security, managing contexts, processing variants, etc. (see Figure 9.20). The set of roles is applied as follows. For every topic, the technical architect indicates a solution, preferably a market solution. Otherwise, the specific technical solution needs to be elaborated. At all times the solutions should correspond to the expectations of the logical architect. If this is the case, the solution will be adopted. The logical architect draws his/her conclusions when creating the logical model. If there is no identified technical solution, the project needs to undergo a concerted effort when it comes to its design. In this case, designing an ad hoc solution starts with logical design.

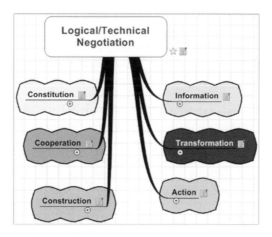

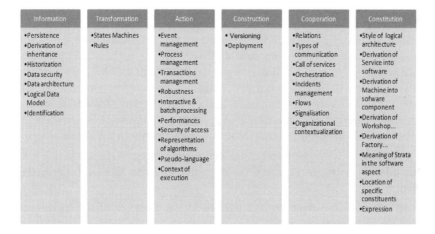

Figure 9.20. *Logical and technical negotiation: overview of topics*

During this negotiation, it is possible to stabilize the procedure of logical modeling and the specification of necessary tools that are often aggregated in a technical framework (see the chapter on tools and methods). Two examples of the results of logical/technical negotiations are explained below:

– Transaction management ranks among the topics of technical architecture: the logical designers only need to indicate by an annotation when a service behaves in a transactional way. The technical framework takes in charge the transactional management.

– Error management can be modeled either in the form of a report that is transmitted in the parameters around the service or as an exception that is specified independently by the follow-up message. The second solution is stricter and requires formal modeling of error management. This is, however, not possible in all programming languages, especially COBOL. If the development is applied to modern environments such as Java, it makes more sense to opt for the logical modeling of the services' signature (UML signals) for error management.

Technical devices can have an impact on the way the modelers work. This is the case for the rules engine. Since the rules of organization are aimed at the rules engine, the logical designer does not need to integrate them into the services. The technical designer creates a formal expression that is compatible with the solution. The solution has been retained in a way that enables it to distribute the services directly. The MDM solution used to manage variants at the lowest possible cost facilitates the logical design. The question of service variants obtains an answer that makes the process involving logical design easier. These examples show that logical/technical negotiation is very important. If this negotiation is not carried out, a project might experience unnecessary expenses.

Logical/technical negotiation has been shown as a single act. In fact, this type of negotiation requires several exchanges depending on the topics' level of maturity. The advantage of this method, proven by facts, consists in the check-list that gives a systematic outline of logical/technical negotiation. This way of working stems from the MDA standard that was mentioned in previous chapters. Moving from logical aspect to software is based on a choice of possible techniques. The technical choices described in a file on technical architecture can be split into two different categories:

– technical devices, software components and solutions from the market are introduced into software architecture to ensure that the technical functions are covered;

– the rules of derivation that are applied to the elements of the logical model produce the software components.

A logical model can therefore be translated into several types of target architecture. It is sufficient for the logical terms to be recognized and transformed in all possible scenarios. This is why an overview of themes for the logical/technical negotiation is of utmost importance.

9.8. Software modeling

9.8.1. *General principles*

Modeling is carried out by dealing with the software aspect. "Not another model!" many experts might object. Not much effort is required to create this model, though. The essentials have already been covered by previous models. Creating a program consists of translating a text (a logical model) on the basis of a dictionary (technical architecture). The technical framework takes on board most of the technical decisions. The derivation of the logical model towards a software solution can be largely automated. Indeed, it is sufficient to link the categories of the software aspect to the categories of the logical aspects. The rules of derivation are simple or mechanical. They can therefore be dealt with by a UML profile.

Praxeme recommends creating a model of the software first and then generating the program itself as a second step. This model corresponds to the PSM (*Platform Specific Model*) level of the MDA standard. The logical model corresponds to the level of PIM (*Platform Independent Model*) of the same MDA standard. This is how the designers express the last technical details around a model that has been obtained via automatic derivation. These decisions are isolated and preserved.

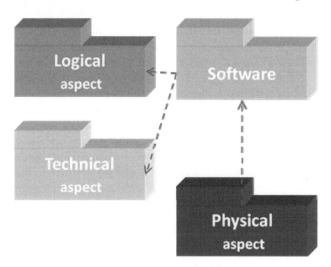

Figure 9.21. *The position of the software aspect in topology*

The software model describes what happens in reality. As is the case for all components linked to each other, programs are created on the basis of this model. The designer works on them in his/her development environment. There is no interruption in the production line under the condition that there is a design and development platform which synchronizes the model with the code. If this type of synchronization does not exist, the software is forced to separate itself from the model. This would limit the software evolution. The model then becomes obsolete very quickly and represents lost investment. As a result, there is a lack of information on the history of the IT developments, which hinders evolution and represents a risk for the company. Model-code synchronization is the key factor of success:

– synchronization allows for the long-term preservation of a realistic image of the software system;

– synchronization forces the software to be updated by its representation (i.e. model) and reinforces the modeling endeavor;

– the model is up to date and the work of refining the software is being carried out. Correcting a certain type of development may be the occasion on which the decision of modeling or factorization might be taken for the respective component;

– it is much easier to provide information on the software, which can therefore be shared and appreciated by many people;

– the feedback from software to model allows for round-trip development. It stimulates the practice of modeling. The modeler no longer produces "paperwork." The model needs to be of a high quality for the program to work. This practice of back-tracking exerts control over the practice of logical modeling as well as upstream modeling. This type of model comes to be a "runnable", at least a "productive" model, which is the aim of the modeler working on semantic aspects.

The software aspect leads to the convergence of methodology and technology. This convergence is mainly obtained with the concept provided by the MDA standard. The technical framework plays an important role when it comes to ensuring this convergence (not only on paper but throughout the teams that are involved). The technical framework benefits from technical expertise and the choice of different techniques. The respective techniques are isolated so that they can be easily changed. The chief information officer's (CIO) projects also benefit from this technique since entering technical decisions into the framework no longer requires the developers to possess detailed technical knowledge.

As the developer receives a formal and detailed specification, he/she no longer needs to acquire a detailed functional knowledge. This knowledge is already conveyed in the upstream models and expressed in the logical model, which will therefore transform into a practicable model. The developer requires the following competences:

– the capacity to read a logical model. This requires a basic knowledge of UML and the terminology of logical aspect;

– the capacity to translate this model and the pseudo-language, into a programming language;

– the capacity to use a framework and to apply the rules of development;

– the capacity to use test models that are associated to every logical component to carry out tests of services in cooperation with the logical designers who provide functional knowledge.

The guidelines on how to use a framework have been created by architects and explain to the developers how to transform a logical model into software. The number of guidelines depends on how detailed the framework is, as well as on how automated the derivation process between the logical model and the software is. The further developed the technical solution, the less detailed the guidelines are for the developers.

9.8.2. *Towards the industrialization of programming*

The developers become specialists in programming once again. They do not need to be familiar with the details of the business knowledge anymore. Creating a program becomes an increasingly predictable activity. This is a big step towards the industrialization of programming. The logical model contains the specification of services in pseudo-language. The programmer therefore receives a formal specification that usually eliminates all functional questions. In practice, it makes sense for the programmer to cooperate with the logical designer to make models more stable, work on tests, implement and carry out maintenance, etc.

Furthermore, when translating logical specifications into a program the programmer might also have to work on a user interface. This happens if the logical model does not define the stratum "Interaction." To deduce graphic components, the developer uses the descriptions of the human-machine dialogue in a use-case, samples of interface and the ergonomic chart. The link between graphic components and services is very simple. The interface corresponds to one, or to a group, of use-cases. Yet use-cases derive from logical machine in the "Activity" stratum. These machines provide the necessary services required to carry out a use-case.

9.9. Benefits of the methodology

9.9.1. *Opportunities*

9.9.1.1. *Cartography of competences*

On the basis of EST, methodology examines and renews the transformation and development process. The first benefit is crystal clear – the organization of competences. Moving towards the industrialization of programming also means the end of a wide variety of universal competences. When computer scientists talk about the "business", they sometimes have problems expressing themselves. If technical experts think about the structure of a system they cannot appreciate strategic evolutions of the company. When modelers refine semantic models they cannot worry about the technology that allows for their ideas to be carried out, etc. The different disciplines in SOA projects require different types of competences, ways of thinking and personalities. This variety does not make work easier. Praxeme solves the issues present between these disciplines. Topology is not only used as a conceptual framework applied to an enterprise, but also as the cartography of competences.

Identifying competences required for SOA and big projects is a prior task before throwing oneself into the adventure. Evaluating different profiles is another prerequisite. Defining the procedures and the methodology helps when it comes to evaluation. To give an example, Praxeme suggests a scale of seven degrees to estimate the UML knowledge and the competences in the field of modeling.

The advent of SOA's provides the opportunity to re-evaluate staff competences and motivation. The wide variety of required competences for new projects satisfies the aspirations of all partners and provides opportunities for meeting their preference for one aspect or another. Overall, this methodology is very strict. It gives a precise outline of responsibilities and the limits of responsibilities. This is required to start up an organization.

9.9.1.2. *Reusing services*

Reusing services is one of the main motivations when investing in SOA. To increase the rate of reuse significantly, good intentions and plans alone are not enough. The following points are stated in the methodology and should increase reuse:

– First, the isolation of the semantic aspect creates a source of reusable services. Indeed, it is not direct actions carried out by user that provide the right starting point, as they are tainted, full of presuppositions, and bogged down by rules of organization and the constraints of procedures. On the other hand, the services that cover the lifecycle of objects are highly reusable as they express the basics of the business knowledge, which are widely shared. A large number of important services derive from semantic models. When deriving a great deal of services from the semantic model, the system automatically restructures itself around a core of highly reusable components.

– Second, the detailed specification of the system in logical terms is independent of techniques. The logical model itself can be recycled as it can be derived towards target architectures in time (changing technology) or space (sharing with other organizations).

– Third, the restoration of modeling as an art and part of the process favors reuse. This cannot be done on the basis of an informal specification. To obtain reusable services, these services need to be designed with the purpose of reusability. It requires a global vision. Only the model allows for this way of thinking.

– Finally, the craft of logical design makes the designer aware of reuse. For a high level of reuse, precise guidelines state how to establish the signature of services. The method recommends to broaden the field of services by working on their denomination, their contract and their parameters.

Furthermore, while promoting MDA, Praxeme favors the decoupling and the separation of concerns, which improves the capacities of reuse. In particular, the dissociation of core business rules (semantic aspect) and organizational rules (pragmatic aspect) is already an important advantage for increasing the opportunities of reusing services.

9.9.2. Obstacles

Even with an involved and supportive hierarchy, the introduction of a methodological approach requires a careful change management. The change is just as important as the lack of a reference method. For several years there has been a lot of confusion regarding the distribution of roles and the identification of competences and procedures of modeling. Especially modelers ought to comment on and justify their choices of modeling in writing. The processes and advantages described above cannot be obtained easily.

SOA introduces radical changes in the attitude towards IT systems. The letter "A" in the abbreviation is not to be underestimated. "A" refers to architecture, i.e. a global approach, a comprehensive understanding of the system. Accepting this global vision means that the software engineers take the time to patiently implement the new structure and wait for the turning point to rework the entire system. This is not a dominant trend in IT.

Semantic modeling seems to be the most difficult task as its methods and practices are no longer used.[8] Looking at the outcome of several experiments in the field of semantic modeling, we observe that a key success factor is the authority and the involvement of the decision-maker. This applies no matter whether the decision-maker is a CIO or a "business" manager. Lacking this type of support, the modelers are confronted with computer scientists who do not understand the challenges of a model, nor its aim. In the best case, they would like to anticipate the software solution even though above all the model represents knowledge. Former methods and outdated slogans from the press are also added to this perception of the model.

---

8. Merise is a method that was developed in France. On the conceptual level, it is the equivalent of the semantic aspect. Methods from the English-speaking world of the same level of abstraction (*separation of concerns*) do not reach such a high level. The perception of business and enterprise can be described as the activity through a process, use-cases or equivalents.

Linked to the situation mentioned above, there is the problem of representing the business knowledge. The semantic modeler asks the required questions and sometimes reveals contradictions. The modeler needs to obtain the source of knowledge. Yet, in many organizations the members of staff that respond are not actors who are directly involved in the activity but are only representatives of the real business actors. They often forget about the actual function of a representative and spokesperson. They give their own opinion rather than collective knowledge. Another critical point resides in the difficulty, for the business actor, to read the model. It is true that the model can also not always be subject to the job actors' decisions even though they are less problematic due to the formal representation of techniques. This hiatus in the communication between the person who possesses the required knowledge (business expert) and the person who creates its form (modeler) is the main cause for the delays in production or the bad quality of semantic models.

What we call "reflow" is a bad strategy, a derivative that has a negative impact on the entire approach. Reflow consists of polluting an upstream model with the considerations that are based on a downhill aspect. For instance, thinking of database implementation, some modelers exclude the use of n-ary associations, even in the semantic model. The detailed description of processes slows down the events of technical inspiration. This tendency represents the following two drawbacks. It ruins the company's interest in creating a model for any other use than IT (e.g. knowledge management). It changes the activity chain that obtains services of a high semantic content. Reflow also has an impact on techniques and logic. Introducing cooperation between two parties is crucial. In this cooperation, a methodology of logical/technical negotiation would be insisted upon.

Part IV

Mastering Existing Techniques

Chapter 10

Tools for Industrializing the Method

A RECAP OF IDEAS MENTIONED IN PREVIOUS CHAPTERS

– The diffusion of SOA requires an enterprise method within a reference framework that is not limited to service-oriented architecture. The previous chapters have shown how Praxeme responds to this requirement with the help of Enterprise System Topology (EST). This framework subdivides the enterprise representations into eight different aspects.

– With Praxeme the possible logical components are referred to as metaphors: factory, workshop, machine.

NEW IDEAS TO BE INTRODUCED IN THIS CHAPTER

– Unified platform for the development of services (UPDS).

– *Virtual Engine for Praxeme* (VEP), technological reversibility.

– Technique for the development of graphic components.

– *Design patterns*.

– Tools for agile software development *Business Rules Management System* (*BRMs*), *Master Data Management* (*MDM*) and the concept of ACMS (*Agility Chain Management* System).

– UML CASE, *Model Driven Architecture* (MDA).

– Test and management of the configuration of services.

10.1. Requirements in the industrialization of procedures

Diffusing SOA and the associated enterprise method is based on several tools that support the model of architecture and work procedures. Without these tools the project teams would intervene manually and could decide that the service-oriented approach is too complicated and too theoretical. Therefore the team might possibly reject the approach. On the other hand, tools that are far too elaborate risk generating unnecessary complexity. In the worst-case scenario, these tools might be perceived as a risk to the job market. Some people might fear that an automation of certain tasks will lead to redundancies. A generation of code that has been developed too far might have a negative impact on the software developer's work.

A detailed study needs to be carried out to enable the correct implementation of these tools. This implementation is a complex project that might lead to SOA being called into question. The art of finding the right number of tools is difficult. Expertise is required on the level of method, techniques and carrying out changes. The main challenge consists of the implementation of a unified platform for the design and development of services. It needs to cover all steps in the fabrication of an information system from upstream with a dictionary of requirements to downstream with the generation of code, managing the program's configuration, tests and implementing production. This project needs to favor teamwork, allow for the tracing of production, manage the levels of authorization, etc.

This chapter will take a look at UPDS. UPDS is a concept that does not function like a off-the-shelf prebuilt package. It is not "ready to go" when it is bought. Commercial SOA-based programs offer partial solutions for UPDS. These solutions are several program units and not a global solution. Even if the orientation is excellent, the functional opening of these SOA suite products remains heterogeneous and limited. Some are specialized in the field of modeling tools (CASE), others in development (IDE) or production, layers or, last but not least, communication (ESB). The company needs to invest in the integration of multiple tools that support service-oriented architecture and methods: modeling CASE (UML tools), IDE and development, management of different versions and the configuration of programs, directory of services to be designed, directory of services that are being used in production, directory of security, rules engine, engine for the management of parameters and reference data (Master Data Management), tools for quality control in the field of developments, tools for integration and tests, tools used for tracing and management of services, framework for services to be carried out, GUI framework, transformation of models, generating code, generating documentation, etc.

UPDS's variety is very impressive, as it contains a maximum of functionalities. It is impossible to describe all of them in detail in this text. This book therefore only takes a look at the most crucial ones. Some of these functionalities, such as workflow, have already been covered above. This chapter will focus on frameworks and modeling tools. The following chapters will deal with mediation (interconnection) solutions such as Enterprise Service Bus or other technical components that will be described in the chapter focusing on the SOA platform.

UPDS needs to be subject to a precise definition of requirements that will lead to a personalized integration on the basis of heterogenous tools that are available on the market. For example, the integration of a version management software (or Software Configuration Management) with the UML CASE is already a challenge. Indeed, these UML CASEs do not necessarily contain a way of managing different versions of models.

Even though some software vendors promote their products as being based on SOA, their tools are often based on proprietary platforms and old generations that have little in common with service-oriented architecture. It is therefore difficult to integrate these solutions with other solutions. The concept of composite application needs to be developed further by software vendors. While this development is taking place, the company needs to focus on the project of integration in UPDS. The cost of this type of integration might be relatively high. Therefore a budget needs to be established early when using an SOA strategy. Furthermore, a detailed plan of the project with different steps of successive validation is required. This plan focuses on prototypes and checks how robust the tools are, as well as their performance. Before defining the key points of the unified platform, UPDS's objectives need to be defined. There are often many objectives that represent different strategies. Mastering these strategies has a major impact on SOA's success:

– Increasing the speed of distributing the method: as previously mentioned, a method without tools is prone to fail. On the other hand, a surplus of insufficiently integrated tools hinders the success of the SOA project.

– Mastering competences: it is not always possible, or desirable, to have the project managed by experts through its entire lifecycle. Methodologists and experienced technical architects provide the necessary ideas at the beginning and sometimes check if operations function as required. They monitor very little though. Experts need to ensure the communication between different parties involved in long-term projects. Communication between the different parties becomes easier if some of the necessary knowledge can be accessed automatically and is part of the tools, e.g. the derivation rules of models.

– Increasing the quality and robustness of deliveries: on the level of modeling, tools that verify the model's form and quality need to be used. This means, for example, that state automaton does not carry out unnecessary transitions or that the structure of information does not go over a certain level of nested data types (generally a maximum of three levels under the root), etc. On the level of the program, the developers use a toolbox to rationalize some technical implementations that can be used commonly. As well as the usual technical framework technique, this text will focus on the concept of a virtual machine for the execution of services.

– Insuring technological reversibility: this method preserves the modeling of requirements in the field of technological evolutions. To achieve this aim, MDA-based model engineering suggests a separation of business models and technical models. Applied to the level of models, this separation also has to be respected by all programs. Furthermore, the business part of the software needs to be protected from the evolution of IT standards and technical choices. In this context, the principles of implementing the software are integrated into the virtual machine of executing (factory, inversion of control) to guarantee separation between the business code and the technical code. The technical code might change depending on the moment in time.

– Rationalizing the costs and avoiding every project bringing up the same questions for the software designer, developer, tester, etc. In addition, increasing the relevance of mutualization also improves risk management.

We have indicated that currently there is no UPDS that could be used. However, UPDS is very likely to be put on the market by IT companies. The initiative of Praxeme, an open source method, might contribute to this new trend. In fact, the specification of UPDS is difficult if the user/client is not familiar with EST. This topology specifies the products to be delivered, which also concerns UPDS. Praxeme aims at an open method based on open source. This is why a progressive integration of Praxeme is to be expected. This integration would not only affect modeling CASE (UML profile, making topology more concrete, rules of quality control for models according to the method used, etc.), but also IT platforms, which would make the work within a company much easier. The following section will show a VEP. VEP is an open specification of services required for the execution of SOA components. The VEP has been updated in the framework of the SMABTP project.

10.2. Frameworks and design patterns

UPDS hides certain technical layers from the developer. These layers have been produced and made available for all projects. These shared developments make up the frameworks. The difference in concept between frameworks and ESB (*Enterprise Service Bus*) has to be emphasized. The framework intervenes when services are being carried out on a platform of homogenous techniques that are not distributed, e.g. in Java or COBOL.

ESB is a solution of a mediation system (interconnection) for the composition of services that are situated in heterogenous and/or distributed platforms. The framework is a toolbox that is embedded in every application in the form of a library of programs. ESB is a unit of infrastructure that is often shared on the level of the information system. Issues in terms of functionality management of performance and security are different depending on the respective concept. The framework depends on the IT platform, while ESB is at the crossroads of heterogenous platforms.

A high level of industrialization of technical layers leads to the parallel use of both ESB and frameworks. The developer has to manipulate the services in a logically and independent way from the required techniques. ESB is used for invoking a service via an intermediate layer, while a framework is applied to cases of local invocation of an application.

There are several types of frameworks, which are used according to the technical layers to be processed. This chapter will provide details on the framework's functions, show how a company carries out services and explain the concept of virtual machines. Framework functions used for the production of a human-machine interface will also be explained. Other types of frameworks will not necessarily be dealt with in this chapter, as this would go too far. Managing persistence for object relational mapping, communication, security, XML serialization, etc. will therefore not be covered in this chapter.

10.2.1. *From services framework to virtual machines*

Service-oriented architecture leads to the design of logical components that expose the services. In the Praxeme method, these components correspond to machines, workshops and logical factories. They are situated in the stratum of organization or business and respect the strict rules of communication that favor loose coupling.

When the developer receives the functional specification of a component, the aim is to limit his/her workload in the production of the business code. Technical elements enable the logical component to become part of a program. These elements work automatically. This affects the instantiation of a component (its creation), the invocation of a service according to the transport protocol (processing via a programming language or an intermediary ESB layer), the level of logging (trace of all actions carried out by a service), supervision of a service being carried out, etc. All of these aspects are implemented in a way that is transparent for the developer of the service. There are several different advantages to this position. The developer can concentrate on the business code and the required level of competence for the technical code is reduced. The robustness of the program is improved since the technical code is implemented only once and stabilized during the first few applications.

To achieve this aim, a toolbox known as a framework needs to be implemented. This toolbox provides the developer with a set of high-level technical services. It becomes, for example, possible to order the creation of a logical object without knowing its physical localization in the network, its version, its technology of implementation, etc. Several versions of this framework exist, especially in the open source community. Spring is, for example, a very well known framework among Java developers. Three main problems can, however, be identified when using frameworks. These are the lack of alignment with the method of design, a shorter lifecycle than the business code and, last but not least, bad management when defining parameters. These three disadvantages will be analyzed in the following part of this chapter.

10.2.1.1. *Alignment with the method*

Frameworks are created by technical experts and often remain independent of the methods of design used by the projects. Consequently, frameworks are limited to offering basic technical services such as the logical creation of a simplified component. The developer does not directly manipulate the different types of logical components provided by the method. This is a weak point. With Praxeme, this typology retains the terms of machines, workshops and logical factories. Using a particular state of this type of framework does not allow for a sufficient link with the method. Therefore and unfortunately, a developer could implement a logical business workshop component as if it were a logical business machine component even though the two concepts are subject to different rules of behavior. The first can be directly invoked by the organization stratum, even though the second is protected by the service interface of the logical business workshop.

The framework's surrounding area aligns the framework with the retained method of design. Reversibility of frameworks also plays an important role and will be covered in the next section of this chapter.

10.2.1.2. *Reversibility*

Like all programs, frameworks have a limited lifespan. This fact is emphasized if they are linked to platform techniques. For frameworks it is often easier to undergo innovation than the business code. It is pretty common for overhauling projects with appropriate budgets to set up software with a lifespan in production of around 15 to 20 years. During this period, a framework undergoes numerous evolutions. Sometimes the different versions are incompatible and the framework might even disappear. Technical experts work on *refactoring*, which means that the business code is realigned to the new versions of frameworks. This type of intervention is delicate since detailed technical knowledge is required as well as regression tests. Furthermore, frameworks are often developed by an open source community or external provider. The company therefore needs to put up with the different versions being introduced into its IT system. The company has to find a solution for this issue. It would therefore be useful to isolate the framework from the business code.

The introduction of this isolation requires a layer of abstraction on a framework's highest level. This layer needs to be aligned with a concept that is being retained. This approach responds to the first two issues, which will now be described in further detail. These issues are alignment with the method (previous section) and lifespan. If the method used for design is open, as Praxeme recommends, the alignment of a framework with a method is immediately made open through the method. This abstraction of the framework is inspired by the concept of virtual machines that execute components. Due to this machine, the developer directly manipulates the logical components that are created in the design process. The virtual machine verifies that the components communicate with each other while respecting the rules that have previously been established by the method. The developer cannot produce code that does not comply with the architecture principles.

As the virtual machine is a layer of functional abstraction of frameworks, it favors technological reversibility. This can be referred to as an act of sustainable development. For the same specification of virtual machines, the experts have different techniques of implementation at their disposal. These techniques are based on different types of frameworks.

In the case of Praxeme, a virtual machine has been specified. Known as VEP, it is an open source specification. [BONNET and LAPETINA, 2007] describe the service interfaces of the virtual machine. Its implementation can be based on a variety of frameworks in multiple technological platforms, e.g. in Java Spring, PicoContainer, in Microsoft .NET or also specific implementation, etc.

10.2.1.3. *Adjusting parameters*

Another problem of frameworks concerns the quality of parameter management. The developer is familiar with every component in the form of a logical abstraction that masks several technical parameters, such as physical localization in the network or different versions. This configuration data is generally stored in XML files. These files can be manipulated manually and do not allow for the management of versions or the implementation of a process for the validation of modifications. Some frameworks, when using Java for example, authorize the definition of parameters directly in the code. This possibility could be replaced with an XML standard that would enable experts to add a business tool that would take over the administration of configuration data. These parameters are often limited to the technical configuration of components and neglect the adjustment of parameters. This functional part, however, has a much bigger impact. To improve the management of adjusting technical and functional parameters, the virtual machine for the execution of services needs to accept a unified concept of parameters. This concept needs to be compatible with the tools that are being developed throughout the management of parameters, i.e. in an XML schema. These tools are based on MDM and provide a business interface for the administration of configurations. These tools also integrate governance features. The process of validation, profiles of authorization, management of different versions, etc. is part of this governance. Adjusting the parameters of components can be affected. Whether this is the case depends on the nature of the parameters, development teams, teams in production, as well as teams working on the functional side of things.

10.2.2. *Frameworks and human-machine interfaces*

The development of human-machine interfaces is based on the UI framework that ensures the following functions:

– the composition of pages, i.e. the fusion of data with the model of pages. For example, an XML of client data undergoes a fusion with a page of presentation regarding commercial situations;

– navigation between different pages. The navigation needs to remain technical, as the business rules on the selection of pages are the responsibility of services;

– invoking a layer of services by an intermediary of the virtual machine which carries out services.

Other functions and technologies are rather delicate and also need to be specified. This especially applies for the context of data, the data mapping, the Web 2.0 and the presentation technologies. The following section will take a look at these functions and technologies.

10.2.2.1. *Managing the context*

The properties of SOA show how services function according to a stateless architecture (Chapter 4). Consequently, the layer of management for the human-machine interface must consider the preservation of necessary data during the navigation between different screens. This data is generated during the user's sessions. On a technical level, an http session is, for example, used for preservation. The UI framework offers technical services to store and recover data in a context. At this stage storing and recovering data is easily carried out.

The designers often forget that the context is associated with a lifecycle that describes the update of certain event-based applications. Updating, cleaning and producing temporary copies are some examples of these applications. These events are functional and their specifications require an intervention from the designer. Technical architects need to deal with the necessary devices in the UI framework to act on the content of the data's context according to these events. The function "update the context" is carried out if the data on the screen has to be updated as a result of the user's actions. For example, a page consists of two parts (*portlets*). The first part is a synthesis of the accident file that shows the accident's state (currently running, being analyzed, payment to be carried out, etc.). The second part of the screen provides compensation for the accident. Once the compensation has been provided, the state of the accident has to be updated. If this update is not carried out, the part of the screen that represents the synthesis is out of phase. Cleaning up the context is a function that works as a *garbage collector*. It is impossible to preserve all data indefinitely within its context and, in particular, data that is not used when carrying out applications. Without a cleaning up strategy the consumption of resources risks an uncontrollable increase. Several modes of cleaning up are generally used according to the specific needs. These are selective clean up, complete clean up except some data and complete clean up without any exceptions. A temporary copy of the context (sometimes referred to as a defensive copy) is a useful and ergonomic tool. The context is copied (cloned) the moment the user validates the page. This data is available in context and cannot be modified. This backup data is made available to the user in case the validation does not work. Entering data twice is therefore avoided.

An initiative of standardization has been carried out in the domain of WS-CAF (*Composite Application Framework*) for OASIS. This technical standard explains how the context may be shared between several services. This standard also includes the principles of managing transactions on the level of the context. Doing so makes the specification more complex. While waiting for a reliable implementation of WS-CAF, companies use specific approaches in the management of the context's lifecycle.

10.2.2.2. *Data mapping*

The structures of data that have been restored by services and consumed by the layers of presentation do not need to be recycled directly in the pages to be displayed. Decoupling between the different pages and services requirement takes place to allow for evolutions that are independent of both pages and services. On the other hand, a data copy tool has to be introduced. This tool is referred to as mapping. An automatic generation of this part of the program is possible if the description of the structures is available in an XML format.

10.2.2.3. *Web 2.0*

The usual ergonomics of Web applications are based on a rather thin client PC. The navigator does not process any data and all applicable logic is located in the server. This solution is excellent when favoring the centralization of applications and compatibility between different versions of the navigator. The less work the navigator needs to carry out, the higher the capacity of interoperability. It is, however, possible at all times to defy this rule and add JavaScript forms of processing that are carried out by the navigator. This type of processing has to be linked to the human-machine interface, as the services ensure the exclusivity of the organizational and business rules. The layer of presentation cannot replace the services. In other words, developing services in JavaScript is not feasible unless the principles of layer development are no longer applied.

Even though a thin client is a useful approach when rationalizing the development, this approach is not ergonomic at all. Indeed, every modification of a part of the screen requires an exchange with the server. The page on the screen is therefore entirely updated. The user is confronted with a flash effect as the entire page is updated, even if only one data element on the screen requires an update. Furthermore, the traditional use of thin clients does not allow for the parallel and progressive display of several parts of the screen. This would, for example, shorten the time needed to obtain a reply. It would indeed be possible for the user to consult the first level of information while the system processes the display of other parts of the page. The same applies to the display of lists of information that require a system of paging. Every new increment in the paging requires an unnecessary page update.

Web 2.0 was introduced as a response to some technical problems. Web 2.0 is based on the Ajax standard of asynchronic communication between the navigator and the server. Ajax can, for example, invoke a service (on the side of the server) at the moment when the user has left the area in which some item has been selected.

The type of processing mentioned above is carried out and sends the information back to the navigator. The navigator benefits from this information without imposing an update of the entire page. The programming language for the navigator remains JavaScript, which might lead to the problems of interoperability described above. Apart from layer-based development, this is the main reason why Ajax and JavaScript are better off being limited to processing data that stems from the management of the human-machine interface. In this case there are no problems with interoperability.

10.2.2.4. *Choosing a presentation technique*

The level of the techniques' maturity for the development of human-machine interfaces remains weak. Several approaches, such as frameworks, standard *Java*

Services Faces (JSF) and Ajax, stop each other from functioning correctly or complement each other according to different experts' opinion. Even an entire book could not explain the benefits and shortcomings of the different possibilities. This study would also have to take a look at technologies that are used by a fat client. Instead of doing so, this chapter will take a look at an interesting approach suggested by Google and point out a possible return to the technology of Java applets.

The latest initiative has been suggested by Google and is known as the GWT (*Google Web Toolkit*). GWT is a visual CASE of page modeling, which allows for event-based programming in Java. This mode of development was well known at the client/server era during which everything relied on behavior when dealing with a thin client. GWT introduces a compiler that translates Java programming code into JavaScript and Ajax, which allows for traditional Web applications to be maintained. The use of this technology still allows for the model of layer development to be respected. Business rules do not need to be localized directly within the events of the human-machine interface and is limited to services calls.

Another interesting trend is the return to Java applets. This return responds to certain needs in ergonomics. The increase in networks' power makes it possible for the applet to be downloaded on the client's PC (an applet requires no more space than a digital photograph). For example, if the user would like to carry out a manipulation based on multiple hierarchical axes, a drag and drop, then application of Java applets would enable the user to do so without any difficulties. The aim is not to create a human-machine interface with this technology, but rather to complement the use of HTML and even Ajax.

It is likely that the stabilization of techniques, standards and development tools in the layer of presentation might require several more years of research. Until stabilization is reached, technological reversibility cannot be guaranteed for developments on screen. Once again, this reinforces the need to develop a program in layers, which insulates the technology of presentation and therefore separates it from the services. Redeveloping the pages and management of the associated context does not have an impact on the services. Specifying the layer of presentation for the use of formal UML modeling as a basis allows for the automatic generation of part of the program. The designer describes in UML all the UI components and the logic: data structures that are displayed on pages, navigation between pages, the lifecycle of the data context and orchestrations of services that are invoked by user-based events.

10.2.3. *Design patterns*

Internal architecture of frameworks retains the principles of design that are referred to with the generic term of design patterns (model for the design). The most widely known ones were created by the GoF (*Gang of Four*) [GAMMA, HELM, JOHNSON, VLISSIDES, 1994]. Among numerous models of existing designs, the most familiar are facade and interface, factory, inversion of controls and proxy. For readers who are unfamiliar with these models, they will quickly be defined in the following sections. The following sections will also point out the principles of SOA, i.e. loose coupling, technological reversibility and the management of different versions.

10.2.3.1. *Facade and interface*

The facade is an object that unites all services and ensures the implementation of services that are supposed to be hidden. In Praxeme, a logical component of the workshop can be equipped with a facade that implements the services that are exposed to other logical components. During their implementation, these services rely on other private services in the workshop's scope. The facade and the interface are not to be confused. The facade implements services while the interfaces present the signature of these services without providing access to their internal codes.

The facade contributes to the implementation of an architecture marked by loose coupling. Every logical component exposes its facade, which unites the services to be presented via the interface. Without the concept of the facade there is the risk that services that should be hidden are presented. These services would be of a high value for their consumers said Craig Larman [LARMAN, 2005]: "Usually the facade must not expose low level operations. On the other hand, it is beneficial if the facade exposes a small number of high level operations, i.e. services of a high granularity. If the facade exposes a high number of low level operations it tends to lose its cohesion."

10.2.3.2. *Factories and the inversion of control*

The factory is a technical object specializing in creating instances within other objects. Design patterns with logical components and the factory in the Praxeme method are not to be confused. For Praxeme, the factory is a package that represents either an organization (organizational factory) or a domain of objects (business factory). On the level of design patterns, the factory hides the mechanism of instantiation of the components that exposes the invoked service. Praxeme's virtual machine for the execution of services, for example, creates a logical component with the help of a factory. This factory hides the technical services that ensure instantiation: physical localization on the network, passing via ESB or not, using a pool of instances, automatic running of pre- and post-conditions of the service, etc..

The developer no longer needs to worry about the technical code when creating instances for the components or when invoking services. The factory ensures the industrialization of the code. The concrete implementation of the component is decided on the level of the factory. The factory sends the consumer back to an interface that has been linked to different implementations. The factory has access to the context of carrying out an application that enables it to decide which type of implementation is to be linked with the interface.

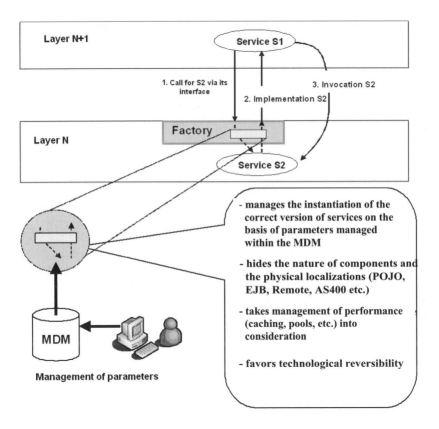

Figure 10.1. *The principle of the factory linked to MDM*

The context is based on the configuration file, which prepares the different cases of carrying out services, e.g. versions, multi-channeling, partners, environments, dates. These configurations are generated in the MDM. The factory separates the consumer and the strategy of implementation that was created by the provider. This procedure favors technological reversibility. The provider can change the implementation of services without this impacting on the consumer. The only condition is that the service contract has not been changed, i.e. the services interface remains the same.

The developer exploits technical services from the factory to create instances within the components. This is why there is adhesion between the business code and the factory. Reducing this adhesion takes into account the initiatives that are trying to standardize the functioning of the factory. In practice, these standards cater for specific needs (WSIF). If this is not the case, they are not yet mature (SCA):

– WSIF (Web Services Invocation Framework) is an implementation of an open source factory based on the movement of XML Web services (Apache community). WSIF allows for the instantiation of a Web service component, which is independent of an underlying technology. These components are SOAP as well as EJB (known as IIOP-RMI), XML in http style (REST style), JMS, JCA and even native calls in Java. Use of WSIF requires that the services are invoked with the help of an XML interface via WSDL (Web Service Description Language). WSDL is necessary for components to be accessed locally, i.e. Java without a transport protocol. This passage is generalized by a WSDL interface which limits the general use of WSIF for the invocation of distant components.

– SCA (Service Component Architecture) is a recent initiative based on the SOA alliance that unites the main players in the IT industry. SCA is the suggestion for a standard for assembling components within service-oriented architecture. SCA specifies the way in which the components are instantiated but does not impose WSIF's properties. According to these properties, the interfaces have to be declared in the WSDL standard of Web services. A developer can base his/her work on SCA when creating instances of a component that is natively exposed to Java, C++ or others. SCA is a more global approach than WSIF and should be chosen as its successor.

Favoring the isolation of the business code with respect to the factory requires that complementary technical principles such as IoC (Inversion of Control) are taken into consideration. They are favored by the majority of frameworks, such as Spring or PicoContainer in Java.

10.2.3.3. *The proxy*

The proxy is a procedure that intercepts the invocation of a service to add a pre-processing procedure. In the same way, when the result of the service is being sent back the proxy allows you to add a post-processing procedure.

The use of a proxy allows, for example, for the externalization of the management of transactions of the service code. At the moment of invoking a service, the proxy checks that it is a transactional service that stems from a file described by sets of parameters. This file needs to be administered by MDM. If necessary, a transaction is started (*begin*). When the service is returned, and if the execution is nominal, the proxy closes the transaction (*commit*) or otherwise cancels it (*rollback*). Services can therefore be recycled and used in different transactional contexts.

10.3. Tools for increased agility

Service-oriented architecture will offer considerable advantages under the condition that technical components that favor agility are considered. The method of adapted design also needs to be implemented (see Part III). Without these technical components, there is the risk of creating a rigid SOA with services that cannot be easily adapted to different contexts of execution. The extended SOA's level of maturity has to come into play at this point, as has already been mentioned in previous chapters. In particular, the use of the rules engine and the system that manages reference data have to be integrated carefully. The next section will show how these two constituents are used when increasing agility.

10.3.1. *Rules engine*

10.3.1.1. *The SOA model and the use of rules*

Contract-based design, on which SOA is based, leads to the specification of a service according to pre-conditions, body and post-conditions. This model is applicable to all categories of service from organizational to elementary services, as well as business services. It does not matter whether a service is exposed to a consumer in XML with an SLA or not. Every service needs to respect the principle of contract-based design (see Chapter 5). Pre- and post-conditions provide the rules of management that are presented in the service contract. The consumer of a service is familiar with these rules. The body of the service contains rules that are private and can only be accessed by the service provider. Variations on management rules essentially take place on the level of pre- and post-conditions and correspond to differences in behavior that respond to specific consumer needs. These variants cannot alter the service's main body (adding multiple "if", "then" conditions to the programs) as this would make the service more complex, generate difficulties for tests and, last but not least, slow down the process of variants. The rules that form pre- and post-conditions are therefore better externalized in a business rules management system. Doing so allows for the parameterization and declaration of new rules that would describe the new behaviors according to the execution contexts of services.

In the Praxeme method, use of the rules engine mainly takes place on the level of the stratum's "organization" services. Indeed, the pre- and post-conditions are systematically situated in the business rules management system. This is a universal principle of architecture and not a choice of design that depends on how complex the rules are. Organizational services absorb the variations linked to the organization, i.e. they depend on different contexts of consumption. The code of every pre- and post-condition of organizational services contains an invocation of the rules engine. This invocation undergoes a flow of data that corresponds to the information that has been manipulated by the logical component. This component exposes the organizational service in question. In Praxeme, this component is of the "logical machine of organization" type (see Part III). The flow of information is sufficiently large for the creation of new rules and does not systematically require maintenance of services. If the flow is not large enough, every rule that manipulates unplanned data in the flow requires a modification of a call transmitted to the engine to communicate this additional data element.

In addition to this flow, the rules engine receives information on the context. This information enables the rules engine to determine the set of rules that need to be carried out according to logical components, the consumer, the channel of use of the service (Web, Internet, call-center, etc.), the version, the date, etc.

Note that the service is unfamiliar with the set of rules that are executed after invoking the rules engine. It is important to know that the services and the rules engine are loosely coupled. The behavior of rules can be modified, the sets of rules that are invoked can be adapted depending on the execution contexts of services without modifying the services programs.

Even if every organizational service is capable of invoking the rules engine, it cannot be guaranteed that for a precise configuration of logical components all invocations are actually useful. The configuration data might or might not validate the effective invocation of the rules engine without having to modify the programs of services.

A simple set of parameters allows for a decision to be taken for every organizational service on whether or not its pre- and post-conditions invoke the rules engine.

```
<?xml version="1.0" encoding="UTF-8" ?>
<rulesActivation>
    <categorie name="CTR">
        <niveau name="SOR">
            <component type="MLO" name="MoGererArchives">
                <service name="demanderArchivageInit">
                    <preconditions active="false" />
                    <postconditions active="true" />
                </service>
                <service name="demanderArchivageValid">
                    <preconditions active="false" />
                    <postconditions active="false" />
                </service>
```

Real call for BRMS

No call for BRMS =
emulated response as
if the BRMS returns
any errors

Figure 10.2. *Extract from the configuration file of the rules – SMABTP project*

From a technical point of view, the interception of the rules engine's invocation can take place via a proxy (parameterization facade). The XML configuration file is administered by MDM, which ensures the centralized management of all reference data and sets of parameters, including those used for the configuration of the rules engine.

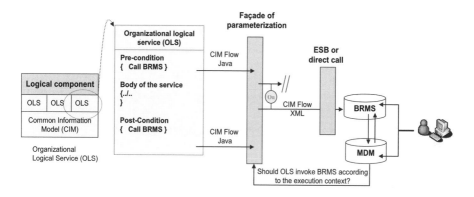

Figure 10.3. *Use of the rules engine in SOA*

The number of rules may be relatively high. This number needs to be urbanized according to the same criteria as those used for logical architecture. Packets of rules are linked to logical components, in particular logical machines for organization. The "MoDeclareaccident" machine (see Figure 10.4), for example, is associated with a packet of rules applied to use cases in the declaration of accidents. The rules of this machine are applicable to all organizational services of this machine. For every organizational logical service there is a packet of rules.

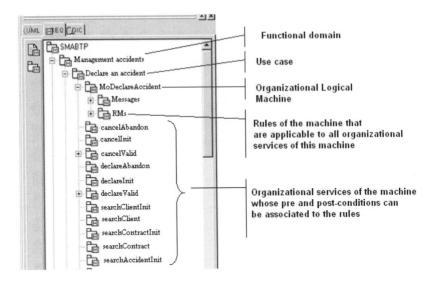

Figure 10.4. *Organizing packets of rules (here in UML CASE)*

The differentiation between rules that are applicable to pre-conditions and those that are applicable to post-conditions is carried out directly in the expression of rules in the form of a test (see Figure 10.5).

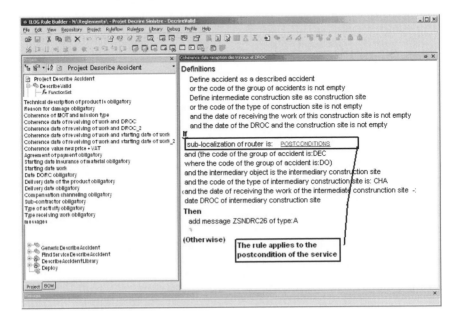

Figure 10.5. *Example of the ILOG JRules – SMABTP project*

The rules for tests can also be externalized, which determines if the context of invocation concerns pre- or post-conditions or the body of the service (see Figure 10.6). This procedure allows for the recycling of a rule, if necessary in several contexts of pre- and post-conditions and the body of services.

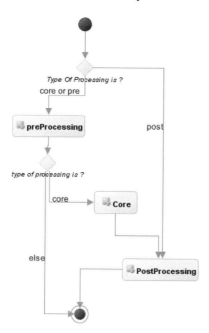

Figure 10.6. *Context of invocation of rules in SOA –Copyright ILOG*

10.3.1.2. *Other cases of using rules*

Apart from the SOA model of using rules, the designer can decide that some services of the stratum "organization" should also benefit from the rules engine on the level of their body, by completing pre- and post-conditions. At the same time the designer could decide that certain services of the stratum "business" have to be based on the rule engine. This way of using the rules engine is established during the process of designing and, first of all, depends on the following needs:

– rapid modifications of rules without the systematic intervention of IT specialists;

– visibility, by business actors, of rules implemented in the program. Using natural or nearly natural language for the presentation of rules favors a better communication between the business and IT specialists;

– audit of how the system is being carried out, based on rules. Every rule is subject to complete traceability when being carried out (identification of the consumer, results, etc.);

– reuse of rules;

– managing the rules' lifecycles: right of consultation, modification, display, managing different versions, etc.

10.3.1.3. *Towards a Business Rules Management System*

The rules engine needs to be robust and of high performance. The rules engine on its own, however, does not allow for a strategy of rules to be displayed on the level of information systems. Functions for the administration of rules are required to do so. A Business Rules Management System (BRMS) therefore applies to the level of information systems. These administrative functions allow for the creation and update of rules, as well as the management of different versions, the lifecycle of models and associated data, carrying out tests, etc. The repository of rules is secured by the user profiles that grant the right of consulting data as well as updates.

The rules management systems can also be used as a repository of rules without many of them being carried out by the engine. This is therefore a solution in the field of knowledge management. In this case, the use of the rules management systems needs to be evaluated with respect to requirements in certain modeling CASE tools, especially in UML. Rules or requirements (the terms are interchangeable) need to be linkable to the UML models to guarantee traceability between the expression of rules and the modeling. This traceability also has to be possible between the repository of BRMS and UML models. Otherwise, an interface between the modeling CASE tool and BRMS needs to be created to avoid two different repositories having to be administered manually.

10.3.1.4. *The link between MDA and the rules engine*

The previous chapters have already shown that the procedures of SOA's production are based on an MDA standard. Due to this procedure a better alignment of the program and models that formally evaluate the requirements can be guaranteed. However, the production line of a program based on models is not easy. Mastering this production line requires the developer to be extremely strict during the modeling process. High stability in the process of generation is also required. In practice, it is impossible to restart this code production line for every evolution in the program. The developer needs to be able to be more flexible. Interventions need to be able to be carried out rapidly without the risk of destroying the system's architecture. How can this goal be reached without challenging the idea of MDA?

The company's rules engine is strategically situated and functions as an addition to MDA. The idea behind this procedure is as follows: the stable parts of the system are generated on the basis of an MDA chain. The variable parts are added via a BRMS.

The fixed part which has been generated in MDA corresponds to the framework of the system, in particular the skeleton of the logical components with the signature of services, error structures, data models (including those that are used by the rules engine), etc. The variable part corresponds to the rules of organizational services, in particular pre- and post-conditions that are included in the MDA generated framework. Adding and modifying these rules does not require the MDA production line to be restarted.

Without a rules engine, the MDA production line would be counterproductive. This type of production line would impose a generation of code for every single modification of requirements, which would be too tedious and handicap agility.

10.3.1.5. *A business solution*

The software editors of SOA technologies suggest solutions with several components marked by a high number of functional laps. The rules engine in particular presents a potential usage in several environments within this type of architecture. Its application for pre- and post-conditions has been shown earlier in this text. The rules engine is, however, also useful for the following use cases:

– specialized rules in a business domain such as price setting, client scoring, etc.;

– the rules for the transformation of data, especially for those used in the layer of communication such as ESB;

– the rules for monitoring the production, e.g. to calculate the prioritization of services according to the IT resources that are available in production;

– rules of navigation between different screens;

– rules of calculating steps in a process based on BPM.

It is impossible to use as many rules engines as cases of applications since doing so would multiply technologies, make efforts of integration unnecessarily complex, risk the duplication of certain rules, face different grammatical issues concerning rules, etc. This duplication of technology is even more delicate if there is no mature standard for the grammar of rules. Software engineers can therefore not count on interoperability between different engines. The company needs to agree on a single solution for the management of rules. These rules need to be independent of different types of component-based techniques, which are sufficiently open to respect SOA standards (service-based communication, use of XML grammar, etc.) to be integrated easily into different cases of application.

10.3.1.6. *Towards the management of reference data*

Rules manipulate reference data and parameters. These rules and parameter valorizations are also subject to administration. A rule that, for example, verifies a maximum number of files needs to function for different value thresholds depending on how the service is consumed (headquarters, subsidiary, partner, type of product, etc.). This rule needs to manipulate a parameter (the threshold), which depends on the context of execution. It cannot be written with values of an encoded threshold since adding a context would automatically imply that a test for the rule would also have to be added. These parameters complete the use of the rules engine. The use is based on a reference data management tool known as MDM, which centralizes the reference data and the parameters to be used in one single point. These points are applications and services as well as other components in the system such as the management of rules, BPM, edition, authorization, etc.

The integration of BRMS with MDM is a key factor for the agility of the information system. This topic has already been covered in the concept of ACMS (*Agility Chain Management System*) described in the chapter on SOA's properties.

10.3.2. *Reference data management system*

10.3.2.1. *Defining reference data*

Defining reference or master data works as follows:

– A data element is shared between several functional silos or services. The value of this data element is applied while several different processes are running. "Client type" data, for example, is fixed at certain key moments of the client's lifecycle, particularly at the moment of its creation. This data would be used in several processes, e.g. the suggestion of commercial discounts, distribution of revenue, management of litigation, etc.

– A data element whose value changes according to the use cases. The rate of discount, for example, has a range between 10% and 30%. According to the country of distribution this rate might vary within this range, e.g. 15% in France, 18% in Germany, 25% in Japan. Another example concerns the adaptation of a UI (User Interface) for different languages. Every label on the screen has a different value according to the respective language.

At all times the value of this type of data has to be updated and validated while it is used and exploited by numerous processes. This quality requirement is fundamental to the integrity of the system. Respecting this required level of quality is not always easy in information systems that are subdivided into functional silos, as the data may be duplicated. With SOA, the multiplication of the context in which services are carried out leads to a multiplication of valorizations of the same data according to the respective context. This adaptation requires a tailored solution to guarantee that the values are exact. Two cases of application can be combined. These are duplicating data and context based multi-valorizations.

There are multiple categories of reference data. They contain business data such as the catalog of products, typological classification of clients, party and role, data on the marital status of people, etc. They might also include technical data such as parameters of databases, ESB, security, etc., as well as labels for screens and ergonomic style guides. They contain all parameters; many of them in SOA, as this improves the agility of services.

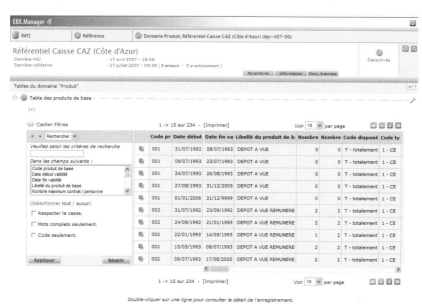

Figure 10.7. *Screen for the administration of data (EBX Orchestra Networks)*

The reference data and parameters have to be managed in a secure repository controlled by a MDM tool which offers advanced data administration functions (see Figure 10.7).

10.3.2.2. *The functions of MDM*

MDM is a data warehouse. It contains values of reference data and parameters. MDM is not limited to storing descriptions of data structures and links with other databases. The filling of data is carried out by several employees in the company and follows the production cycle and software development. The following teams are involved: development team, test team, a team in charge of the production, as well as the users that act on certain functional parameters without actually undertaking an IT-based intervention.

During development, the rules of validity control, authorization, versioning, etc. have to be respected. Given the high number of actors that are implied in this management process and the extent of the reference data and parameters, it is impossible to rely on only one technical tool.

The manual update of XML configuration files, Excel files, Java parameters or the simple use of administering tables in DBMS is no longer feasible. A tool of the highest level is required. This tool needs to propose user-friendly features with a unified UI for both business and IT users.

This tool has to offer advanced functions for the management of access rights when it comes to modification, consultation, traceability, updates, workflow of modifications, reporting, etc. Another key function of MDM concerns the lifecycle of data. Similar to a version management tool such as CVS, versions of the repository need to be created more easily. These versions would be linked to different branches.

Figure 10.8, for example, shows the branches per environment. Every branch can be found from (N) to (N+3). They can respectively correspond to environments of development, integration tests, qualification and user acceptance tests.

In every environment, intermediary versions (*draft* 1, *draft* 2, etc.) can be created. Then the fusion of different versions with the main version can be carried out.

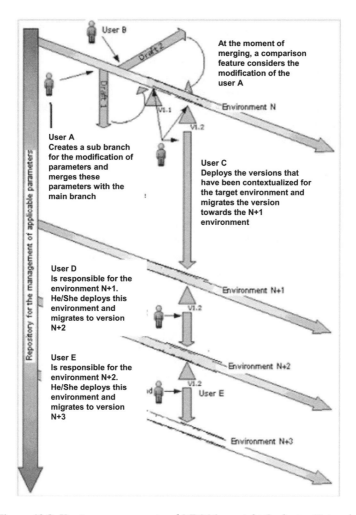

Figure 10.8. *Version management and MDM (copyright Orchestra Networks)*

SOA leads to the service variants being considered in a formal way. A service needs to be recyclable in different processes and adapt its behavior to the respective requirements. The service needs to be able to do so without any heavy IT development and therefore reduces the amount of time required to deliver a service.

This idea has already been presented in the contract-based object design by Bertrand Meyer [MEYER, 1990]: "The aim of composability is directly linked to the problem of recyclability. The aim is to find a means to design elements of a program that carry out previously defined tasks and are usable in a wide variety of different contexts." When used with the right method, SOA responds to this aim and favors the specification of service variants depending on the respective context, especially the design of a parameter-based model that is associated to each service. The service algorithm and the rules situated in the rules engine rely on the parameters, especially of the pre- and post-conditions of organizational services. Numerous parameters are therefore specified and processed according to multiple requirements. These requirements could be functional and technical or concern exploitation, security, etc. These parameters are managed by the MDM.

10.3.2.3. *Exposing services via MDM*

The reference data stored in MDM are published via reading and updating services. The services are accessible to the consumers according to the modes of invocation that will lead to an increasing interoperability with Web services, SOAP-XML and even native calls such as Java. The data needs to be manipulated simultaneously according to both the unitary and the regrouping mode (a group or cluster of objects respond to the criteria of the filter). For a flow of high volumes of data, MDM exposes import and export services of files under multiple formats such as XML, CSV, etc.

MDM uses ESB to publish the subscription services, which enable the consumers to subscribe to events. A consumer can therefore be notified that data has been updated in MDM.

When the company deploys several physical repositories of master data, the ESB's routing function hides the existence of storage from the consumer. The consumer only requires access to the reference data and does not need to be familiar with the physical organization of repositories. For performance reasons, certain repositories can be duplicated to split the impact of consultation between several machines. Based on routing tables or with help from a production monitoring tool, the ESB directs the search entries of consumers to the right physical repository. In this type of scenario, the duplicated repositories of master data have to be able to synchronize themselves to update the master repository and obtain a duplicated physical repository.

The services of MDM respect SOA's property of being stateless. The services therefore do not save previous executions. The moment an MDM service is invoked by the consumer, the consumer provides a context of data, which serves as identification. If necessary, this context is created with functional data that will be recycled while running subsequent services.

When accessing the reference data the consumer contacts the logical component that is responsible for this data element. The consumer does not directly contact the MDM services. SOA's principle of isolation is, in this way, respected. This principle states that data is hidden on the level of services. MDM is situated on the level of data, which are hidden by the services on the highest level of logical architecture. Accessing tables of codes and labels, for example, requires the implementation of a specialized logical component in the management of codification that exposes services for labels based on the code, verifying the existence of a code, etc. This implementation also respects the context of execution such as language, version, organization using the service, etc. This component of codification invokes services of the MDM.

Having an MDM compliant with services is vitally important to SOA's success. Doing so allows for a maximum unification of reference data and parameters. Furthermore, MDM has to be capable of invoking services and other technical components at all times of the management cycle. When receiving a request for creation of a client, for example, MDM invokes a cleansing service that is exposed by the solution of quality management. Similarly, at the moment of modifying reference data or parameters, MDM ensures invocation of services for the control of that data's validation process.

10.3.2.4. *The different types of MDM*

Implementing a data warehouse is not a new idea. The companies know Datawarehouse and Datamart well and have already done so to respond to the needs of consolidating information, interrogation according to the multiple axes of hierarchies, etc. These repositories make up decisional systems and function with denormalized data structures that optimize the performance of consultation. The process of denormalization leads to diverse strategies, e.g. star schema. If decisional systems have already implemented repositories, why would others need to be added? Why would new technologies be required as has been suggested in extended SOA? Analysts, especially Gartner Consulting, identify two types of approaches: analytical and operational MDM:

– Analytical MDM: the goal of analytical MDM is to implement a decisional system whose scope is the same as the scope of the reference data. In case of having several hierarchical axes, for example, a catalog of products can be consulted. The catalog can therefore be accessed by using the following search categories: type of product, regions, distribution channels, etc. Using Datawarehouse or Datamart technologies implies that a denormalized model is being used even though this is not imposed in the case of this application. Indeed, the volume of manipulated information for the reference data is inferior to the production data. This pointless denormalization prevents the limitation of the implementation of referential integrity constraints. This implementation is mandatory for updating data. This is why analytical MDM is dedicated to consultation functionalities. On the whole, analytical MDM is similar to a Datawarehouse or Datamart with a limited functional scope of reference data. There are therefore neither functional nor technical innovations. This type of solution has been used by companies for a long time.

– Operational MDM is different from analytical MDM. The data model on whose basis it functions is not denormalized. It is a model that respects the referential integrity constraints. It allows for filling data associated with validation rules taking into account the referential integrity constraints defined when designing the data model. The denormalization of the data model does not impose itself. In fact, the volume of information handles by the MDM is lower than that of decisional systems.

When faced with the need to rationalize existing data repositories and the management of the parameterization services, "operational MDM" is required. Due to the way it functions and with help from a normalized data model relying on referential integrity constraints, the updating of data is completely secure and reliable. Moreover, as previously mentioned, operational MDM offers advanced governance functions for versions of management, display, data approval workflow and the lifecycle of data (create, delete, update), authorization, etc. Operational MDM also offers advanced consulting functions. These are based on the creation of hierarchical axes, as is the case in analytical MDM.

Even in the case where a functional requirement is expressed in only one dimension of analytical MDM, it makes sense to place it into operational MDM, as this would allow evolution towards a global management of reference data and the parameters of services. Operational MDM has to accept all kinds of data, whether functional or technical, and so all reference data is unified via the same tool. This includes the management of all reference data and parameters on the level of the information system, e.g. catalog of products, client repository, organization, authorization, style guide, codes and labels, variants of services, ESB parameters, etc.

10.3.2.5. *The integration of MDM into SI*

The technical integration of MDM with applications leads to two possible scenarios, depending on the maturity of SOA:

– In cosmetic SOA, MDM feeds the production database before moving on to the exploitation of services. In this case, the services interact with the databases without being aware of the existence of the MDM repository. This option is interesting as it is not intrusive to the existing databases, especially if software packages (ERP) are being used.

– In overhaul SOA, MDM can used by services directly in production. The old reference databases, parameters and other configuration files are therefore replaced with the repository based on MDM.

The SOA platform assembles different technical components to support the architecture (ESB, directory, service monitoring, security, etc.) so that MDM is able to find its place immediately within the cosmetic SOA. The platform's components deal with a high number of functional and technical parameters that are administered by specific tools. These tools are often not very ergonomic, which makes the management of access rights for modifications and configurations, as well as helping those who are not experts in the field, a rather difficult task. This multiplication of tools used for adjusting parameters and the absence of a management system for the lifecycle of the platform's configuration leads to high risks for the deployment of services. The parameters are not reliable and cannot be reproduced; it is impossible to generate a version, etc. To solve these problems MDM has to be integrated into the SOA platform for it to benefit from the unified repository of technical and functional parameters. This criterion determines the selection of the SOA platform.

10.4. Representation tools

The method is based on a modeling CASE tool, a procedure for the formal specification of services (pseudo-language) and the tools of model engineering. This section describes the essential principles of solutions, with the exception of the tools used for designing tests, which will be described later.

10.4.1. *Modeling CASE tool*

The choice of the CASE tool modeling is vitally important because it must allow for implementing the methodology. This implementation is very efficient when it comes to the vigilance that will be covered in this section. Vigilance is a condition for the success of the method's instrumentalization, which includes unified notation, the repository of requirements and traceability, team work, the management of different versions, UML profiles, quality control, testing and, last but not least, new forms of notation.

Dealing with model-based engineering is also a form of vigilance when selecting a modeling CASE tool. The extent of this theme will be covered in the next section of this chapter on MDA.

10.4.1.1. *Unified notation*

The modeling CASE tool has to cover all steps in the production of the software. These stages start with the expression of the requirements and end with the automatic generation of a part of the software. Different types of tools and notation between different phases in software production should be avoided, as rationalization of these tools reduces the costs and emphasizes the approach of model engineering. As already seen, the Praxeme method and its EST on eight aspects (semantics, pragmatics, geography, logical, software, technical, physical and hardware) reinstate the art of modeling.

The use of UML notation at all times is highly recommended. Due to its homogenity, the transformation of upstream models into models of logical architecture is easier and traceability between different kinds of models can be guaranteed. Furthermore, the modeling of the process based on the activity diagram can provide a reference of the modeled data with the help of a class diagram.

10.4.1.2. *The repository of requirements and the traceability*

The modeling CASE tool needs to integrate a repository of requirements, i.e. the administration of the requirement's nomenclature captured during the fabrication of the system. UML models are linked to the requirements in order for them to benefit from a complete trace of the presentation of requirements and their translation into models. In the case of Figure 10.9, the semantic operation "describe" is derived, at the level of the logical architecture, with help from three logical services. Amongst these services, the logical service "describeValid" implements the rules RG2067, RG2068, RG2069 and the messages M2067, M2068, M2069.

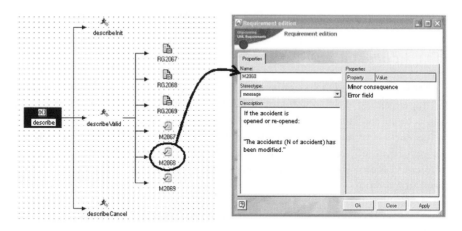

Figure 10.9. *Link between UML and the requirements (modeling CASE tool)*

The traceability of requirements and models is fundamental. It is a good means for increasing the legibility of upstream models and justifying their existence when faced with requirements. This is very useful when it comes to verifying that all requirements are in the right place within the models. Traceability links are also used to follow up on the derivation between upstream models and program engineering. Xavier Blanc insists on the importance of these links [BLANC, 2005]: "The diversity of possible models as well as the possibility of expressing the traceability links are decisive assets when it comes to the management of complexity."

10.4.1.3. *Group work and the version management*

In overhaul SOA projects, it is not uncommon for the volume of models to reach several hundred megabytes, or even gigabytes, if work is being carried out on several different model versions at the same time. The number of people involved can be very high, since the modeling CASE tool is used at all levels of the Enterprise System Topology. It is used by designers of the business and the organization, by logical designers, technical architects, software developers (at least in a reading mode but also for the automatic generation of a part of the code), data administrators, production teams, etc. Furthermore, SOA encourages sharing of knowledge and recycling of services. It is normal that the people involved in several project-based models use those models at least for consultation. The number of users therefore increases very quickly. The modeling CASE tool therefore needs to support the access of several dozen actors with the appropriate access rights for consultation and the required updates. Parallel access and updates are protected by mechanisms that allow for a secure sharing of models (*check-in*, *check-out*). Overall, the modeling CASE tool is a real teamwork tool.

Version management devices for models also need to be considered. This is often a weak feature of the modeling CASE tool. The following functionalities need to be available, even with the integration of another group of tools:

– based on a reference branch, the possibility of creating working branches on which the versions of models are labeled;

– comparison between two versions of a model, i.e. presentation of modifications taken from the models;

– tools which support the fusion between a branch and a reference branch to synchronize the updates and moves from one version to the next;

– reporting on the modifications carried out on the model from an identified version.

The scopes of comparing models, fusion and reporting have to be decided upon by the user of the modeling CASE tool. The tool must not impose a systematic and mandatory work scope on the entire modeling repository.

10.4.1.4. *UML profiles*

The UML CASE tool needs to integrate the concept of profiles.[1] This is not always the case and therefore needs to be checked. UML profiles are a standard of OMG. OMG favors the specialization of UML uses. It is a way to distribute or limit the notation to adapt it to a particular use case. A UML profile assembles stereotypes, which enrich the definition of standardized notions, annotations, limitations and transformations. UML profiles are a way to inject the method into a modeling tool. Every discipline can set up a profile that expresses its terminology and rules of work.

The Praxeme method, for example, is based on a UML profile that deals with certain specializations in notation to provide details for the logical components of service-oriented architecture such as logical factory, logical workshop and logical machine.

10.4.1.5. *Quality control*

The default use of the modeling CASE tool allows for extensive exploitation of UML's notion. The method restricts this notation and is based on strict rules of modeling. In the Praxeme method, for example, it becomes impossible for a logical component of the "business stratum" to interact with a component of the "organizational stratum". The communication takes place exclusively from the outside (organization) to the inside (business) of the system.

The design tool needs to define the rules of quality control. This helps the designers to verify whether the methodological framework has been respected. There might be a high number of these rules (several hundred) covering all topological aspects of the enterprise system (semantics, pragmatics, geography, logical, technical, physical, hardware). They provide the knowledge base for the method. Their automation in the modeling CASE tool is the best means to improve the quality of the design teams.

The more a method follows the trend of model engineering, which is the case for Praxeme, the greater the interest in capitalizing on the rules of quality control. The model production line requires early detection of errors in modeling and architecture as these could, due to the derivation of different models, reproduce themselves throughout the cycle of fabrication.

---

1. The principle of UML profiles was invented by Philippe Desfray: *Using UML 2.0 profiles for supporting the MDA approach* – OMG days 2003 – P Desfray.

10.4.1.6. *New forms of notation*

UML notation is currently in version 2.x of its development. is the more remarkable new concept is introduced with the help of the "component" that replaces the use of packages for the representation of a logical component. As opposed to packages, the component contains classes (structural parts) and use-cases which are represented by the concept for "parts". The assembly of components is done with help from parts. A part unites one or several interface services either at the output (the component exposes services), at the entry (consumption of services that are exposed by another component) or a mixture of the two approaches is used. One main interest in using parts is the possibility of setting up several configurations for the same components, from the beginning of the design of the architectural graph of the system. The same component, for example, can be recycled in several projects and could present two different parts. This would personalize the services to be presented and used for each one of the projects.

Note that the UML profile for SOA that has been created by OMG is referred to as UPMS (UML *Profile and Metamodel for Software Services*) and based on components and parts. When this book was first published in French, this profile was at the state of a preliminary response by OMG.

10.4.2. *Formal language (pseudo-language)*

UML notation allows for the modeling of the architecture's framework, interaction between services as well as data structures, but does not suggest a clear solution for the specification of service algorithms. The use of OCL (*Object Constraint Language*) for the expression of issues might be possible, but its grammar is often seen as too complex for it to be used by designers who are responsible for functional specifications. OCL is also inadequate when it comes to expressing actions. In practice, the most widely used approach in the description of algorithms remains informal, i.e. natural language is used. The translation of this type of specification into a program is not implemented immediately. Numerous ambiguities or interpretation difficulties can appear and the developer is forced to plan an intermediary step in the detailed specification before coding. The developer needs to be sufficiently familiar with the functional domain so that the detailed specification agrees with the initial expectations.

An alternative approach consists of specifying services in a formal way through the use of pseudo-language. The designer expresses the content of services with a minimum of ambiguity by using a standardized style of writing, which is shared by all teams. This specification takes place on the level of logical design at the moment when service-oriented architecture is being created.

Figure 10.10. *Example of French pseudo-language –*
the grammar has been suggested in Praxeme

Logical designers require lots of discipline and motivation to describe the group of algorithms in a detailed way by using pseudo-language. This description cannot be classed as a form of programming, but the level of subtleties shows how close this description is to the program. Logical designers can entirely understand and seize this approach if they are able to use a tool that has been adapted to pseudo-language.

This tool needs to offer functionalities which are just as advanced as those of programming tools, e.g. automatic completion when naming data and services, control of whether the grammar of the pseudo-language has been respected, color-coding to emphasize the key words of the language, search functions, replacement, printing, management of different versions, analysis of differences, refactoring, etc. Unfortunately, not all forms of UML CASE tool deal with an editor that is well adapted. In the Praxeme framework, the pseudo-language is suggested in the form of a grammar expressed as BNF (Backus-Nor Form). If the developer prefers an informal description to pseudo-language, at least the well-structured form of notation for data handling needs to be kept, as it states what data is being manipulated in the algorithms.

This well-structured form of notation allows for identifying directly from the data model (class diagram) without any ambiguity. The cost of a compensation for an accident is, for example, expressed with reference to a data model:

InfoSinistre.lstdommage[idDommage].cout[2]

An informal expression such as "take the cost of the compensation and add it to the list of compensations" would be insufficient when the developer is supposed to select the information at the right place within the data model. Formal notation also requires the logical designer to be a lot more precise.

The choice of using pseudo-language depends on the organization of work retained in the logical design and development.

There are two possible approaches:

– On the one hand, the objective is to delay the moment when developers need to get the functional knowledge. In this case, the use of pseudo-language allows for the logical conception to be extended so that the developers only take on the role of translating the pseudo-language into the implementation language. In theory, the developers do not need to be familiar with the functional domain. In practice, the different steps in a test and the correction of bugs require teamwork and collaboration between the logical designer and the developer.

– On the other hand, logical designer and the developer could be twinned. These teams would have to be created at an early stage of the logical design. In this case, the logical designer is limited to expressing the service's specifications in a textual way while taking care not to be ambiguous and adopting the structured form of notation for data handling. The developer uses the informal expression and translates it into an algorithm with the use of pseudo-language for complex cases.

10.4.3. *MDA*

The importance of the MDA standard has already been mentioned in previous chapters (capitalization of knowledge based on models, exhaustiveness of design, automatically generating parts of the code, etc.). In practice, using an MDA production line is delicate, especially if not enough attention is paid to certain key points. [ROQUES and VALLÉE, 2002]: "Do not underestimate the cost and the risks of a tool which generates code. The development of a generator is a project within a project that requires the same criteria of follow up: running the project based on risks, development based on increments and construction around the model."

---

2 InfoAccident.1stcompensation[idCompensation].cost.

The worst-case scenario consists of having to regenerate the models and the code at each modification of the system. In some projects the modification of a simple data structure requires the process of regenerating code to be carried out over several days. In this case, the MDA chain slows down the flexibility of the teams' work. This is by no means acceptable. To be prepared for such difficulties, the main aspects favoring MDA's success will be explained in the following sections. These are the generation of service signatures, the competition of models, and the development of model transformers and code generators.

10.4.3.1. *Generating the service signatures*

The transformation of models or the generation of code at each change of parameters that compose the service signatures is not required. The stability of these signatures, especially in the first phases of design and development, cannot be guaranteed. If this change of signature imposes an update of the design model and the adjustment of all logical components that consume a service, the cost of the design by models may become too high.

Using an implicit passage of parameters with the use of a complex type of data therefore makes more sense, as it preserves the service signatures. For example, the following signature:

– calculateCost(in_accident: InfoAccident): InfoAccident

is preferable to:

– calculateCost(in_idAccident: string, in_date: date...): long.

In this case, InfoAccident is a complex type that unites all parameters that define the accident. If a parameter of this complex type is to be added, the signature of the service is not to be altered and there is therefore no update in the models of service-oriented architecture that are used except for the definition of the complex type. Reading services (accessors) also deal with banalized signatures. The reading services are therefore not multiplied, which reduces unnecessary requests brought forward to the MDA chain.

10.4.3.2. *Management of variable codes*

The MDA chain has to be used in the process of generating the system's framework, i.e. its most stable parts. Its applicative logic that represents high variation over time is exported into the business rules management system, which is independent of MDA. Once the service skeletons have been implemented, especially on the level of the "organizational" stratum, the generation of code is no longer necessary each time a new rule is added to the rules engine. As explained earlier, every pre- and post-condition of organizational services is linked to an invocation of the rules engine. Without the rules engine, every modification of the system's behavior requires a regeneration of the models and the code. This comes at a rather high price.

At the same time, the services are specified in a generic way to absorb variants of behavior via the adjustment of parameters. This leads to a decrease in the solicitation of the MDA chain. It is impossible to implement the MDA approach without using the rules engine and a strategy or adjusting the parameters of services.

10.4.3.3. *Competition of models*

Conforming to the MDA standard PIM (*Platform Independent Model*) is not to be confused with PSM (*Platform Specific Model*). An error that is regularly observed in these projects consists of the use of functional models to control the generation of code. In this case, the developers start to enrich the functional models with technical directives that slow down its functioning. In the long term, updating functional models becomes impossible and a competition of models takes place between the different teams of designers and developers. This competition provides huge difficulties for managing models and versions of these models over time.

MDA's success requires the transformation of functional models (PIM) into other models at the software level (PSM): PIM is the designers' property; PSM is the developers' property. The cost of setting up and managing the transformation chain of models is an obligatory condition of the success of MDA. Without this condition it makes more sense not to use the model engineering approach.

10.4.3.4. *Development of transformers and generators*

The modeling CASE tool has to accept UML profiles. These profiles are indispensable for models which allow for the transformers and generators of code to function.

An MDA project needs to be identified by the implementation of a dedicated team that deals with the methodological and technical competences for the design and the development of transformers for models and generators of code. This complex type of processing absorbs the know-how of the production line of models which represent a high-value asset. Xavier Blanc also insists on the following point [BLANC, 2005]: "The importance of transformation of models cannot be underestimated. The transformations provide the methodological process with intelligence for the construction of the application. They are strategies that are part of the enterprise's know-how or the organization that carries them out as they contain the rules of quality and the development of applications."

If the company uses Praxeme's open method, compatible MDA might become available on the market. The generation of code for services particularly needs to be part of the implemented framework to provide the linking between software components that have been generated and the technical services exposed in the framework. Praxeme is linked to VEP, which has been described above.

10.5. Tools for tests and management

Designing tests is often neglected by projects for several different reasons, such as lack of means, lack of tools and low motivation of the teams. In the best case, the projects create functional tests that act on the level of the human-machine interface. The SOA framework requires very thorough tests, since the interactions between different services are richer and more complex than the communication between different functional modules. Ideally, every service should arrange its own bank of tests with a complete description of the associated set of data. These services may operate with a graphical interface, but the majority are program-based and situated in the business and organizational strata of logical architecture.

Successive versions of services need to be packaged with other IT resources such as databases and technical components. A configuration management of these packages is needed to control the interdependences between different versions of these groups.

10.5.1. *Non-regression tests*

As soon as cosmetic SOA is introduced, an approach and tools for testing are required, as they will automatically verify new versions of a service do not produce by regressions. Recycling a service, e.g. consultation of a client in different contexts (portals, organizations, versions, etc.) implies that when modifying and adapting a program to a specific context there are no regressions. When maintaining a service, non-regression tests have to be automated. When adjusting the parameters of variants according to context, especially in the system of rules management and the reference data manager limits regressions as the code of services has not been modified (see the chapter on SOA's properties). In overhaul SOA non-regression tools are used all the time, as the number of services increases simultaneously with the interactions between them.

The automation of tests is available for unitary tests of a service as well as for tests of integration. Every actor responsible for a service or a component that exposes several services needs to be able to carry out non-regression tests in a unitary manner. Calls to other components are therefore simulated with the help of mock objects.

Step by step, the integration of services and components, due to the removal of the mock objects, moves on to non-regression tests. The tools are used to manage the chains of tests and produce reports on the quality of tests. In Java, for example, solutions such as JUnit and Maven allow for the implementation of a type of integration known as continuous integration. Other tools such as cruise control add, on top of Maven, more management layers. This creates a real continuous integration.

The chain of automating tests needs to be flexible and high performance. On one hand, it allows for the automatic creation of a chain including several tests and also accepts the launch of the call for a test or a group of tests according to specific requirements. This flexibility imposes that the underlying technical framework used for the execution services, especially for the case of a virtual machine (such as the VEP), is not re-initialized at each launch of a test. Furthermore, the passage from mock objects jack mode (simulating the function of an invoked service) to a mode of invocation by passing through a real service takes place. This mechanism is provided by a simple adjustment of parameters without intrusion into the program. Factory-type procedures and the inversion of control have been mentioned above and allow for implementing this mechanism.

10.5.2. *Designing tests and test data*

Designing tests is a task that requires investment. Rationalizing this work while keeping up the designers' level of motivation requires flexible tools when entering sets of data and different scenarios of tests. A basic textual description of these tests is not sufficient, as it is impossible to automate the generation of programs and test cases. This approach to testing would not allow for synchronization with the data structures and the service signatures that are modeled in the modeling CASE tool. In this case, a modification in a model should be reported manually with the textual specification which could be rather complicated and lead to the generation of errors. Furthermore, the designer must deal with advanced query functions used for test data that are analyzed during the process of impact analysis. In the case of modifying the format of a data, for example, the tests to be used need to be easily identified in order for them to be modified. These impact analyses are impossible to implement in combination with the textual approach of the specification of tests.

These findings present the modeling CASE tool as a possible solution when entering data sets and test cases. The modeling CASE tool deals with the description of data structures and signatures of services (entry parameters, response parameters, list of possible errors). The modeling CASE tool needs to offer a module dedicated to the filling of test data and test cases when accessing sets of data and test cases. At a minimum, the modeling CASE tool has to accept a specific development on the screens needed for entering and implementing query functions as well as impact analysis. As a next step, from the design of test data and test cases an automatic generation of tests must be available . In Java this is, for example, the generation of JUnit, a tool aimed at the automation of programmatic tests.

10.5.3. *Different levels of tests*

There are three different levels, which require different tools such as human-machine interfaces, programs and performance.

10.5.3.1. *The level of human-machine interfaces*

As the screens are based on recyclable graphical services (select client, enter circumstances of the accident, etc.) unitary tests can be implemented for every single service. Specialized tools allow for the simulation of action on behalf of the user on the screen to store different scenarios that are played back automatically later on. The data from these scenarios has to be externalized in databases to create several test cases on the basis of an initial scenario.

The tools need to be capable of establishing differences in behavior on the level of the screen and restore reports on errors in tests. The tool could even present differences visually, which would enable the tester to analyze the reasons for these errors. This tool is used by IT specialists as well as by users when testing the functional acceptance and for enriching existing functional test cases. When the user acceptance test (UAT) is applied to every new test scenario, it enters the test base and could be re-run later during the session of non-regression tests. Figure 10.11 shows an example of a gap analysis at the screen level for the management of accidents (insurance company). These gaps are analyzed by an operator to determine whether they represent a regression of the service's behavior or not. On the right hand side of the figure the expected state of the screen is shown. On the left hand side is the screen that has effectively been obtained during the test. These differences are emphasized by sets of color and highlights.

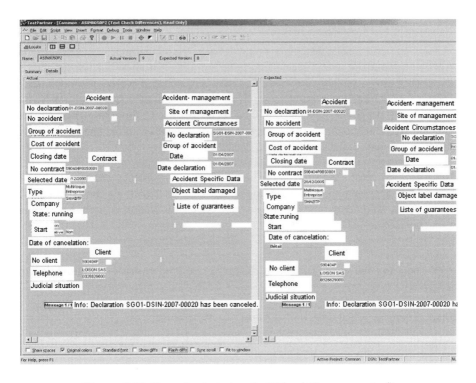

Figure 10.11. *Example of a test on the UI level (Compuware tool)*

10.5.3.2. *The program level*

The aim here is to proceed to tests of services that do not have a graphic interface. These might be services that communicate in XML, *Web services* (SOAP-XML) or in a native programming language. For this type of exchange there are different types of tools. For XML and Web services there are specialized tools that are able to proceed to automatic comparisons between an expected data flow (test data) and the data flow obtained after the test has been carried out. This comparison has to be sufficiently intelligent to filter certain types of technical data such as *timestamps* that vary from one test to another without this variation being significant for the validity of the test. For Web services, the tools work on the level of the XML SOAP message by distinguishing the header (technical information) and the body (business information). The tester does not need to be a specialist in the SOAP standard to ensure that the test is acceptable.

Note that other test tools exist. They are embedded into the BRMS, in some BPM, as well as in solutions such as semantic mapping of data (transforming the format). These solutions will be described in Chapter 12.

10.5.3.3. *The level of performance*

Tests on performance take place on the level of the human-machine interface and on the programmatic level. Specialized tools are used that allow for the simulation of user scenarios, e.g. using screens, delay between each new screen or simultaneous access of users. For programmatic services, flow injection robots based on XML, SOAP or a programming language need to be used. Programs need to be implemented which automatically generate sets of test data with the aim of obtaining sufficient volumes of data injected into databases.

Last but not least, the tester should benefit from complementary tools, which will help with diagnosing the consumption of the systems resources. Interpreting the results leads to collaboration between the teams of technical architecture and production.

10.6. Tools for the management of different versions and the configuration of programs

10.6.1. *The level of versions and variants*

The chapter on SOA's properties has already shown the difference between the concepts of versions and variants. The version intervenes if the code of the service (its program) is being modified. The variant of a service is created by the simple setting of parameters, data or rules without any modification of the program. The combinations between versions and variants of services may be numerous and even increase as the system's agility personalizes the behavior of services very easily. This personalization is based on the users' demands. The configuration of versions and variants cannot be satisfied by a program's form, which is based only on standard strategies of configuration management of the program. These standard strategies usually come into play at the level of components used for development and production (source files and runnable packages). In this case, the program's form would lead to duplications of the code and packages and difficulties when installing it in production environments.

Furthermore, this approach is not flexible enough since changing a version of variant in the use contract for the service implies a lengthy process. This process also includes a new and heavy generation of a new runnable package. Therefore this type of traditional management has to be linked to another type of configuration for the program, which intervenes directly in production. This form of configuration dynamically chooses the right versions and variants of services according to the context required by the consumers.

The moment the user invokes a service, the provider needs to choose the right version of the service's facade. This facade might be different when several versions of the same service is possible (cohabitation of versions). Figure 10.12 shows that the call by the consumers is carried out on the context which specifies all parameters. This group of parameters has been laid out in the service contract and defines the right service to be launched depending on, for example, the organization that consumes the service, the technical environment (development, tests, training, production, etc.), starting date, functional segmentation, version, etc. The version might also be determined directly by the consumer if the provider opens up this possibility in the service contract. In Figure 10.12, arrow [1] shows that the repository of parameters managed by MDM delivers the physical name (concrete implementation) of the service's facade. This service is to be launched according to the context of invocation expressed by the consumer.

This procedure illustrates a mode for the management of versions on the basis of a physical router that indicates the facade of the service to be executed. The provider can therefore publish the same service with different signatures, e.g. differences in entry and exit parameters.

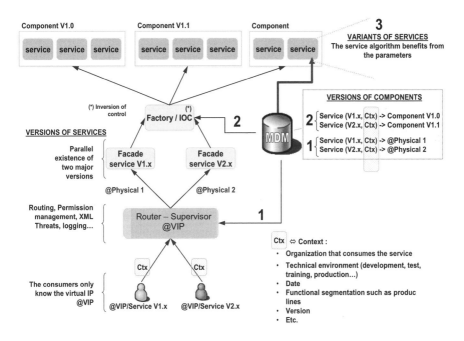

Figure 10.12. *Example of version management and the configuration of services*

Once the facade has been launched it sets off a mechanism for invoking components that executes the service (factory, inversion of control). Arrow [2] shows a new request to the MDM, this time for recovery of the right version of the component to be executed and depending on the context of the execution. The example used in the figure shows two different versions of the same component that have been invoked according to the consumer's context. When a service is executed the version has been identified. The service may call for an MDM to recover the parameters and reference data that enable the service to adapt its behavior to the context of execution (arrow [3] in Figure 10.12).

This example also shows how to manage chains of versions from a demand that has been expressed by the consumer, the service's facade and the component. This form of managing configuration does not take place at the level of the program's sources but at the level of the components to be exploited. This form of managing configuration for exploitation is an important point in SOA that is not to be confused with the management of configuration of components used in development.

The chain of versions needs to be handled with care. Just as a component is likely to be recycled and used in different projects and by different consumers in the form of a different version. Each of these versions can require particular versions of other components and services. This interdependence of versions needs to be administered carefully as they are the most precious reference data in SOA. MDM naturally imposes itself as a tool, as it allows for a secure administration of the repository.

10.6.2. *The level of delivery packages*

The SOA project can be organized around two modes for the delivery over time:
– around significant functions for the user: each delivery package absorbs all necessary components to be used in the production of a functional scope. Design and development of components is strictly limited and only considers parts that are necessary for the design of the scope;
– around well-identified components that are not linked to the functional scope.

With the first approach, the users are in a better position to validate the system, as they have to deal with all functions. With the second approach, IT specialists are in a better position to develop the software as every component is processed on the entirety of its scope. The delivery around significant functions for the user is most commonly used. The parallel management of several functional delivery packages needs to take into consideration the sharing of certain components between these packages. Once the delivery approach has been decided upon, the types of delivery packages are defined. They will contain elements of design, programs and the test cases. The following types of delivery packages are needed:

– "Delivery package for the specification of a component": these packages contain the component's design, logical design, test cases, sets of data, the list of services to be invoked to other components and sets of data associated to the tests.

– "Delivery package for a component software": this package contains programs of the component and its test case (e.g. code for JUnit in Java for pragmatic tests).

– "Delivery package for the database" with the schema of the database, associated sets of data and procedures to manage the database.

– "Delivery package for each technical component," e.g. for the virtual engine (technical framework used for the service execution), technical modules of editing, etc.

The management tools for configuring components of development and exploitation, e.g. Rational ClearCase type, work on this level. They create references for these components and manage their links and interdependences. These management tools are added to the dynamic management of versions and variants that have been described in previous versions.

10.7. Benefits of using tools in the method

10.7.1. *Opportunities*

Making service-oriented architecture available without the shared tools of UPDS is very risky. The range of functions and techniques has briefly been covered and shows the amount of work teams might face if prior consideration and a continuous investment in the platform do not take place. If well prepared, UPDS is an excellent vector for the changes within teams. SOA is perceived in a more concrete way as it has been instrumentalized by a group of integrated and coherent tools. The training of these teams is therefore much faster and the robustness of the developments increases. The industrialization of SOA finally takes place.

Given the cost of UPDS, it is useful to carry out a financial study at the level of the information system (mutualization of needs and means). Technological reversibility as well as open source should also be kept in mind.

10.7.2. *Risks*

10.7.2.1. *Mastering the unified platform for the development of services*

As indicated at the beginning of this chapter, there is no unified platform for the development of services (UPDS) that can be bought "ready to go." The company therefore has to deal with the project of integrating the platform, choosing from several offers, completing certain functions via specific developments, etc. Since all SOA projects will rely on the UPDS, both for the building up and running of services, it is vitally important to set up a sustainable organization to manage this platform. This organization would accompany the teams during the use of the platform and its maintenance. The required level of technical and methodological expertise is very high and it is not always easy to obtain an expert on a long-term basis. This is why it is better not to use specific approaches, but, as previously indicated, rely on the open method that ensures a sustainable return of investment and the continued existence of the platform.

The standard approach also allows for a more economic contribution of subcontractors. With Praxeme's public method, groups of consultants now exist at different IT service providers.

10.7.2.2. *Model-based engineering*

When it comes to model-based engineering several risks have to be taken into consideration:

– The computer engineer is no longer familiar with modeling. Even worse, with the recent disappearance of historical methods, such as Merise in France and SADT, other techniques have taken over the process of constructing systems. The computer scientist is therefore an expert in programming but hardly works with UML notation and does not know how to model a requirement or architecture.

– Producing models. Yes, but which method should be used? Establishing models requires the use of a methodology that describes procedures. UML is a notation that defines the possibilities of representation but does not indicate their use. SOA might be slowed down by in-house methodological initiatives carried out by each company. How can companies efficiently communicate if they define their own and diverging typologies of services and the associated rules of modeling?

– Weakness of interoperability of the production line. The available interoperability at the level of technological standards such as XML does not have any equivalent when it comes to models. The procedures of decorating models (UML profiles), transformers of models and generators of code, are essentially a specific and often locked-in software offering. Using a modeling CASE tool implies the risk of being dependent on the software vendor. The use of the XMI standard does not correspond to the interoperability of the model transformers or code generators.

– Increase in the requirements for tests. Models have to be precise and exhaustive to allow for a generation of code. This code is necessary for the model's execution. A lack of modeling generates malfunctioning at the moment of generation and the software cannot be obtained. There is a lot of upstream effort in modeling. Between the time of generating a model and obtaining the final product it might be necessary to proceed to manual techniques of adjusting parameters in the production line. These parameters are not always flexible, especially during the regeneration due to the evolution of existing models. Consequently, it might be better to specify the test data and the test cases at the same time as modeling to deliver the required information to prove the models. The ideal solution would be to test a model even before generating the code. A virtual UML machine needs to be available to do so. This machine, however, does not yet exist on an industrial level.

Chapter 11

Systems Integration and Common Information Language

A RECAP OF IDEAS MENTIONED IN PREVIOUS CHAPTERS

– Cosmetic SOA: exposing services on an already existing system

– Overhaul SOA: rewriting existing code in a service mode

NEW IDEAS TO BE INTRODUCED IN THIS CHAPTER

– Service Bus

– Functions of ESB (Enterprise Service Bus)

– How far can we go with XML?

– The modeling of exchange data

Communication between systems is a challenge that occurs as soon as the cosmetic SOA is deployed. The aim is a better integration of cosmetic SOA into existing systems. This integration goes further with overhaul SOA as exchanges become intensified. Interconnected systems integrate existing applications in the form of services, software packages, new developments, technical components in infrastructure (security, editing, rules management systems, management of reference data, etc.), etc. These systems are also based outside the limits of the information system to enable communication with subsidiaries, partners and other third parties.

In the past, communication between systems has been based on EAI (Enterprise Application Interface) solutions, which are specialized in the management of communication and exchange. Looking at the situation now, companies realized that the cost of development and maintenance of these communication systems was not decreasing. Several books have been written on this issue, e.g. [KRAFZIG, BANKE, SLAMA, 2006]: "In many cases, middleware such as CORBA was only used to solve point-to-point integration problems on a per-project basis, instead of being established as a global software bus; as a result, many enterprises now have nearly as many incompatible middleware systems as they have applications". This chapter will show that the reason for this failure is to be found in an approach that is far too technical when it comes to the interconnection of systems.

In SOA, ESB (Enterprise Service Bus) replaces EAI. ESB recycles the concept of EAI and uses new standards in XML at the same time. Rather than creating exchanges between systems based on a proprietary protocol (EAI), the open source standard of XML has been chosen. Is it therefore sufficient to replace EAI with ESB to lower costs? We have to warn the reader at this point that the answer to this question is "No". Even if XML is useful for these exchanges, this standard remains very technical. If the data to be exchanged has not been modeled correctly, the cost for these exchanges will not decrease. Data has to be modeled to put an end to modular structures which are redundant and not aligned with the business requirements.

The service-oriented approach will revolutionize the way in which systems provide data. These systems have to move from an approach exposes flat data to the exposition of services which requires the modeling of exchange data, also known as the common information model. The modeling significantly reduces the costs of integration between systems but will also impose a supplementary methodological effort.

Whether EAI or ESB with XML is used, the lack of a business-focused approach during the modeling of the common information language makes rationalization of the cost and quality improvement of the exchanges very difficult. Unfortunately, it is still possible to create rigid systems that are not very reliable for data exchange, even if they are created with XML. The teams in charge of EAI or ESB cannot be isolated from the business teams. The business teams have to contribute to the modeling of the common information language. Currently these teams often only fulfill a technical role within companies.

11.1. New requirements in communication

11.1.1. *Increase of data flow*

Information systems are not homogenous blocks. They consist of multiple silos of applications, software packages, services, technical components, etc. situated on heterogenous production platforms. Exposing services does not really change this complex production of systems. However, the exchange based on a common language and SOA's logical architecture might be better urbanized and therefore less redundant. However, a more reactive and faster process requires an increase in data propagation speed in systems that restore information for the user. As real time treatments increase, communication between services situated in different production platforms also increases.

In future, the Internet of objects will significantly increase the flow of exchanges between systems. RFID (Radio Frequency IDentification) technology enables companies to tag all physical objects (contracts, machines, manuals, conference rooms, etc.) with sensors that send and receive information. RFID technology does so at a very low cost. These new sources of information will be transported into the network and provide the company's databases with information. Information systems need to be adapted to these new requirements. David A. Chappell, vice president of Progress Software, gives an interesting example of the use of RFID when controlling goods in large warehouses. This type of tracking moves from the carton level down to each single product; [CHAPPELL, 2004]: "The increased granularity in messages due to item-level RFID tags can also be a problem for applications that were not designed to handle data at a granularity beyond the carton level."

When dealing with this increase in data flow, the company needs to pay attention to the modeling of the common language that will rationalize the exchange. If the exchange includes unnecessary information, it will slow down the development cycle and increase the risk of the exchanged data being of a very low quality. The higher the data flow, the slower the cycle and the worse the quality.

11.1.2. *Considering the business*

In recent years, companies have dealt with the issue of exchange between systems from a technical point of view. These exchanges were mainly designed on the basis of data flow that had been organized in a stable and modular way. Data from different business objects is often mixed in the same message. Filtering this data on the basis of use is very difficult. The contract business object, for example, is diluted in the client business object but it is impossible to filter this data contract for by contexts of consumption (header of the contract, history of the contract, events linked to the contract, etc.). In this situation the exchange of flat data files takes place. Messages are no longer urbanized.

EAI solutions have not improved the situation, as their approach is purely technical. EAI has been taken over by IT specialists who have not left enough space for the business. Systems providing data have preserved their aspect of exposing modular and stable flow. Therefore, EAI teams develop often complex programs for the transformation of data to restore the information and deliver it to the appropriate consumer system. The EAI teams, however, do not deal with the business knowledge and then the specifications of the transformation of formats remain unclear. The quality of the exchanges is therefore reduced and the cost of integration too high.

With SOA, a new paradigm appears. SOA will favor the business in order to normalize data exchanges. The exposition of services leads to providers overcoming the rigid simplification of data that obliges the consumer or the EAI team (now ESB) to undertake the necessary efforts to understand the content of data flow, to extract only the useful parts while verifying the quality of received data, etc. Indeed, exchanges become more intensified and the context in which SOA is used (versions, channels, subsidiaries, partners, etc.) leads to consumers requiring a definition of normalized exchanges. This definition cannot contain any redundancies and needs to be of a high quality to rapidly absorb the evolutions. The providers are therefore obliged to consider a project of modeling exchange data, that is to say a Common Information Model. This modeling is done with the consumers of data and will allow for streamlining data exchanges. Without this global approach there is a risk of implementing specific data messages for every context of exchange and makes ESB's work unnecessarily complex. This situation is to be avoided, as the maintenance of exchanges would be rather heavy, as well as there being a risk of incoherence when publishing data. Defining a common language is not an easy project, as the providers and consumers do not always share the same idea of data structures and the semantics of information.

The business is also favored by an evolution of ESB and the associated tools, especially the management of transforming data and the directory of services. These tools are now less technical than the previous generation of EAI. They may be considered by users to consult, or even specify in certain cases, the rules for transforming a format, versions of services which use these transformations, associated tests, documentation of data structure, etc. Communication is therefore more easy between teams in charge of ESB or business teams.

11.1.3. *Take the bus!*

The term ESB shows the need for a service bus whose objective it is to share some functions in the infrastructure that are necessary for communications between systems. This bus is made up of specialized programs for the exchanges as well as material platforms, which represent the points of passage. These points are required to enable communication between consumers and providers.

Another approach consists of letting participants communicate directly with one another. This method is referred to as point-to-point protocol (PPP). In 2000, Web services emerged and PPP was state of the art. However, companies realized very quickly that, at the current state of technology, PPP does not share the necessary functions of infrastructure for the management of exchanges such as transformation of data, security, counting of flow, supervising, etc. It therefore makes sense to "take the bus" for systems that connect consumers and providers. The same applies when using the standard of Web services.

11.2. ESB's functions

ESB is useful when it comes to the management of communication between distant and/or heterogenous systems. ESB is not necessary within a domain of applications or a group of services that are situated within the same technical platform. For example, ESB processes lead to an exchange between MVS, AS400 and Java platforms but are not used for communication between services when they are situated within the same execution platform. Nevertheless, the perimeter of ESMBuse also has to consider the performance of an exchange flow in XML. The question that arises is then: up to what point should XML be used?

11.2.1. *Use perimeter*

11.2.1.1. *Up to which level should XML be used?*

ESB is based on XML standards to rationalize the technical layers of communication between different systems. This is a very interesting step forward in terms of interoperability and independence from software vendors. All ESB solutions are implemented with the same XML standards. Therefore they increasingly become IT commodities such as SQL databases. Given the current technical limitations, XML standards might lead to problems in performance if overused in the lower levels of an information system. The natural use of ESB's perimeter might be more adapted to communications between distant and/or heterogenous systems. In practice, choosing the level of use of the XML standard is rather difficult. Two examples will be given below.

In a company which organizes its management of IT around an MVS mainframe, several AS400 systems and Java applications by business domains, it is easy enough to decide on the zones in which an XML standard is to be used. In this case, XML is used for communication between these IT platforms and exposes services to the outside of the information system. However, the decision of whether to use XML also has an impact on the exchanges between components of infrastructure such as the workflow, the editing process, rules engine, management of reference data and parameters. If the level of performance allows for communication in XML, XML is beneficial as it leads to better interoperability, decoupling between components and recycling of the common information language. A flow of XML data taken from AS400, for example, may undergo a fusion of complementary XML data generated by MVS. Due to the use of a common language, all of this data could be sent to the rules engine for a validity check and later on to editing and printing. This type of unified communication in XML also enables the implementation of a unified tool that controls the data flow of production independently of IT platforms, operating systems, protocols of communication, etc.

However, if the rules engine and other constituents of infrastructure are invoked too frequently, it is possible that the delay of replies will become too long and no longer acceptable with XML. A form of communication that is closer to the language of implementation will therefore have to be used. For a development in Java, for example, the rules engine would be invoked directly by the Java service with the flow of exchange, which consists of Java objects instead of XML structures.

The second example concerns a company that exploits IT used in trading rooms for the management of movements on the stock exchange. The company's job imposes a real time coordination of important events in several domains of applications, some of which are exposed in the form of services. For some domains this type of coordination by services has not yet been implemented. In this situation it is unclear whether the use of XML might be the best solution given the possible problems of performance. The event-based communication and the high number of requests favor an EAI solution, as its proprietary implementations might be of a better performance than XML standards. This statement is, of course, based on the current state of XML technology.

EAI is added to ESB in exchanges that require a specific solution to preserve performance control. Ideally, there is a single solution for the infrastructure that covers both XML exchanges (ESB) and native calls (EAI). Neither ESB nor EAI can substitute a virtual machine for the execution of services (see Chapter 10). This virtual machine works from within the perimeter of a unified IT platform. It has to guarantee a high level of performance, as this machine is responsible for the interaction of a large number of services at the lowest level of applications.

Finally, ESB does not challenge ETL (*Extract Transform and Load*), whose use is limited to processes that supply large amounts of data, e.g. migrations of systems or injection into *Datawarehouses*. There are situations in which ESB and ETL might compete with each other. However, ESB specializes in real time exchanges based on an invocation of services while ETL specializes in the exchange of large volumes of data in batch mode without a necessary use of services.

11.2.1.2. *The pre-applicative zone*

With XML exchanges it is easy to add processing of interception and exploitation of XML flow on the level of ESB. This can, of course, only be done with the respective access rights. An XML request to consult a contract could, for example, be intercepted at the level of ESB before being sent to the contract provider's system. This interception might be completed by processing according to the needs of business and techniques.

Some business data could, for example, be completed by transforming the format of the data, carrying out calculations, etc. This type of processing creates a zone of execution in the system known as the pre-applicative zone. Intercepting XML flow and processing this data in the pre-applicative zone are possible for both the flow of responses emitted by the consumer and the flow of answers emitted by the provider.

Due to this principle of interception, XML standards can be implemented. WS-Addressing (W3C), for example, enables the consumer to add the network address from which he/she would like to obtain a response to the XML header. When the provider sends the reply the infrastructure benefits from this information to steer the reply to the address entered by the consumer. Another example concerns agents which supervise the data flow in production. Their functioning is based in the same principle of interception and introspection of messages to observe the exploitation of services.

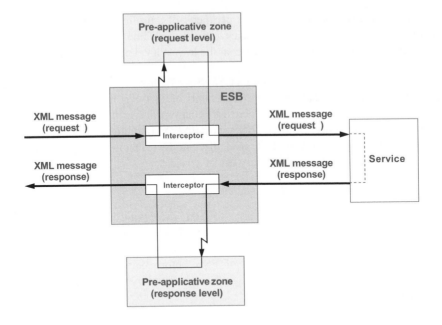

Figure 11.1. *The principle of interception in XML (pre-applicative zone)*

The company might extend the XML header to include all directives that might be necessary when directing certain types of processing to the pre-applicative zone. If, for example, the number of requests sent by each consumer has to be counted, a form of logical identification is required for each user. In this way, the infrastructure would be able to process this information (counting). These specialized forms of processing are considered such as *plug-in* and added step by step. They factorize certain actions on the level of IT infrastructure. The use of this device needs to be handled with care, as malfunctioning at the level of the pre-applicative zones should be avoided. Plug-ins have to be justified and managed by a team who specialize in this type of architecture.

11.2.2. *ESB's components*

The main function of ESB is the transportation of messages between the consumers' systems and providers' systems. In this perimeter, software vendors find that their solutions become less rewarding as XML standards are unified implementations. As companies are confronted with other needs of interconnecting systems, software vendors use ESB for several functionalities, such as orchestration of services, modeling of processes, transformation of data, governance of services in design and production, rules management, management of reference data, etc. At the end, ESB is distributed in a global approach of an SOA platform and commercialized in the form of an SOA suite of programs.

These SOA suites are a new trend and will develop further in years to come, as the components of these programs are often collections of different functions with several overlaps. These functions already exist but a logical homogenous architecture still needs to be created. These SOA suites need to be developed further to respect SOA's properties, which have been described at the beginning of this book. Tight coupling is still to be found between functions. An SOA software suite, for example, could integrate different business rules engine on the level of the ESB and the level of the data mapping solution. If these engines cannot be recycled for other purposes in the information system, the company could end up with three different types of rules engines. The editors need to be challenged on the question of the framework for their SOA platforms. The internal teams of a company often do not have the necessary competences to work on this aspect. Unfortunately only a use case on a real life scale can indicate possible difficulties.

Due to its main function of transporting messages through the network, ESB is organized around technical components that have been used in traditional solutions such as EAI. The new trend is the use of XML standards, which unify the implementations offered by the software vendors. Not all of these standards will be mentioned here; only a few will be explained to illustrate XML standards. For a detailed overview of all standards, please take a look at the websites of organizations dealing with these standards, such as W3C and OASIS.

11.2.2.1. *Invocation of services*

The way in which the developer invokes services has to respect a standard which avoids a coupling of the program with the implementation of ESB. The standards of WSIF (*Web Service Invocation Framework*) and SCA (*Service Component Architecture*) might be able to ensure this independence. These have already been covered in the chapter on the method's tools.

11.2.2.2. *Reliability of exchanges*

The transportation of XML messages has to take place independently of the underlying transport protocol, in particular HTTP. This standard is not a "reliable" communication protocol, as it does not guarantee that no message is lost during the exchange. Due to this reason, a complementary XML standard, called WS-Reliable Exchange (OASIS) has been set up. With help from this XML standard, the ESB can use a counter of XML messages situated in the XML header (SOAP header) in order to check the number of exchanges between a provider and a consumer. This counter provides the number of messages that have been exchanged between the consumer and the provider. ESB is therefore able to detect messages that might have been lost or sent twice.

11.2.2.3. *Asynchronism*

The model of transporting messages according to a synchronized communication is the standard. The consumer waits for an answer from the provider. More flexibility can be achieved by using asynchronous exchanges. In this case, the consumer sends a demand without waiting for an immediate response. The consumer asks the provider to send the response in the form of an event that informs the consumer when the actual return message will be available.

A group of XML standards is available for ESB to identify the events in messages and manage the notification of consumers. WS-Eventing (W3C), in particular, sends an event to a participant in the exchanges. This participant is localized at an address in the network due to the XML standard of WS-Addressing (W3C). The event is described in an XML format and interpreted by a standard form for all ESB. As for all other standards, the consumer and the provider are not obliged to use the same technology and software vendors. Exchanges are possible if both respect XML standards.

11.2.2.4. *Security of exchanges*

XML messages are secured by standards such as WS-Security (OASIS), which allow for the definition of authentification, signatures and encrypting data. WS-Security only formalizes the descriptions used by the security tools. This standard does not replace, for example, encrypting algorithms. On the other hand, WS-Security provides an XML grammar standard to declare algorithms and security guidelines to be used.

11.2.2.5. *Transforming the protocol*

ESB needs to be capable of instantly transforming a communication protocol such as SOAP over HTTP into another protocol, e.g. CORBA. Due to this transformation several protocols can be used at the same time.

11.2.2.6. *Routing*

On the basis of a service's virtual address and its logical name, ESB is capable of determining the physical address of a service, as well as its physical name. The virtual address and logical name are known by the consumer, but this does not apply for either the physical address or the physical name, which are exclusively owned by the provider. ESB stores its translation information in routing tables that are administered by a business tool. Here the aim is to reuse the *Master Data Management* (MDM) tool, which has been described in Chapter 10.

If the routing process also considers changing needs, such as version management, it might be useful to deal with a rules engine. The rules engine provides supplementary intelligence during the translation process. If, for example, the service is invoked by a certain type of consumer, its physical address corresponds to the service in a specific version otherwise the physical address is the current version. These rules of routing are numerous and also integrate the requirement of load balancing. Furthermore, a service that is known to the consumers by its virtual address can have several physical implementations on different servers, which lighten the weight of exploitation. We might have the impression that this procedure exceeds the main functions of ESB, moving on to complementary functions of managing production services, especially the management of SLA (*Service Level Agreement*). This issue will be explained in detail in Chapter 12.

11.2.2.7. *Index management*

Current information systems are often structured around silos of applications that lead to data redundancy. In cosmetic SOA this redundancy needs to be hidden from the consumer of services. In overhaul SOA, redundancies should be reduced to a minimum. A consultation service for a list of contracts per client, for example, might require access to a database situated on the mainframe as well as to another database situated in AS400. These two systems exist for historical reasons and process different types of contracts. The consumers of a service would like to access all contracts at the same time without having to worry about the existence of both mainframe and AS400. A common data language enables the consumer to do so as the structures of information within the two systems are very different from one another. The principles of designing a common language will be explained in the following sections. To enable the unification of data which stems from two different sources of information, ESB has to use an "index base" which provides the name of the services to be invoked and also, if necessary, the client identifiers, as they might be in two different systems.

As soon as identifiers (primary keys) are present in the index base, synthetic data can be added to allow for the construction of consultation services and search functions that do not systematically invoke distant systems. The index management solution can therefore be extended. The index base is updated simultaneously with other systems. It goes hand in hand with the business tool so that the administrators can manage the lifecycle of this index base: versions, query, consultation, validation rules, manual updates, etc. These administrative functions are found in MDM, which was described in Chapter 10. The aim is always to retain a single tool for the same requirements. Managing an index falls into the category of managing reference data.

11.2.2.8. *Logging*

ESB traces the exchanges with help from the standard of shared logging between systems which communicate with each other. This might be the XML standard CBE (*Common Base Event*), which suggests a unified logging of the applicative events. A tool for correlating these traces might be implemented as it obtains, if necessary, a total overview of the logging. This overview includes the consumer's system, ESB and the provider's system.

11.2.2.9. *Continuity of services*

If ESB comes to an unplanned standstill the process of interconnection between different systems would block the entire information system. ESB is a crucial point in the system, which needs to be secured with methods such as clustering and load balancing. In the latter scenario, ESBs are able to cooperate. They also are distributed. The company therefore installs several ESBs that work independently. Every ESB works in a precise functional domain while ensuring a certain amount of autonomous functioning. These ESBs are capable of communicating with each other if processes of different functional domains are to be dealt with. If one ESB stops working, only one functional domain is affected. Distributed ESBs know how to back each other up in case one stops working. If this is the case, the responsibility of another ESB increases and temporarily takes over the functional domain of the deactivated ESB.

11.2.2.10. *Connectors*

For proprietary or specific systems and software packages, data is exposed in the form of XML messages; it is necessary for connectors to be available. These are generally installed at the source of systems and allow for the translation of data from proprietary formats into XML messages. Many connectors on the market respond to very great needs, e.g. EJB, Excel data, DB2 databases, Oracle, flat files, VSAM files, CRM and ERP software packages.

11.2.2.11. *Towards the components of an SOA platform*

The following components are added to ESB to create an SOA platform:

– orchestration of invoked services between systems;

– follow-up of processes with BAM (Business Activity Monitoring);

– governance of services with registry and repository of services;

– follow-up of contracts of service in the production;

– mapping of data (transformation of a source format towards to target format);

– management of reference data (MDM);

– rules management.

The following chapter provides a detailed presentation of these components. Orchestration has already been dealt with in Chapter 10, which was entirely devoted to this subject.

11.3. Integrating ESB into SI

11.3.1. *Towards a common language*

Communication between systems becomes far more economical if they are using the same language. This applies to data structures and semantics. This common language is also known as a common information model or simply data exchange. It is not reliant on the physical structures of data. It unifies the way in which data is exchanged between systems.

In practice, companies are confronted with two constraints when implementing a common language. First, existing systems are not always able to produce data under this common format. Processes to translate messages into the common format have to be available. These processes cannot be intrusive and are executed at the moment when messages are transported under the control of ESB.

The other constraint is the definition of the common format. It is rare that a company deals with a modeling of exchange data. It would make sense that EAI would provide the basis for the creation of these languages. This is, however, not the case. In several situations EAI has been implemented by technical teams that have not been trained in the modeling of common languages. This is why there are so many data transformation processes at the EAI level that have problems in terms of robustness and maintenance. Every exchange between the provider and the consumer leads to specific translation requirements to enable this dialogue. This is a sort of point-to-point connection between systems.

The emergence of ESB is a good opportunity to restart a business approach. Even if the idea of a common language already existed in the past, given the implementation of SOA it can now no longer be avoided. From the first steps of cosmetic SOA onwards, services have to carry data issued from a unified modeling that is independent of existing physical structures of applications. If this type of modeling cannot be ensured, there is the risk of producing services that cannot be recycled as the data carried by services will be specific for every system. The consumer of a service, for example, cannot understand why the structure of a postal address is not the same for the consultation services for the clients, providers, experts, etc. It makes more sense to provide a common format for postal addresses.

Another benefit of a common language is the reduction in the number of translation processes that are necessary for exchanges. Rather than making one process per exchange available, it is sufficient to provide one translation process into the common language and another into the target language of the consumer. In a system of six participants the point-to-point approach provides nine necessary translations. The approach of a common language only requires six.

11.3.1.1. *How can we use a common language?*

Once the common language has been implemented, the use policy needs to be decided upon. This policy includes principles that are sometimes contradictory:

– limit the intrusion into existing systems of providers and consumers;

– limit the complexity of processing transformations of data situated on the level of ESB;

– reduce dependencies between systems of providers, consumers and ESB. Care has to be taken that a modification of a data format in one system has the smallest possible impact on other systems.

There are some contradictions in these principles:

– It is impossible to limit the level of intrusion on the side of providers and consumers while reducing the level of complexity when processing and transforming data situated in ESB.

– A common language cannot be imposed on all participants within the exchange while reducing the impact on the participants if the common language is developed further or transformed.

The goal of imposing a common language into all systems is therefore hard to achieve. A common language needs to be shared without being intrusive to existing systems and without creating complexity at the ESB level. Furthermore, tight coupling between participants is also to be avoided. This aim is impossible to achieve. Therefore a compromise has to be reached and this compromise depends on the context of each company.

11.3.1.2. *Modeling a common language*

Common language cannot be reduced to a simple dictionary of flat data. It corresponds to an information model that is built in terms of semantic modeling, which has been described in the chapter dealing with the method. This type of UML modeling is derived from the form of an XML schema that can easily be shared between different systems.

As a common language is necessary to ensure communication between services, its modeling needs to be linked to cosmetic SOA. Doing so enables services to benefit from this common language immediately. If using overhaul SOA for the design of a common language, the first services need to be redesigned to be compatible with the common format. These changes of data structure would not be appreciated by the consumers.

When working on data exchange, necessary semantic modeling does not have an impact on the entire information system. Work is carried out on around 20% of the data, i.e. the data that participates in the existing exchanges and might be involved in future communications.

The common language does not need to be modeled around business objects that correspond to the aggregates of information. Every business object deals with a stable part to be used in the exchanges and other variable parts that depend on the context of consumption. The business object contract, for example, contains a descriptive header which is stable. Then the variants "content of contract" and "history of contract" are identified. This is complementary data of the header. According to the context of consumption, the contract uses one or other variant. The exchanged messages are constructed on the basis of a fixed part, and other variables are added according to specific needs. This flexibility in creating messages is important to avoid transporting large volumes of information that is not always required. On the other hand, this procedure does not mean that a specific message has been created for every exchange. This would lead to an inflation of messages that would be difficult to manage in terms of maintenance. It makes more sense to use the compromise of a stable header and variants that are chosen according to context. This allows for a relevant granularity of exchanges.

During maintenance of common language, an increase in backward compatibility is to be favored. This means that the consumer of a message expressed in the common language V(n) could also receive the same message in the common language V(n+1) without requiring modifications within the consumer's own system.

Companies can use semantic modeling based on the models published in certain industries. These are generally UML models that accompany XML schema, e.g. SID (*Shared Information and Data*) for operators in telecommunications, ACORD for insurance, FPML (*Financial Product Markup Language*) for finance, H7 for the health care sector, OAGI for the canonical model of data for several different sectors. Such a model may be a useful point of departure for the negotiation of a common language. It might be that for one business object different opinions exist on how it should be modeled in terms of data structure and semantics. Using an internationally standardized model to start off is a huge advantage in the process of creating a common language.

11.3.1.3. *Validation rules*

Common language is a rich model that defines typed data (integer, string, date, etc.) as well as rules of validation (mandatory and optional data, enumeration, threshold, data control, etc.). To increase the robustness of exchanges, the rules might be executed at the moment of sending messages. This would allow for error identification before the message reaches the consumer. It might become apparent that a message emitted by a provider lacks a compulsory data element. In this case it would not make sense to send the information to the consumer. This error therefore needs to be dealt with immediately. The higher the number of validation rules, the more reliable the exchanges.

A new issue has emerged in the modeling of a common language. Some rules for validating messages can be personalized according to the context of consumption. A data element in a message, for example, would be mandatory in one context and not necessarily required in another. The rules can therefore not be linked to the definition of data structures without personalizing the context. The use of a rules engine then makes sense at this level. When receiving a message, ESB finds information on the context in the message header. The message and its context will be forwarded to the rules engine. The rules engine determines the packet of rules to be carried out. This packet might vary according to different contexts of consumption.

11.3.1.4. *Reference data*

A common language also has to include reference data that participates in the exchanges. From cosmetic SOA onwards the reference data used by the services has to be identified. A warehouse of reference data should be exposed to existing repositories that have often been duplicated and are heterogenous. The warehouse of reference data increase the quality of data and ensure its homogenous and secure values. This solution is based on MDM (Master Data Management). These repositories might concern several categories of data, such as product catalogs, organizations, clients, third parties, real estate or translation tables, as well as functional and technical parameters. The outlines of MDM have already been described in Chapter 10.

11.3.1.5. *Which level of coupling should be used between the provider and the consumer?*

As previously shown, the introduction of a common language on the level of ESB is the first step in rationalizing data processing. However, it has to be decided whether this language is made available to providers and consumers. Several approaches are possible and can be used at the same time. The service provider is likely to work in two modes. The service provider could emit data under the format of a common language. In this case, ESB would not ensure the processing of transformations at the reception of the message, as the exchange is already in the unified format. This requirement is often intrusive for the provider's system. The provider's system therefore has to respect this common language during development and take the unified format on board when a new system is being created.

Another approach enables providers to emit data in their own language. In this case, mapping of data, situated at the level of the ESB, carries out the transformation towards a common language. Consumers, on the other hand, might prefer to receive the message in their own language or in common language. All of these situations are possible scenarios which depend on the level of intrusion in the systems and the expectations of both providers and consumers.

However, an additional decision needs to be taken. This decision concerns the level of coupling between the participants in exchanges. Must the common language be used within the same systems or does it remain subject to the data to be exchanged? If the common language is used within systems, an evolution of the data structures in one of these systems leads to modification of the common language. As several systems produce and consume the language, efficient governance needs to be implemented under unified format. In this situation, tight coupling between the participants is created. Another possibility is to use common language only on the perimeter of exchanges; every participant is then responsible for translation of the common language into their own language.

A solution with ESB can be negotiated so it becomes responsible for the translation at the moment when the exchange takes place without intruding into the participating systems. In this case, the coupling between participants is loose, but supplementary forms of processing have to be considered due to the translation of data into the common format. When using the unified format within systems, it is important to deal with a development chain which is as automated as possible. The modification of the common format spills over to the new version of the XML schema. This schema has to be injected automatically into the systems of both provider and consumer. This injection goes hand in hand with the development of participants that are not obliged to consider the new version in unified format.

11.4. ESB's benefits

11.4.1. *Opportunities*

Mastering the exchanges between provider and consumer systems is the key element in SOA. The more reliable and structured the common language is (unified format is associated with the validation rules) the more possible it will be to link the systems at a very low cost. The rationalization of interconnections between systems is strategic due to the raising of real-time exchanges and extended processes beyond the boundaries of companies.

The technical standardization of exchanges, due to XML, which cannot be obtained when using EAI, leads to ESB being increasingly perceived as a basic technical solution that lowers the cost of acquisition and generalizes the associated competences. This situation has not been reached yet, as the XML standards, especially around Web services, still have to reach a higher level of maturity. However, a reduction in price of ESB platforms compared to EAI solutions can already be observed.

ESB is also an important opportunity for focusing on the communication of systems in an approach that is more business-based than EAI. The aim is the implementation of a common language for the exchanges. However, this is not a new idea. Some companies have already done so on the basis of EAI. As EAI is a technical tool it does not usually favor dialogue that is intensive enough and takes place between the business and IT. This intensive dialogue would enable the design of a common language. Unfortunately this dialogue is diluted in technical and proprietary developments and is often too complex when using EAI tools brought forward by ESB have benefited from an additional level of abstraction that improves the dialogue between functional and IT teams. Processing the translation of data, especially into unified format, has been developed with the help of ergonomic tools that are not reserved for experts in the field of IT. These are visual data mapping tools that go further than the first generations of these types of tools. The new generation integrates functions of work groups, user-friendly visualization of mapping, integrated tests, management of versions, etc. These tools will be covered in the chapter on SOA platforms, which also describes the technique of *Semantic Data Mapping* (SDM).

The quality of managing these exchanges in unified language, respecting XML standards and a high-level tool for the transformation of data are the key factors for SOA's success.

11.4.2. *Limitations*

ESB remains a technical tool. To benefit from this tool, an entire organization that is adapted to the aim of defining and administering a common language needs to be implemented. The modeling of this language requires a detailed knowledge of the business. The person responsible for this language has to negotiate with the participants in the exchanges to reach a compromise on a unified version of transporting data. This form of transportation applies on the level of data structures as well as in semantics and in the rules of validation.

The functional perimeter of ESB goes much further than the basic functions. This chapter has shown that the software vendors mainly look for other necessary components in SOA, which leads to the concept of the SOA platform. A management tool for service contracts might be required. This tool could control the system's resources on the level of ESB and therefore check whether they have been distributed according to the service contract. The acquisition of ESB needs to be distinguished from its basic functions. If ESB does not deal with basic functions, its integration with other components into SOA (service repository, management of the production of services, service orchestration, etc.) has to be studied in great detail. On the other hand, if ESB overlaps the components of the SOA platform, the functionality of these components needs to be applied to more than just the ESB's perimeter. ESB specializes in the management of exchanges between systems. It is based on standards that allow for interoperability, i.e. XML. On the other hand, the use of ESB is not recommended inside a system. A domain of use, such as the management of accidents, that has been developed in Java and installed on only one platform for exploitation has no interest in using ESB for the communication between services within this perimeter. If the same domain was, however, spread out over several platforms for exploitation, the exchanges would have to take place via ESB. XML standards might create performance problems if they are to be used inside a system. In this case, the benefit of interoperability is less important since within a system technology is homogeneous. The medium-term XML standards will be of a higher performance, and it will be possible to use them within every system to homogenize the procedure of development and exploitation.

Chapter 12

SOA Platform

A RECAP OF IDEAS MENTIONED IN PREVIOUS CHAPTERS

– Unified platform for the development of services (UPDS): technical components for tools used by the methods

– Enterprise Service Bus (ESB): interconnection between distant and heterogenous systems

NEW IDEAS TO BE INTRODUCED IN THIS CHAPTER

– SOA platforms: global vision of technical architecture. This vision includes UPDS, ESB and other technical components required in SOA.

– SOA test card: tool used for SOA's technical audit.

– Semantic Data Mapping (SDM), directory and registry of services, security, traceability of services in production, Business Activity Monitoring (BAM) and Complex Event Processing (CEP), Business Intelligence, editing.

– Mastering performance, exploitation and maintenance.

Chapter 10 described the technical components used in the modeling procedures and development of services. The features of UPDS provide the framework of the designer's and developer's workstation. Chapter 11 showed ESB's functions in the management of distant and heterogenous systems. These tools will now be analyzed in the larger context of technical architecture. Other components which have only been mentioned briefly will be analyzed in detail in this chapter. All these components make up the SOA platform.

12.1. Requirements for the global vision of technical architecture

It is difficult to provide an overview of all the technologies that are required by SOA. These technologies include registry of services, BPM, BAM and ESB tools, virtual machine for services execution (e.g. VEP – Virtual Engine for Praxeme), UI framework, rules management system, Master Data Management, test tools, modeling CASE tools, IDE, etc. Not all of these components are necessarily needed in the beginning. When implementing cosmetic SOA, ESB is required as its connectors provide access to existing systems in a service mode. Furthermore, a UI framework is required for building up recyclable graphics components as well as a modeling CASE in UML. This CASE allows for modeling the first processes orchestrating services. An editing tool is also required and needs to be flexible enough to be integrated into the process in the form of services. If the company decides to link surface SOA to devices favoring agility and data rationalization (extended SOA), a *Business Rules Management System* (BRMS) as well as *Master Data Management* (MDM) have to be added. When introducing overhaul SOA, the SOA platform is used and completed by other components such as the registry of services, SLA (*Service Level Agreement*), etc.

The implementation of SOA described above is a possible scenario for the use of technical components. Every company creates its road map, which includes details such as the level of maturity for cosmetic, overhaul and extended SOA.

When producing a road map the business requirements and availability of technical components have to be considered. References are provided in an "SOA test card"[1], which contains eight main axes. These are fabrication, orchestration, execution, ESB, human–machine interface, repositories, security and production. Every axis is subdivided into three levels of implementation. These are known as basic, evolved and strategic.

The SOA test card is a tool used in several situations, e.g. for the technical audit of the information system, technical audit of software packages, audit of SOA's software vendors, choosing technical components of cosmetic, overhaul and extended SOA.

---

1. This test card was created through a collaboration between Orchestra Networks and DPM Services. DPM Services is a specialist in strategic marketing for the IT market (http://www.dpm-services.com/).

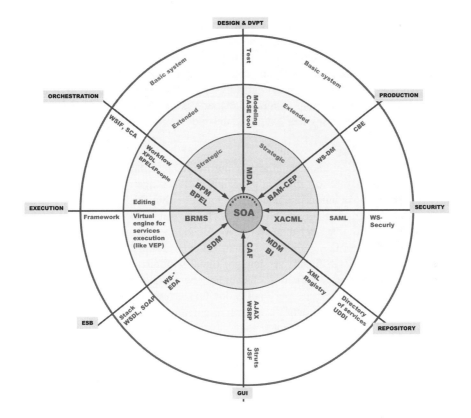

Figure 12.1. *SOA test card (technical components of the SOA platform)*

The majority of technical components in the SOA test card have already been shown in the previous chapters. New components on this card have been mentioned briefly. These new components will be explained in detail in this chapter.

12.2. New technical components

12.2.1. *The transformation of data*

As opposed to the technical tool of data mapping (transformation of data), which can only be used by specialists in XML or Java, SDM increases the level of abstraction and models transformations even if data structures are rather complex. SDM is particularly useful if there are many complex transformations that require a high level of optimization in their performance. The transformation of data is necessary, as the common language (or unified language) used for the exchange between systems cannot be implemented in all systems. Even in overhaul SOA, common language might not be integrated very well with the composition of services to avoid tight coupling between the consumer and the provider. If the consumer and provider share the same data format, an evolution of this language in the provider's system would automatically have an impact on the consumer's system. The requirement of a common language is not called into question but it needs to be decided to what extent a unified language should be used (see Chapter 11).

Translation into common language at the moment of data exchange is always required. The structure of a client's business object agrees with the common language for a service but has to be expressed differently to be understood by a third party. These transformations require a functional specification and their development is not to be neglected. When modifying data structures, the processing of associated transformations also has to be updated. If ESB tolerates the parallel existence of several different versions of data structures describing the same business object, these versions have to be managed when processing transformations. In some cases personalization on the level of transformation is also to be managed to adapt the data flow of requirements to the consumer. Some types of data have to be filtered or adapted to the format used for numeric data. Business rules are added to validate the structure of the data source for transformations and verification if the obtained response agrees with the anticipated results. Process transformation is not limited to a simple correspondence between columns in a source structure and in a target structure. SDM centralizes the knowledge on data transformation and integrates all necessary functionalities for its management. SDM becomes a key component in the SOA platform. If processing transformation is not industrialized, with dedicated project management and adapted tools, an increase in the cost for integration tests and a low quality of exchanges can be observed. As the transformation of data is also applied to exchanges with partners and third parties situated outside the information system, malfunctioning might pose a strategic problem.

SDM has to be ergonomic enough to be used by non-specialists in XML and programming transformations. This tool is not to be used by the end user, but functional validation should be obtained via a modeling of transformations. As transformations are often carried out during the transportation of data, non-intrusive to the applications, one might believe that the ESB teams have to work on SDM. This, however, is often not a very good solution as these teams are not familiar enough with the business to deal with different cases of transformation. It makes more sense that the teams working on the business modeling also take care of SDM. They can use SDM as a tool. The use of UML is insufficient in this case as the modeling of multiple transformations between data structures and the target is impossible. A connector between modeling CASE and SDM allows for exporting data modeling to the transformation tool. A description in an XML schema (XSD) can also be exported directly to the SDM tool.

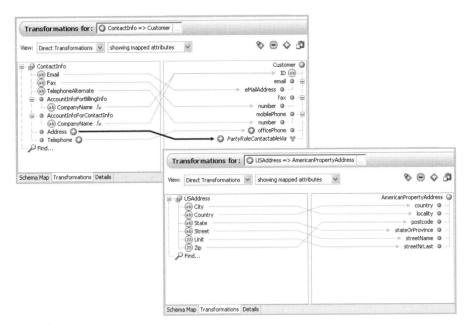

Figure 12.2. *Semantic Data Mapping tool (copyright Progress Software)*

On the basis of this modeling, the tool processes transformations and ensures better performance. Doing so requires the use of a programming language such as Java or XSL/Java rather than a native transformation in XSLT. Processing transformations have to be organized in the form of reusable services. A test tool is integrated into the transformation process to check the behavior of transformations independently. An analytical function for the differences in results that have been obtained makes tests on non-regression run automatically. This testing tool has to manage versions of processed transformations as well as models in common language (unified format). Configuring versions means precisely describing a version of processing transformations that is linked to a version in common language.

SDM is required as soon as cosmetic SOA is implemented, as services must rely on the common language at the level of ESB. During the cosmetic SOA, this language is not used inside existing systems because this SOA is not intrusive. However, if this stage of common language utilization is neglected, the implementation of overhaul SOA might create evolutions in the data structures that will penalize existing services and then consumers. SDM has another important advantage due to the reuse and industrialization of developments. This advantage lowers the cost and time needed for developments.

12.2.2. *From a directory to a registry of services*

Making services visible to the consumer is a first that is not always a sufficient argument for investing in a registry. The simple description of services is not sufficient, as the consumers do not find enough information on how to actually use the service. For software engineers, a pure description of the services is also insufficient. Indeed, the following aspects are also to be described: data structures which are transported by services (entry message, response, errors), pre- and post-conditions (i.e. rules on the use of a service), associated SLAs, documentation (UML models, textual descriptions etc.), versions, etc. All of this data cannot be stored by a single UDDI (*Universal Description, Discovery and Integration*) standard. UDDI is a very popular component for service directories. It only deals with the referencing of services of an added value in the classification system (taxonomy) and automatically notifies the consumers when there is a reference of a new service, etc. It is therefore different from all descriptive properties of services that have been mentioned before. This chapter will now move on to the registry of services also known as *Registry XML*.

Based on a UDDI model, the "services registry" tool has to accept extensions that link services to other components such as data structures and other types of documentation. Each of the components deals with a version and has to manage the configuration of versions according to the dependencies between them. This configuration also includes other components that deliver services, especially processing transformations of data and invoked services in the provider's system. Consumers are, for example, familiar with the service "list-contract" and have to use the service AS400 "RPAS400-LSTCTR". The service "list-contract" processes the data transformation of "SDM-CONTRACT". A registry of services is a routing table, i.e. a management index similar to ESB's functions (see the chapter on the interconnection of systems). The extensions linked to UDDI can also respect two other standards. These standards are ebXMLrr (registry and repository) for referencing data structures (XML schema) and ISO 11179 for the documentation of every data element in the XML schema. ISO 11179 provides the metadata for the documentation of data, e.g. registry name, definition, example, user name, version, administrator status.

The registry of services does not contain all services. Its perimeter of use is limited to the services exposed to the consumers situated outside the company's information system and between systems that work in different domains. The registry of services is therefore used around the borders of enterprise architecture fixed by the company. It relies on loose coupling and interoperability often due to XML. The registry takes up an average of 20% of the information system's perimeter. The services within this perimeter are of a high interoperability and part of the registry of services. A team responsible for the management of contracts in AS400, for example, adds XML services for other domains in the information system to the registry. A team in charge of the overhaul of management of compensations could use the registry to describe links between services and those invoked by AS400 during orchestration. These links allow for the management of configuring versions. This configuration is important for the synchronization of developments and maintenance between overhaul and AS400 teams. An analysis of the impact of modifications in AS400 on overhaul services could, for example, be carried out.

Services published into the registry are also described in the CASE (UML) when modeling them. The modeling CASE tool is a registry of services within itself but does not allow for easy configuration of versions. Apart from services in XML, all other services in the system are described in the modeling CASE. There are more services in the modeling CASE that are not part of the XML registry as they cannot be shared by different teams situated in different domains of the information system. The use of a CVS or a sub-version version management tool is sufficient, given that there is good integration with the modeling CASE. Search functions of services can be carried out in the modeling CASE via queries. Not all services have to be part of the registry. The registry of services and modeling CASE can be added to each other. The registry of services allows for the configuration of versions between components that are shared by different domains in the information system or even located outside the information system. It does not allow for designing services. Modeling CASE is a repository which designs services. Its perimeter is subdivided into different projects. If a team working on one project decides to make a service available to other teams or a third party situated outside the system, then it uses the registry.

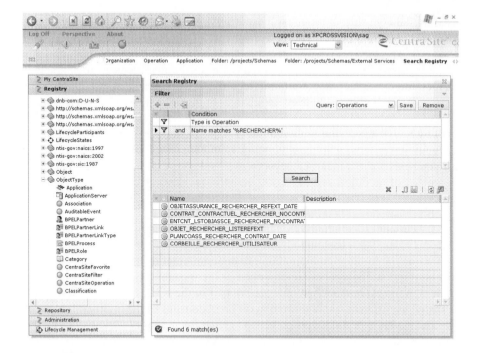

Figure 12.3. *Example of a registry (copyright Software AG – WebMethods)*

The registry of services can be implemented when using surface SOA, as configuring versions of services requires an ergonomic tool that can be used for team working. The registry also exposes services to the outside of the information system in a standardized form, i.e. a catalog of services.

12.2.3. *Security*

Technical components for security management are integrated into the SOA platform and based on XML standards. Security devices are often expressed in XML and can be combined with security systems that already exist in companies, such as password-based identification or certificate-based identification, e.g. PKI (*Public Key Infrastructure*).

Among the standards mentioned above, WS-Security (OASIS) is currently the most popular. WS-Security manages different features of security, particularly usernames, passwords and certificates. These are transported by XML messages in the header of the XML flow with the SOAP protocol for web services. Due to this standard, the security infrastructure reads the header of the XML flow and obtains the required security features, e.g. a password. WS-Security also contains devices used for the signatures of messages (XML-Signature) as well as encoding (XML-Encryption).

The difference with SSL encoding is that XML is able to encode pieces of data selectively. With SSL the encoding process is applied to the entire flow, which might lead to problems in performance and makes the use of several keys in the same flow of data impossible. Access rights to services are managed by the XACML (*Extensible Access Control Language*) standard, which defines the rules of authorization. When a service is invoked, these rules determine if the consumer has the right to use it or not. The rules are based on the data of the context, which can be found in XML's request. These rules are based on *assertion* and respect the SAML (*Security Assertion Markup Language*) standard. A service used to buy products "price of product" would, for example, be transported in SAML for the invocation request. A rule XACML will be executed and check if the user of the service has the right to buy a product with a price higher than what has been stipulated in the assertion "price of product". This form of control is carried out when the XML request is being transported and before the actual service is started. If the user does not have the right to buy the product, the service is not carried out and an error message is sent to the consumer. This way of functioning is not intrusive at the level of the services and leads to high flexibility in the management of authorizations.

XACML is currently not used very much as companies need time to adapt their authorization systems. Furthermore, the tools used for the management of XACML rules are not advanced enough. Rules often have to be written directly in XML, which is rather complex. Solutions for the management of the rules' versions and tests, etc. are also not yet advanced enough. The positioning of XACML's execution engine in relation to the BRMS is still unclear. If a BRMS is used, the rules of authorization are written in the language used by the rules engine and therefore differ from XACML. As is the case for XACML, these rules provide, or do not provide, access rights to services according to the context of consumption. The rules also manipulate *assertions* which are administered by MDM. The link between BRMS and MDM provides advanced administrative functions, application in different types of environments, tests, etc. The integration of this solution is done in the same way as is the case for XACML. The XML request is intercepted while the message is being transported. This procedure does not hinder the actual services. For graphic components an XML ID card can be produced. This ID card defines the access rights on the screen, i.e. whether certain menus, buttons or columns appear or not, according to the user profile. The management is done with the help of an MDM tool, which is also based on reference data.

SAML is also used for the identification of consumers, i.e. SSO (*Single Sign On*). Many other XML standards for security are being specified and address evolved requirements such as managing access rights in an organization's subsidiaries, unifying the management of PKI on the basis of XML, etc.

12.2.4. *Traceability of services in production*

Service contracts on use mainly collect information on the conditions of exploitation, e.g. availability, delay of response, back-up processing, priorities for execution. All this data forms the SLA. Managing resources in production has to be compatible with the conditions of exploitation. The main goal is to improve the position of SLA by a better use of the available resources.

XML grammars exist for traceability of services in production, especially WS-Management (Microsoft) and WS-Distributed Management (OASIS). Supervision starts when XML messages are transported through the network. They are intercepted during transport so that the control system can check parts of the messages and calculate delay of response, frequency of requests, etc. This data is then sent to a central administrator, which verifies if SLA's conditions are being respected. If this is not the case, the administrator decides on the exploitation of resources by setting new priorities of the processing of invoked services. If, for example, a problem with the delay of response is detected for a particular service, the consumers of a weaker SLA will have low priority. Doing so improves the situation of other consumers. The central administrator is also familiar with the interdependences between services and infrastructure. The infrastructure resources are also considered as services and are controlled by XML. A database, for example, regularly emits XML messages so that the administrator is updated on the database's state of availability. If a database stops working, the central administrator knows which services are affected and intercepts these requests to redirect them or send an error message to the user.

Designing SLAs is rather complex as they are combined with the composition of services. A service "subscribe insurance" (on the level of the process), for example, leads to a chain reaction which sets off several business services such as "select client" and "select contract". The process's SLA has to remain compatible with the conditions of execution described by other SLAs. If the service "select client" requires a minimum of two seconds for a response, the process cannot be expected to provide a response any faster than that. The conditions of execution make up a knowledge base of several rules and parameters. The tools for supervising services implement internal solutions for rules management, sometimes also parameter management. However, they are dedicated to the context of supervision and do not provide administrative functions of performance such as BRMS and MDM, which are in particular used for the management of versions and tests. It therefore makes sense to study the possible integration of this supervising tool within the infrastructure of BRMS and MDM.

Supervision is linked to a system of logging for the audit of the services' behavior during execution. This logging system also exists for distributed architecture. A service is, for example, executed on a Java platform and invokes a service that is managed by ESB. This service invokes two other services in the mainframe and on AS400. These two services invoke other services situated outside the information system. This chain reaction is very complex. When a problem is diagnosed, the invocations between services have to be traceable throughout the entire chain (see the CBE standard in Chapter 11).

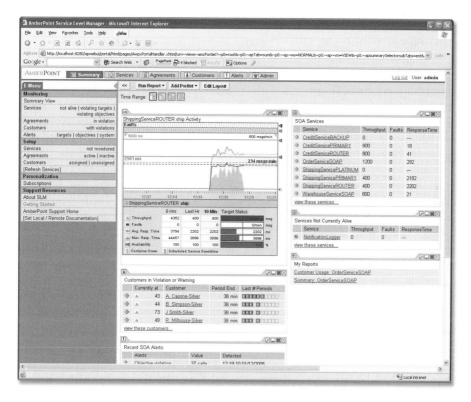

Figure 12.4. *Example of a tool for the traceability of production (copyright AmberPoint)*

In cosmetic SOA, if the SLAs remain simple and unpersonalized by the consumer, a solution for the production management of service might not be needed. However, also in cosmetic SOA, the increase of services might even at an early stage require automatic management of production. In overhaul SOA, personalized SLAs emerge. Their services are flexible and able to adapt to different contexts of consumption. As a result, the use contracts need to provide more detail. When linked to CBE the logging system has to deal with cosmetic SOA. This combination of solutions diagnoses malfunctions in the chain reaction of executing services as soon as cosmetic SOA, and further with overhaul SOA.

12.2.5. *BAM and CEP*

Tracing the execution of processes implements the *reporting* tools situated on the level of BAM (*Business Activity Monitoring*). These tools intervene on the highest level of the service composition, i.e. the workflow (human-oriented BPM) and orchestrations localized in ESB. The exchange of data flow controlled by ESB is often strategic, especially for communications with a third party located outside the information system. BAM adds data to a database of indicators that trace information on the behavior of the process, e.g. starting time, identification of the consumer, errors, stop and restart of the process, start of sub-processes. These performance indicators provide an overview of all processes. Some functional overlap can be identified due to reporting functions that have been integrated into management tools for the production of services (previous section).

BAM's functions go further than simple reporting. BAM deals with artificial intelligence, which has an impact on the execution of the process. The principle is to analyze the indicators in real time to make an automatic decision on invoking other services. This could, for example, be done to stop a process, put it on hold, set off another process, notify the user, etc. The decisions are expressed with the help of a rules management system that offers a high flexibility when it comes to adjusting parameters. This device, based on BAM, has an impact on the concept of CEP and business EDA (*Event Driven Architecture*). This type of EDA is not to be confused with technical EDA that introduces XML standards for event-based communications such as WS-Eventing (W3C).

BAM should be introduced when using cosmetic SOA as it manages the composition of services, even if they are not put into context as they depend on quality of the existing IS. In overhaul SOA, BAM is required to trace processes and their variants of execution. CEP is a possible form of architecture which emerges once overhaul SOA has been introduced. CEP has to be treated with great care and introduced in limited zones of the information system as the methodological framework for an entirely business and technical event-based system has not yet been developed. Entirely event-based systems will be introduced in the future and added to logical SOA without calling SOA's existence into question.

12.2.6. *Business Intelligence*

Quality and speed of decision-making are decisive factors in the success of organizations. Quality can only be ensured if the information is reliable and immediately available. This type of information reflects the different responsibilities of each actor. Despite the efforts made with *datawarehouses* and *datamarts,* the decision-makers always wait for the results of the best performing tools before making a decision. To avoid this wait, the level of integration of decisional tools in the information system has to be improved. SOA will provide the key for this new form of integration. The increase of data and associated redundancies leads to errors, which lower the quality of information and therefore the quality of the decision-making process:

– several values for one data element. There is no single truth for a data element but several. This fact makes it difficult to interpret business situations;

– misunderstanding a data element. The value of a data element is correct but its significance remains ambiguous;

– lack of version management. The significance of a data element may change over time to follow evolutions in the applications. The decision-making process is falsified if data from the wrong version is used;

– difficulty of ensuring the referential integrity constraints between duplicated data. A data element should, for example, not be deleted if it has been listed as a reference by other data even across several physical databases. If this data element is deleted by accident the decision-making process might become impossible. The user has to find the deleted information, which is difficult and takes a lot of time; old reports, histories and archives have to be consulted.

Adding duplicated data to a datawarehouse risks injecting bad quality information into the decision-making system. As the information is of mediocre quality, this system is limited to the creation of statistical reports and does not allow for operational decision-making. At this stage the decision-making system is not reliable enough. Increasing reliability requires the negative effects of the duplication of information to be corrected by the implementation of an operational datastore. These operational datastores unify and guarantee the quality of reference data, i.e. the information shared between several applicative silos or services. To do so, MDM has to be used and linked to a tool for quality data management, which would, for example, remove duplicated information. Therefore, adding data to a datawarehouse is done on the basis of data that is available in MDM. Adding data to a datawarehouse increases the quality of the decision-making system and favors operational decision-making (see Chapter 10 for details on the MDM solution).

The speed of decision-making also has to be worked upon. Companies are no longer satisfied with an asynchronic update of data used in decision-making processes even though production processes increasingly work in real time. As information circulates rapidly, a better integration of Business Intelligence in the system has to be reached. Doing so requires the layer of integrating data to be used when adding data to MDM (ESB/ETL) and adding information to datawarehouses and datamarts in real time. The tool Business Intelligence defines service contracts so that users can subscribe to information. This subscription states whether the information is updated in real time, i.e. once it has been modified in the production system. This modification might also take place regularly, such as every night, once every week, etc. If the user of Business Intelligence has the right, they can configure their own performance indicators by stating the required number of updates. Therefore, in SOA, the Business Intelligence tool is able to invoke services to update the repository of data according to the contracts agreed with the users. The more varied the service used for accessing data is, the stronger the capacities of integration into the production systems. Without SOA it would be very difficult or even impossible to introduce these subscriptions to information updates.

Figure 12.5 shows a screen which is updated every ten seconds and represents major events that have taken place. The update of data is based on an XML web service described by the comment "Get Info from web service". The response is shown in the form of a report. Creating these kinds of performance indicators requires the modeling of a process that contains several services and interacts with the decision-making system. The example given below is Web FOCUS created by Information Builders.

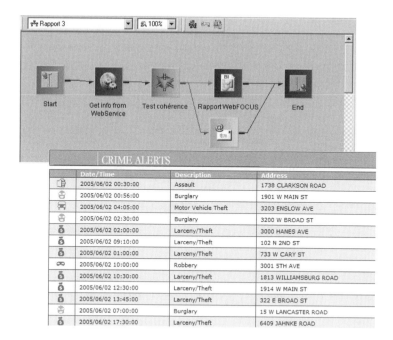

Figure 12.5. *Example of BI and SOA (copyright Information Builders)*

12.2.7. *Editing*

The production line of mail has to be integrated into the composition of services. Within a process it has to be possible to set off editing in service mode by attaching it to flow of information. This data flow has to be sufficiently large so that not every piece of information that is added to a new piece of mail or new version implies a modification of the existing flows of information. The flow contains business data as well as the context of execution that states the consumer which is emitting a demand, the version of the service, the language used, the type of mail, etc. This data describes the contexts and enables the editing system to make the right decisions in the production of a piece of mail. The type of mail enables the editing tool to determine other reference data which provides details for the adjustment of parameters such as the format (portrait or landscape), displaying a logo or not, adding a particular expression of politeness e.g. yours sincerely, number of copies, etc. The existence of similar or other relevant letters might also be checked. The parameter adjustment repository of the editing tool works on the basis of reference data and parameter repository, i.e. MDM . The principle of using the same tool for the same type of requirement is respected as the editing tool is managed by MDM.

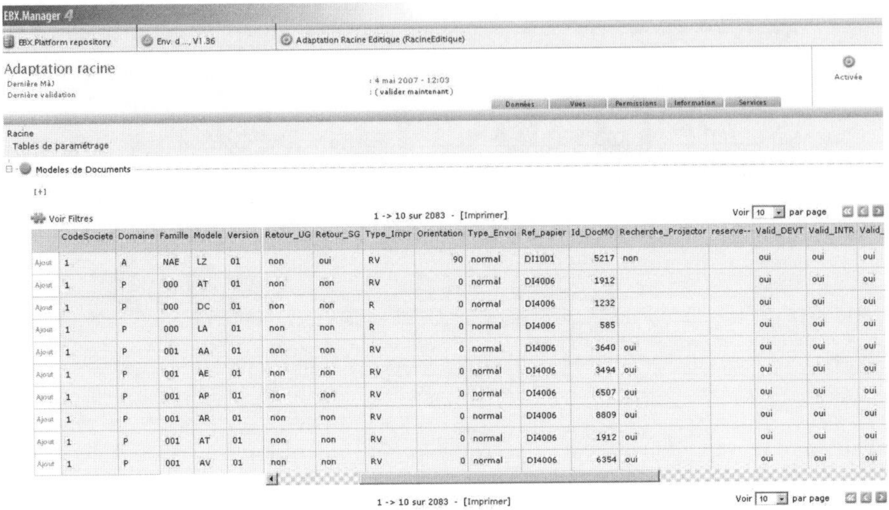

Figure 12.6. *French editing repository managed by MDM (Orchestra Networks)*

Due to MDM, the parameters used for editing can be managed by functional teams who have the right to update some kind of reference data and parameters. IT teams working on production have different access rights and could also safely intervene on the technical adjustment of parameters. This is a considerable advantage compared to the situation in which these parameters have been managed with technical tools such as SQL's level, Java files, text files or directly in XML. With MDM a business UI allows for the functional management of reference data and parameters without having to worry about underlying data persistence strategies (see Chapter 10).

Editing tools should also be able to invoke other services within MDM to obtain labels on the basis of codes taken from the flow of information to be edited. If necessary, the editing tool can also invoke business services to enrich the flow of information that has been received at the moment of invocation. In some situations the user might have to complete the flow of information with the help of a graphical component.

Services communicate directly with the editing tool in XML, which allows loose coupling between applications. Using ESB is of greater interest for a direct interaction of the service with the editing tool, as it allows for different modes of asynchronic functioning. The user might send a request to the editing tool without having to wait for the response, which will be sent out in the form of an event, i.e. an email or via a graphical component. As the XML flow is compatible with a formal data structure (the XML schema corresponds to it) and contains descriptive elements of the version,[2] technical components required for the editing process can easily control the quality of flow before moving on to the process of editing.

As soon as the level of cosmetic SOA is important to benefit from editing to enrich services that have been revamped without intrusion into existing systems.

12.3. Managing performance

12.3.1. *A new order of things?*

Performance is a standard issue in projects. Sensibility towards this issue has, however, increased with the emergence of SOA. The service-oriented approach should not reinforce this trend, as SOA remains a form of logical architecture which does not require the use of specific technologies. It is possible to apply SOA to an outdated technical environment, since the technology of this environment is fully understood, e.g. a mainframe without the use of XML. New technical components such as BRMS, MDM, BPM, etc. bring a lot of added value and also new performance issues. However, SOA does not depend on them. BRMS, MDM and BPM can be used without logic-oriented services. Also note that a language for service-oriented programming does not exist; there are therefore no new problems on the level of abstraction for SOA programming, nor any problems in terms of compilation. COBOL, a programming language, remains valid as well as Java, C#, etc.

It is true that overhaul SOA often leads to the implementation of a technical system such as UNIX with object-oriented programming languages, particularly Java, on a large scale. Therefore, the question of performance for these new IT environments is opened. SOA contributes to a better performance of these technical systems, as its services are stateless as opposed to a more traditional approach. In the traditional approach, the object system is oriented towards a stateful architecture in which each object preserves its data from previous executions (see Chapter 5).

Particular cases of using XML standards also have to be studied. It is important to use XML in areas where interoperability between providers and consumers is required. If the IS enterprise architecture is well done, it concerns 20% of the calls between services. The other invocations take place in other technologies of higher performance than XML, e.g. calls in Java. If the nominal perimeter of use for XML is respected, unnecessary problems that penalize performance can be avoided.

---

2. Due to XML namespaces and attribute versions.

SOA does not bring about a new approach for the management of performances. New environments such as Unix/Java have to be dealt with. These environments, however, do not rely on service-oriented architecture.

12.3.2. *Best practice*

Stateless architecture tries to ensure that the consumption of resources does not increase proportionally to the increase in the use of services. This is one of SOA's basic properties, which was described in the first chapters of this book. However, a data context management is needed to keep information across several service invocations; this is known as a working session. In an interactive application, this context is often managed in an http session. The performances of the management for this context's lifecycle are to be handled carefully. The context might contain a significant amount of data as opposed to stateless systems. Stateless functioning, however, cannot be called into question. It is the only approach that guarantees the increase in cost when dealing with an increase for the consumption of services.

XML messages have to be of limited size in order not to penalize the processing of manipulations (*parsing* XML, *data binding* towards the programming language). If the levels of nesting XML data types must not be higher than three, XML messages are limited to about a hundred pieces of elementary data. When managing lists of information, an exchange protocol is needed that implements paging with adjustable parameters according to the constraints of exploitation.

For interactive applications, uploading pages has to benefit from the principles of asynchronic functioning now available in Ajax. While the user is consulting part of the screen, another graphical component is being uploaded. This is possible due to asynchronic communication with the server.

The management of transactions is situated at the level of organizational services in logical architecture. This type of management prefers a reserving strategy that does not block any resources.

The software components form deployment units (executable collection of components) which can be set up in different machines depending on the level of performances and production constraints. A Java component, for example, is executed in a simple mode (POJO: *Plain Old Java Object*), i.e. not distributed. This component can, however, at all times be reconfigured into a remote EJB (*Enterprise Java Beans*) and used by another machine without having an impact on the services that are consuming this component. This type of isolation has been ensured by the principle of invocation via a factory or the inversion of control (see Chapter 10). Reconfiguring a POJO into EJB is carried out by an MDA. This is an automatic production chain.

12.3.3. *Testing performance*

The theoretical analysis of consuming resources during production and in distributed environments is a very difficult task. Production teams are looking for *capacity planning,* i.e. a calculation which anticipates the required resources. This type of calculation implies a specific and complex know-how. It often takes several years before a company is able to manage its IT consumption when using environments such as UNIX or Java. The technical components that are added to execute services make the task of establishing consumption even more difficult. The level of consumption has to include numerous components such as the rules engine, workflow, BPM applications, framework, GUI, etc.

In practice, the company is best to invest in platforms that focus on testing performance and cover all technical systems. This total coverage of all systems is, however, difficult to obtain. For example, tests are to be carried out on the performances of Java-based SOA applications which invoke via ESB/Unix, a service exposed by an AS400 system with a rules engine located on a windows server, a transaction on a mainframe and the editing process carried out in Linux. In this case, it is difficult to deal with a sufficient number of production platforms. A compromise has to be found and certain systems would have to be blocked or used in shared environments when testing performance. Test platforms do not have to be of such a high performance as is the case for production platforms. However, it makes sense that these programs always use the same configuration machine when testing performance. The aim is to carry out tests on a monthly basis during the stages of development. During stages of optimization and industrialization of the software the frequency of tests has to be increased to up to once a week.

On the basis of regular testing it becomes possible to refine the delay of response and the levels of IT consuming resources. This improvement, as well as *capacity planning,* makes it possible to anticipate how production services will behave.

12.4. Managing exploitation

Production teams have to be involved in the process of installing SOA so that they are familiar with SOA's basis. These teams ensure that from an early stage onwards decisions are made which favor successful management of exploitation. As a high number of technical components are needed, they have to be introduced in stages. These stages depend on SOA's level of maturity, first with cosmetic SOA and then with overhaul SOA. In overhaul SOA it makes sense to clearly establish these stages.

Performance tests require the participation of production teams. These tests are the occasion for production teams to judge solutions and different types of optimization. The increase in competence has to be formalized to create guidelines on the exploitation of infrastructure.

Services that supervise the technical components also have to be tested carefully. Every component has to be able to emit a warning in case of a problem. At this level the management of production, WS-M or WS-DM, has to be chosen. This choice has to be made in terms of production when expressing requirements. The logging tools for applications have to be made available to development teams as well as production teams, as it will help them in the process of troubleshooting. A batch orchestrator has to be implemented as well as tools used for logical design that configure batch processing.

Implementing applications and services in different environments also has to be dealt with carefully. This applies to the following examples: development, integration tests, training, user acceptance test (UAT), pre-production and last but not least production. Whenever a software component is introduced into one of these environments, a series of functional and technical parameters has to be available so that the service functions securely with previously identified databases, appropriate ESB connectors, etc. If the adjustment of parameters is carried out manually by modifying SQL databases, XML files, Java files, text files, etc. without checking authorization, validating data and managing versions, errors may arise, as well as ambiguities regarding who is responsible for this parameter adjustment. The adjustment of parameters has to be unified with the help of Master Data Management, which has already been used in several SOA issues. MDM manages authorizations and distributes tasks of parameter adjustment between production and development teams. The lifecycle of the parameter repository is managed by the functions that take care of the different versions as well as the import and export of data.

The company also has to adapt to new profiles of technical architects. These technical architects have many capacities when it comes to the system and production as well as experience in working within the software development team. From the start of the SOA project, technical architect is the link and communicates with the chief information officer when it comes to issues in development. This architect is familiar with all competences in production and has to mobilize them during different stages of the project's lifecycle.

12.5. Managing maintenance

The efficiency of maintenance depends on the quality of its architecture. With SOA, the effort ensures the level of logical architecture and its formal derivation into software components has to improve maintenance due to the following facts: loose coupling between components, respecting the principles of different layers within a program (separation of concerns with UI organization and business issues), externalizing management of transactions, use of virtual machines for the execution of services, creating variants of services due to parameter adjustment without changing the code, etc. There is, however, the risk that maintenance is no longer flexible. This might lead to problems of regression within the software if a quality approach is not introduced. The following aspects have to be handled very carefully:

– The orchestration of services may be complex, especially for micro-processes (use cases) and the lifecycle of business objects (state machine of the business stratum in logical architecture). The cost of modifying orchestrations has to be controlled, especially when it comes to integration tests. The use of a specialized tool for orchestration (BPM engine) has already been mentioned. This tool is equipped with a high performance *debugger* and is more efficient than specialized developments.

– Decomposition into different services leads to a higher number of components in a piece of software than in the modular or silo approach. Even though the services are put into groups of components that interact with each other according to the rules of loose coupling (in Praxeme's terminology these are logical workshops and logical machines), the communication between these services remains very complex and rich. When controlling these interactions it is important to make sure that the system's documentation is updated and that the rules of architecture are respected during maintenance. If the virtual machine for executing services is well constructed, the service calls are automatically detected when maintenance is being developed. This is an efficient means to ensure the program's quality.

– The ergonomic approach favored by overhaul SOA is often more rich than the implementation of outdated systems. The user chooses the business objects on which he/she would like to work. Then a decision is made on the order in which business operations are carried out. This flexibility in navigating between different business objects and operations is very powerful but requires complex management of UI and the data context used by the screens. When maintaining this part of the system, it is vitally important to ensure that rules of architecture and modeling procedures are respected, especially when it comes to the lifecycle of the data context (update, clean-up, delete, etc.).

– The wide variety of technological components that make up the SOA platform might lead to difficulties when it comes to integration. The execution chain of functionalities can mobilize several software layers, e.g. UI framework, virtual machine of executing services, human-oriented BPM (*workflow*), application-oriented BPM, rules management systems, parameters and master data management, interconnection of systems (ESB, EAI, ETL, *middleware*, connector, *back-ends,* etc.), mapping of data, access to databases, security, etc. The teams working on maintenance benefit from new developments such as logging tools for the execution of the system, i.e. unifying the traces of applications in different layers of the program. This logging tool provides diagnostics on the execution of the system. Without a very high availability of logging the efficiency of maintenance decreases.

If the aspects mentioned above are not taken care of in the cycle of maintenance, problems of regression appear in the software. These problems slow down the delivery of functional evolutions and increase the cost of the entire system. The agility favored by SOA would therefore be at risk. There are means to lower this risk. Programs have to be designed carefully for both development and maintenance. Teams are often confronted with difficulties when managing the stage of transition between development and maintenance. In particular, the software engineers who designed the program are often less motivated when it comes to maintaining it. Unfortunately, the budget for a new team working in maintenance is earmarked before development and is often limited. This is why there is little transfer of competences between software engineers who designed the program and those who take over and carry out maintenance. There is a risk of losing know-how on certain procedures of modeling and developments. This lack of transferring competences could lead to a decrease in the quality of maintenance. If the development of the software is a success it might lead to a feeling of disappointment when it comes to making a supplementary effort for maintaining quality in the long term.

Errors in outdated information systems, which have been shown in Part I of this book, should be avoided. These systems often lack up-to-date documentation and unified architecture. A state-of-the-art SOA system does not guarantee this unified form either, since it is subject to many modifications during its lifecycle. This is why software engineers try to make it as economic and flexible as possible. This attempt is based on SOA's agility. If these modifications, however, infringe on SOA's procedures during construction, the system will lose its quality. SOA would then be just as inflexible and slow as outdated systems that are still being used today.

Judging the level of quality in SOA in the long term is very important and requires a definition of SOA's aims. These are recycling, rapid creation of a new process from existing services and the creation of service variants based on the adjustment of parameters. Feedback of at least one year of maintenance is required to manage the exploitation of these measures as well as reporting tools:
  – ratio of anomalies corrected per period;
  – ratio of functional evolutions carried out per period;
  – number of regressions set off per anomaly;

– number of regressions set off per functional evolution;

– rate of recycling services according to the stratum presentation, organization and business;

– number of up-to-date tests that are available for every service;

– level of alignment between models and software (study carried out by a team ensuring quality). This indicator is important when judging the quality of the MDA chain and whether it has been respected or not. MDA ensures the alignment between models and programs;

– number of rules in a business rules management system compared to the rules that are directly hard-coded in the software. Organizational rules have to be located in the rules engine and may not be implemented by another programming language, as this would falsify the system;

– number of variants of services created when adjusting parameters, i.e. via Master Data Management.

Maintaining quality in the systems imposes careful handling of the risks of regression that may be triggered by modifications. On this level the logical designer is the first one to act. The logical designer has to observe the evolutions of the logical design, such as changes in behavior of a service, extension of a service's signature, modification of unified language, etc. All of these issues to be observed do not necessarily lead to regression. To ensure the surveillance of software, the logical designer uses the modeling CASE tool for the process of designing; a powerful impact analysis tool enables him/her to judge the risks of regression.

12.6. Benefits of SOA platforms

12.6.1. *Opportunities*

Due to the SOA test card, technical architecture and its components are clearer. It allows for deciding calmly which components should be used in cosmetic and later on in overhaul SOA.

With its composition of services the new dynamic SOA has led to an increase in the requirements for successful management in exploitation. This successful management now includes more than just making sure that all transactions used in the same context have the same delay when obtaining a response. With SOA the production has to be adapted to new processes produced by a composition of recycled services in different programming languages, ergonomics, versions, organizations, etc. The management has to satisfy the consumer by optimizing the exploitation of IT resources. Modern management tools for production also use these new XML standards to improve the supervision of how IT resources are distributed to ensure the position of the SLAs.

12.6.2. *Limitations*

Bear in mind that the technical components used in SOA sometimes represent functional overlapping. The teams might observe several rules engines, several parameter repositories, several engines of executing processes, etc. The more functional overlapping that exists, the more the software engineers have to learn unnecessary knowledge that could be avoided. In this case, the aim is to push the SOA project towards a shared use.

Chapter 13

Rules Management at the Scale of the Whole Enterprise

From the principle of Agility Chain Management System (ACMS): "no process without rules and no rules without reference data and parameter", we will detail in this chapter one of the major components of ACMS: the Business Rules Management System (BRMS). We will cover also how BRMS brings agility for deploying a Sustainable Architecture, thus deploying it at the enterprise level within an extended SOA.

13.1. Overview

Let us start by defining what a business rule is and how the use of a Rule Engine and a Rule Management System are bringing the backbone of agility into ACMS. Business rules are expressions of business policy in a form that is both comprehensible to business users and executable by a rule engine. From a business perspective, a business rule is a precise statement that describes, constrains or controls some aspect of the business. A business policy like: "Only claims related to a valid insurance policy and reporting an accident in the state of California are eligible for payment", is constraining the applicability of the claim payment. To implement this policy, the traditional approach is to code a set of if statements within a method in class or a function in a procedural language like COBOL. Supporting all the rules related to claim eligibility for payment leads to hundreds of

Written by Jérôme BOYER, ILOG Software.

rules hard coded in software layers which present a rigid application that takes a long time to deploy changes.

Migrating to a BRMS helps to externalize the business decision and the business rules in a rule repository, manage the rule as a standalone element outside of the core business application and deploy a set of rules (RuleSet) in a form which is executable by a rule engine. A rule engine at run time parses the RuleSet and processes the transactional data by applying a pattern matching algorithm to objects, data elements or XML documents. The following figure outlines this concept. On the left side is the traditional implementation of a rule embedded into the business application. On the right side the decision logic is externalized as a set of standalone statement persisted and version controlled in a central repository.

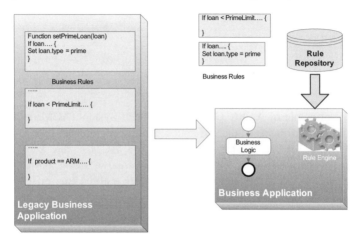

Figure 13.1. *From legacy to agile business application*

13.2. Deep view

BRMS includes a set of components working together to provide all the management functions needed to manage business rules as a corporate asset. Each rule has its own lifecycle outside of the core business application and can be shared between environment and RuleSets.

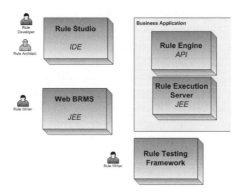

Figure 13.2. *BRMS components*

When building a RuleSet the development team starts by using an IDE like a Rule Studio to define the structure of the rule projects, to develop the object model used by the rules, and to implement the integration of the rule engine into the application. This kind of IDE is integrated in what the developer uses on a daily basis to develop the business application. Rules can be expressed using a high level language, decision table, decision tree or scorecard. They are orchestrated using a rule flow, and can be exposed behind a Web service. Below is a view of ILOG Rule Studio. On the left side is the project structure and the organization of all business rule elements. In the center is a dedicated editor, like the rule flow graphical editor.

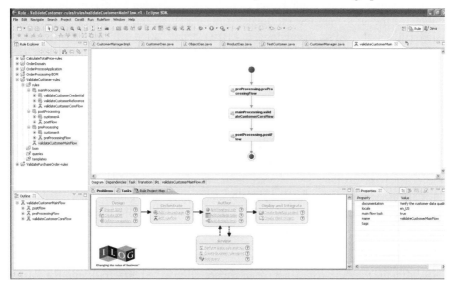

Figure 13.3. *ILOG Rule Studio with project structure*

The second component of BRMS is the Rule Engine: it can be integrated as a low level API and used within the implementation of a service, or it can be deployed as a monitored component in a JEE or .Net container.

One of the most powerful examples of use of a BRMS is to develop "what if" analyses. The Testing Framework component also enables us to define key performance indicators to assess the rule set performance, to present data sets in XML, Excel or data elements, and finally to execute rules against those data so that a business analyst can evaluate what impacts on performance (Key Performance Indicators) the changes are causing.

With a BRMS in place in the IT architecture, business users may author, test and hot deploy rules without stopping the core application. This can be done to support quick deployment of rule, like for example, on some auction websites where a business user can define a rule to flag an item for sale as suspicious. Rules can be deployed at that moment in time without impacting the website. Before detailing the BRMS within the ACMS, it is important to address the methodology issue related to the deployment of such technologies. Following a waterfall approach for the project implementation will not take into account the agility dimension of technologies that BRMS, MDM and BPM are bringing to the development team. Developers can quickly define application choreography (BPM) and business logic (BRMS) without spending months on design and analysis. Reports can be extracted to explain the rules that were executed against data. Developing a rule-based application should follow an iterative and incremental methodology. Part of the open source Eclipse Process Framework, the Agile Business Rule Development (ABRD) methodology is embracing the agile manifesto to focus on the development of business applications using BRMS and BPM technologies. ABRD details all the different activities to develop a rule set, from rule discovery, rule analysis and design, rule authoring, rule validation up to the rule set deployment and maintenance. The development team will follow short iterations among these activities to grow the rule set so it moves closer to the outcome expected by the business. Rule discovery, analysis and validation activities require active and efficient *communication* between the rule developer, the Subject Matter Experts (SME) and business users. The proposed rule set development carried out per iteration, with its validation step, is based on the evidence that a *working* and *executable* rule set has much more business value than a rule description manual. SMEs who define the business policies and the business rules are *strongly involved* in the development process. All those important values and best practices are described in ABRD and help the project team to efficiently develop a rule set. We will reference some of the concepts brought by this method later in this chapter.

Within the extended SOA approach we are often asked how to design the logical architecture leveraging a business rule approach. As seen in the earlier chapters it is clear that BRMS can implement some business or technical functionalities, exposed as decision services. An enterprise architect has to take care not to consider one of those functions as a black box, and think up-front about service and rule reuse, centralized BRMS, empowering the business user to work on the rules, and to deploy them in the context of a rule maintenance process. New auditability requirements, traceability and change management processes have to be considered across applications. Deploying BRMS at the enterprise level forces the enterprise architect to work on the following dimensions: What are the businesses or technical services which have to leverage BRMS? How can they be reused? Where are the data (business object) structures defined, where do they come from? How can rule cross applications be reused, who can change rules and when? Before detailing the enterprise BRMS we need to understand when to use a rule engine.

13.3. When to use a rule engine

This is a common question IT and business people ask us during consulting engagements. To answer this question we need to come back to the main drivers or needs the business unit wants from their IT architecture:

– Adaptability: measures the ability to change the business logic easily. The motivation may be due to short deadline constraint, frequent small changes or important changes that may occur every day, week, month or quarter.

– Transparency: represents the need to clearly implement the business logic as what was agreed upon between the business unit and the IT teams, in a way that every party understands the logic. This leads to expressing the logic in natural or close to natural language and being able to extract a view – report of a given rule set.

– Auditability: represents the ability to trace from the business motivation to the execution of the policy to better understand what the logic behind a decision is.

– Reusability: need to share business logic across processes or applications and stay consistent across applications/transactions. Business policies have to be enforced at the enterprise level not only on one application.

– Manageability: this variable addresses the lifecycle management of the business logic. Who writes what, and when, and all the questions related to maintenance and evolutions of the rule-based service.

These drivers help us to bring an evaluation framework to compare the different types of implementation for business rules: logical data structure, business process flow, application code, graphical user interface, rule engine etc. For a BRMS platform we have the evaluations shown in Figure 13.4.

Variables	Evaluation
Adaptability	Excellent, using the rule as an external artifact rule writer can change the rule quickly and deploy in a matter of seconds without stopping the business application (Hot Deployment).
Transparency	Excellent, by adding metadata to implemented rule we can clearly link rule to business strategies and policies, and using test and statistical reports we can explain how a rule set is designed, and how rules interact with each other.
Auditability	Excellent and most of the rule engine has a log mechanism to trace what the rules executed on a given transaction were. Rule reports are important to the business as part of the documentation needs
Reusability	Very good if the BRMS use rule repository and the rule analyst design rule project with a sharing approach in mind. The highest granularity of reuse is at the decision service level. (A claim validation service to verify the data quality, a risk quoting service, etc.) Powerful BRMS help at the lowest level to package rules using common rules which are reusable in the context of a rule flow.
Manageability	Excellent as rules are externalized and managed as a standalone artifact. Rule configuration management is complex, and integrity control of rule lifecycle and rule set versioning is not a simple practice. Team needs to develop governance processes on top of the BRMS.

Figure 13.4. *Table of drivers to use BRMS*

During the analysis phase it is often interesting to classify the rules using the rule schema shown in Figure 13.5.

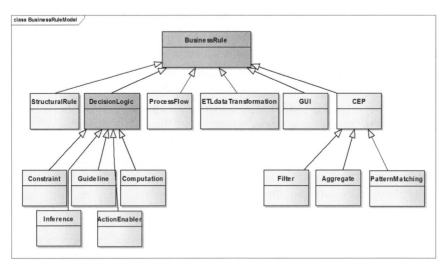

Figure 13.5. *Rule classification schema*

This scheme represents a conceptual breakdown of the different types of rules that are of interest to the business. Structural rules define the terms used by the business in expressing their business rules and the relationships (facts) among those terms. Decision logic is the core of what is typically referred to as a "business rule", it is then decomposed into sub types: Constraint represents a rule that rejects the attempted business transaction (syntax includes terms such as must have, must be in list etc.); Guideline warns about an undesirable circumstance (this usually translates to warning messages); Computation is for mathematical computation; Inference creates new information from existing information resulting from adding a new fact to the rule engine; Action Enabler initiates another business event, message or action when the conditions of the rule match a set of facts.

For Guideline and Constraint it is important to consider what should happen when they are violated. Most of the time the action part will raise an exception or a high priority issue. Process flow rules are rules that purely direct the movement through a process flow (or workflow, etc.). It may be helpful to distinguish process flow rules from the business logic rules that determine the values of the parameters on which the process flow is directed.

CEP stands for Complex Event Processing and supports a category of business rules which apply conditions on a stream of real time events which are themselves part of a time window. An example of such a rule may look like: *Alerts on each <> stock tick with a price greater than 80 within the next 60 seconds.*

Using these tools and methodologies an enterprise architect can work on the logical architecture to efficiently identify the needs, classify them and so deploy BRMS to bring one of the most important building blocks for agility within its IT architecture.

13.4. Logical architecture view

Using a business rule approach to the design of a logical architecture model starts by looking at what exists and what the business requirements to support at the IT architecture level are. As the migration progresses in steps, at the application level the design begins with the analysis of all the use cases, which should help us determine the services required for the deployment. Understanding how each business function is supported by IT applications helps to evaluate the future source of a rule. Depending of the maturity of each business application, the approach may differ. If there is no existing process description, it is interesting to start by studying the lifecycle of the major business object like a Claim, a Purchase Order, a Loan Application, etc. This lifecycle is represented using a UML state diagram (see also chapters concerning Praxeme method and the semantic modeling). From this state machine we can drive the business process that supports the change of each state. Attaching with those changes, it could be possible to find a lot of decisions which can vary in time and complexity. These decisions are referenced in a decision point table and build the future candidates for a rule set. If the architect team is using a business process or use case approach to represent the business needs, the team has to study the description of the process in great detail to find the rule. This evaluation may be done during the rule discovery activity and may lead the team to dig into existing code to understand some business rules and functionalities. Starting from the use cases description or the business process tasks description the analysis team is looking for a verb which involves mental processing or thinking such as check, qualify, compute, calculate, estimate, evaluate, determine, assess, compare, verify, validate, confirm, decide, diagnose or process etc. These verbs are linked to business decision and knowledge, so the underlying activities will most likely have many business rules to discover and analyze.

The utilization of a BRE does not impact the logical architecture and the functional map at the business service level. It supports the implementation of those services. However, the architect has to consider the deployment of the rule management function of the BRMS, and address the requirements related to rule management. The need for a central or distributed rule repository has to be evaluated, as well a central execution server or a distributed one. As explained previously, the BRMS brings three majors components that have to be integrated in the logical architecture: the rule execution server, the rule developer studio and the Web-based rule management component. The diagram below represents a logical architecture for our supporting example, with the management view of the ACMS components and the deployment of their executable part.

At the application level, the component view helps to separate the functions into layers like the presentation (Praxeme's interaction stratum), the business logic (Praxeme's business stratum for core business rules and Praxeme's organizational stratum for organizational rules), the services (Praxeme's logical architecture) and the data layers (Praxeme's technical architecture). In this view, BREs are deployed within the service layer. The service is designed to support business or technical service. No code complexity is exposed to the service client. Design by the interface is now extremely simple and leads to a clear separation of concerns. The service implementation prepares the objects for the rule execution, with any rule set parameters and helper classes, then it calls the BRE using transaction propagation or not. The rules are leveraging a data access layer offering different services to obtain business objects and enumerated domains.

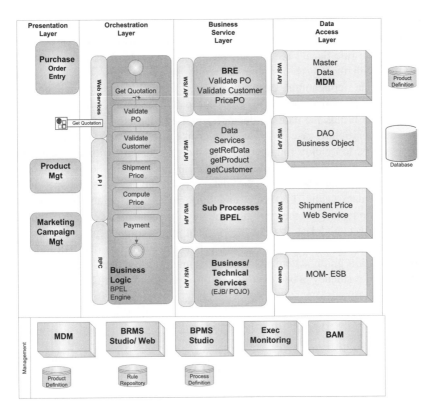

Figure 13.6. *Logical view – purchase order process*

Depending of the type of design, business objects include data access methods or the access is delegated to a DAO layer, and in this case the business objects exposed to the rule act as a Data Transfer Object (DTO) only. There are a lot of interesting discussions on these two different design approaches. Both approaches work, but DTO, DAO and data service can be a better choice if we want to move our IT architecture to extended SOA: moving to the enterprise level leads us to think about defining an enterprise object model to facilitate service reuse, data interoperability, data exchange, and simplify the integration of current applications as well as developing future "mash-up" applications. It is impossible to design an EOM (Enterprise Object Model) upfront. This has to be done by increment. There are a lot of industry initiatives to define standard data model per business area or concern. MISMO, ACCOR, are examples of such standards. Based on XML schema, these models help to define a common vocabulary for applications to exchange data. Architects can leverage these definitions, or at least can apply the same type of patterns for defining their own EOM. To help companies build up or adapt pre-built data models so as to obtain their EOM, they need shared and public modeling procedures[1]. At the rule application level, rule analysts will extract the vocabulary needed for the rule during the rule harvesting phase of ABRD. This vocabulary is reconciled with the EOM. As soon as terms have the same semantic definition across multiple applications, they are migrated from the application scope to the EOM scope. MDM manages them. Once the data sources are evaluated, the DAO design pattern brings the data to the application and the DTO transforms it for the scope of a specific use case or software layer like a service or a GUI. Applying this approach helps to quickly migrate to a common vocabulary without impacting the current application development. The logic to access and prepare the data is externalized and maintained in the data service layer. Rule Engine accesses transactional data using DTO view and through rule set parameters. Sometimes developers, under the pressure of time or due to other considerations, expose an enterprise object model as it is to the rule authoring component to build the fact model. This is bringing complexity when it is not needed. The rule will look like a set of navigation graph statements to access simple terms, like for example, to get the address of residency, a bad exposure of the object model may lead us to write:

```
The  address  of  the  residency  of  the  second  loan
applicant of the loan application...
```

when a rule writer just needs the concept of "co-borrower's residency address". To avoid such an issue, products like ILOG JRules help to define those business concepts or vocabularies and map them to the real executable data model. This is an important facility as it enables us to define and implement the rule according to business vocabulary and not a complex data model.

Common definitions are managed using the MDM component. In the context of a rule, two types of data are considered: the business entities like product, customer, purchase order, etc. and the domain enumerated values. Thus, one of the first natural integration in the ACMS, is the use of MDM to manage master or reference data that the BRMS will leverage. The BRMS is a client of the MDM services. During the rule authoring, rule writers access the enumerated values dynamically from the MDM. For the rule execution the reference or master data used to infer decisions are accessed from the MDM as well as the other data sources. When a BRE needs to enhance his execution context with other type of data it may access other services thru helper classes referenced within the rule engine's working memory.

Once exposed as services the business and technical services using BRMS bring the decision making to the BPM component. BPM is used to orchestrate the

---

1. To find more information about those EOM modeling procedures you can have a look at the community MDM Alliance Group (http://www.mdmalliancegroup.com/).

services, and decisions are made in the BRE relying on MDM for reference data access. This third component of the ACMS addresses a business process efficiency issue specifically around: who is involved? When should they be involved? What do they need to do? BPM supports human and automated actors. At a glance the business logic to implement using BPM Suite is linked to people, tasks, and data to process within a task. When supporting purely automated tasks, BPM is orchestrating the application logic and services. BRMS complement BPM by adding the "why" to a BPM task; why it behaves a certain way, why this decision is done. Changing a business process is generally risky: we do not want to change things that are working well and impacting a lot of different stakeholders in the organization. In fact new policies, regulations or business strategies should affect the decision rules without changing the core business processes. At the high level view, the development lifecycle using those technologies may be tailored so that changes are made more often in the BRMS layer and by parameterization of reference data values via the MDM, then in the BPM, and less into the application code. The following diagram illustrates this timing difference. The business team initiates a change request addressed to the development team. The BRMS is supporting short lifecycle for implementing the change related to decision logic and the MDM also via a friendly user interface allows active reference data value governance such as version management, permission management, traceability, data keying, etc. In some deployment, such as fraud detection, this could be done every hour. BPM process changes will occur once a month or more, and then application updates will most likely support a release plan of one release every six months.

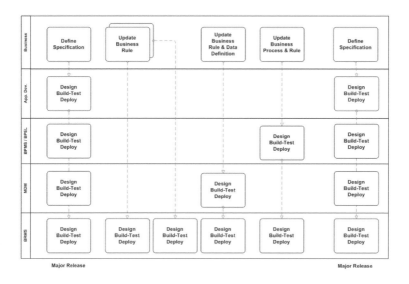

Figure 13.7. *New lifecycle*

We may note that in this model the specifications are handled by a mixture of codes, data models, rules, and processes. Policy changes are supported in the rules and reference data management, process improvement in business processes.

During the analysis phase the team needs to understand how the rules are currently defined, documented, implemented, tested and updated? Who owns the rules within the business organization? What are the different domains of application of the rule? What are the metadata associated with a rule?

In the following business to business order management process, the outcome of the modeling phase leads to this kind of process map (this is a simple case to illustrate the concepts).

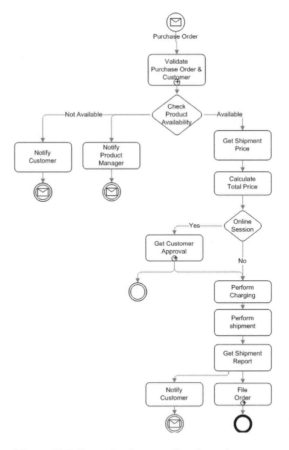

Figure 13.8. *Example of process flow for order process*

The process is initiated when an online customer submits a product order or when an automatic purchase order issued by a well known authenticated customer is received on one EDI link. A customer validation step is executed using customer data and purchase order data. The diamonds are considered as process flow rules, the first one simply checks whether the product is in stock or not. The action is to route the process execution to different paths. If the product is available, the price for the shipment is determined and presented back to the customer. If the product is not available, a message is sent back to the customer by email or Web page error message (if he is still online). If the product is not available, the system also sends an email or SMS to supply the stock for this product. The total price of the order is calculated from the product price, the customer business condition, some marketing loyalty programs… and the shipment price. As there are potentially a lot of changes in this price computation function, we need to implement this function in a decision service using components such as MDM and BRMS. When the charging and the shipment have been performed successfully, the order is filed and the process ends.

Analyzing the activities of this process in more detail helps us to extract the following decision points, candidates for business rule implementation.

Decision Point Name	Description	Rule Owner or SME	Source
Validate Customer Data	Verify the customer data quality and some other testing such as blacklisted customers, customer credentials, etc.	Customer and risk management department	Business Intelligence statistics and algorithm Customer database
Validate Purchase Order	Verify there is no fraud in the purchase orders or on a set of purchase orders coming over a time period. This is to avoid attacks from someone who may have stolen a partner's credentials	Customer and risk management department	BI statistics and algorithm Customer database
Calculate Total Price	As the price may account for a loyalty program, marketing campaign, stock level, and other business dimensions, business rules are relevant here	Marketing department	Customer data Product definition

The owner and source columns are used to manage the rule discovery activities the project team will execute in the early phases of the project. We do not address the rule harvesting process here but merely focus on the results. If we focus on the B2B connection, the typical rules we can find in each decision point may look like: for the "Validate Customer Data":

– the customer name and address match a registered customer's data;

– the IP address matches one of the authorized IP addresses for this customer;

– the customer is not blacklisted;

– the shipping address is one of the possible shipping addresses the customer gave to us at the registration time;

– the IP address is not a blacklisted one;

– the customer does not have outstanding credit with us;

– the name of the "bill to" record is a known employee of the customer company.

For "Validate Purchase Order":

– the purchase order has to include at least one line item;

– each line item needs to reference a known product;

– the quantity needs to be close to a historical quantity this customer is used to ordering for this kind of product;

– the terms and conditions code are not blank and the reference is a known code;

– the person name in the 'purchase order to' record is a know employee of our company.

For "Calculate Total Price":

– the total price includes shipment;

– the total price includes current promotion at the product category level and/or at the product level;

– the total price takes into account a quantity-based discount for a given product;

– the total price takes into account the customer contract, and discount agreement;

– the price of the product takes into account for a seasonal factor for a particular product.

The implementation and deployment of each of these decision points will be designed as services. Each service has a clear contract with respect to the callers. The process is supported by a BPM component calling these services and providing the input data. As most of B2B applications use XML documents to exchange information, the input/output parameters are XML-based data.

There are two types of integration of master data in MDM. One way is static, by getting the values from a XSD or table and is done in one shot when the developer is defining the object model for the rule, or a dynamic way using API to access the reference data on the fly. The following screen shot from a JRules BOM class definition illustrates that the currency domain values are coming from MDM provider, clicking on the synchronize link will reload the data from the MDM service.

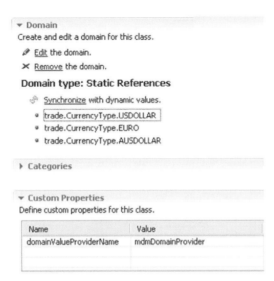

Figure 13.9. *MDM-BRMS connection*

This can be completed at the rule authoring level by adding a value provider API exposed in the rule editor so that the rule writer can get the last updated list of value coming directly from the data source.

The other important elements the BRMS need to access from the MDM data service are the Product, Catalog and Categories elements which can be exposed to the rule engine as objects. Once the XML document is received, the rule service accesses thru API or Web service the MDM component to get reference data. This round trip can also be done at the initialization phase of the rule engine to cache the data. In that last case a publish–subscribe implementation of the cache management is used to update the product definition once the MDM changes it. One other pattern is also to insert into the rule engine working memory (or as input parameters) the reference data, so that the rule developer can write conditions on those objects. To compute the final pricing of the purchase order the rule can leverage an MDM service to obtain the marketing classification of the customer and its negotiated term of business, giving its unique identifier (primary key).

One of the side effects of using an automatic decision service with BPM is that a rule-based system should return a set of accumulated reasons to explain its decision. The outcome of the engine processing can be a Result object (or Issue, Fraud, etc. depending of the business context) which includes a list of reasons (code, description) to explain the decision made by the engine. A typical rule template may look like:

If <conditions> then generate error as: "the purchase order must apply to an existing product"; <change the state of the data>.

This type of rule adds an error as a reason for its decision and may change a particular state within the data it is processing, for example a purchase order state.

This design will help in auditing the decision made by the engine, tune the rule, and look for incoherence. Engine can warn or reject, or generate exceptions. The business process has to route to a work queue for human processing if for example the response includes exceptions. The activities which follow a call to a decision service may look like Figure 13.10.

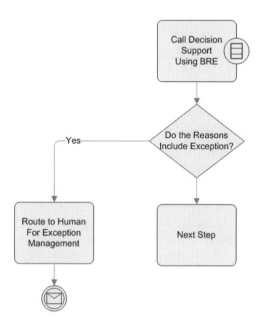

Figure 13.10. *Example of activities following a call to a decision service*

13.5. BRMS and SOA

From the specifications and business requirements the solution architect will design a set of reusable services exposed behind interfaces. The interface defines the contract between the caller and the service. During the application development lifecycle the interface implementation will go from scaffolding code to mockup, up to real linked code. The implementation of these interfaces should hide (encapsulate) the use of a rule engine. In a SOA, BRE deployment is designed within the service tier as a reusable service. The following diagram illustrates the components involved in the implementation of a service using BRE. The Web container can support the flow of Web pages, view preparation and control, and it delegates the business logic to a business interface. The implementation of this interface prepares the data for the rule, obtains a rule session from a session provider and calls the Rule Engine execute (parameters) method. The Rule Engines are pooled and attached to a connection, so the system can handle parallel execution. The pool also helps to support hot deployment of the rules without stopping the application.

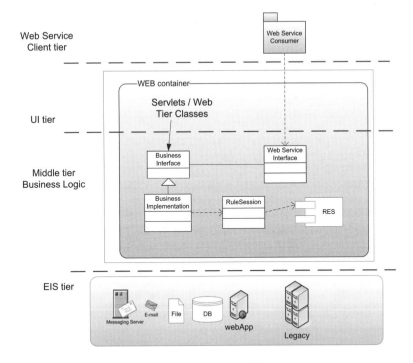

Figure 13.11. *BRMS and SOA*

One major design characteristic of using a BRE is to assume that the rule engine has all the data it needs to infer decisions. To simplify the rule set signature some higher level of container object can be set as the rule set parameter. Then the first party of the rule flow will be to insert in the working memory of the engine the elements needed for rule pattern matching.

When designing a service by contract we may want to consider splitting each service with pre-conditions, core function and post-conditions. A decision service using a BRMS, could have specific rules in the pre and post conditions to take into account different behaviors depending of the caller. The core of the service still uses BRMS but supports the more generic or cross client decisions. One example of such a design was created to support the geography dimension: instead of coding tests within a lot of rules about the origin country of a Transaction, it is better to externalize such conditions in one or more rule package exposed in pre or post conditions of the service. Another case may use a pre-processing package to validate customer profile, where some rules are dedicated to a given customer (or better to a given customer group) for example to apply different contract policies. The main sub-flow includes all the standard corporate policies around customer making authorized to do business.

In the migration of business and technical functions to service-oriented architecture, if we apply a business rule approach supported by an enterprise BRMS, we can migrate sub-parties of the current legacy application. We can start with each decision point identified during the rule harvesting cycle, and externalize them behind a service.

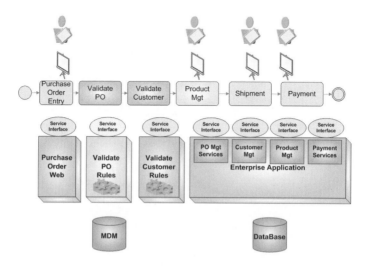

Figure 13.12. *Example of a migration by services*

Figure 13.12 presents this migration by services. A basic SOA approach is to revamp the legacy functions (right side) of the purchase order management, customer management, and product and payment managements. The service interfaces as exposed can be orchestrated from a BPEL engine. The data format will follow some XML schema definition. The "validate customer verification" is a function the IT team have already migrated to use a BRMS to support changeable decision on the customer contract management, as it has a high degree of volatility for change. During this migration, the MDM is deployed to define the Customer and all the master data used by the rules. Externalizing this decision making outside of the process applies a loosely coupled approach: the business process engine is a client of the decision service and calls a defined interface with input and output parameters, all the decision logic is implemented within the service without any knowledge from the caller.

The next function will be related to Purchase Order data validation which has a Web component and a rule component. The migration can be carried out in stages and the BPEL can continue to call this function from the legacy system until the BRMS service is operational. We are moving to the top-right quarter of the SOA maturity matrix. The business process is already implemented using a workflow product which exposes Web-based form GUI to the end user, and manages work items, work queues and XML documents. This case comes from a real architecture migration project; it is interesting to note that BRMS was used at the same time as the BPM deployment to bring the agility needed to change the logic of the validation rules.

We will conclude this chapter by emphasizing the fact that not all business rules can be discovered up front. During the development phase it is common to get up to 60% of coverage. The design of the rule set is an important activity to let the business user know that some data were not triggering any rules, or only some basic ones, and so the data set needs to be analyzed to catch some new cases. The deployment of BRMS improves change management time and control. However, on top of the technology some rule governance processes need to be developed to control who can support the change, who the owner of the business policies is, what the rule lifecycle is, what the rule set lifecycle is and the service lifecycle also has to be designed as part of the SOA deployment.

Chapter 14

Semantic Integration

It is worth repeating that sustainable information systems rely on a strong management of IS referentials. These referentials are structured with help from Master Data Management (MDM), Business Rules Management Systems (BRMS) and Business Process Management (BPM). So far, we have introduced the concept of ACMS (Agility Chain Management System) that defines the link between these three key referentials. Then, we stated that the first stage to regain know-how about the IS is to model master data with *semantic modeling* (see Chapter 8 about the Praxeme methodology). Now, we will show how to reuse the semantic modeling to streamline interconnections between systems. In other words, the semantic modeling is useful to set up MDM but also to streamline systems integration in a sustainable manner.

In this chapter, the term BIM (Business Information Model) is equivalent to the *semantic aspect* of Praxeme and the term CIM (Common Information Model) is equivalent to the *logical aspect* of Praxeme. The derivation rules between BIM and CIM are not detailed here but readers can find more information in the methodology part of this book, including Model Driven Architecture (MDA) used by Praxeme to ensure a formal derivation between models.

Written by Erik STEINHOLTZ, Progress Software.

14.1. Enabling the adaptive enterprise

The contemporary economic environment is known to have an ever-increasing speed of change. Globalization may be the newest of the driving factors, while factors such as consolidation within vertical industries and the increasing importance of information may be more traditional drivers.

Accommodating change in an enterprise is not a trivial task. A company may find a once prosperous market rapidly declining, prompting change in the company's products and go-to-market strategy, or it may find itself acquired by a rival, which induces a series of activities for carrying out the merger.

Below is a survey of a method for enabling adaptability for a company by making use of semantic integration. There are three essential components to semantic integration as outlined in this method:

– a Business Information Model (BIM) – semantic model of the business;

– an IT-level information model, the Common Information Model (CIM);

– tools and systems for putting the models to use in integration projects.

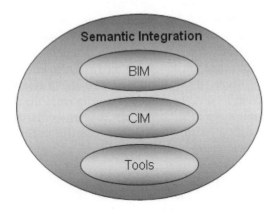

Figure 14.1. *Components of semantic integration*

Moreover, two essential aspects of the models are that they are dynamic and that they are actually used.

14.2. Inhibitors for change

To understand the power of the adaptable enterprise, we first need to look at a few key reasons why some corporations are not ready for change. The change inhibitors present in a corporation at any given time may include:

1. Lack of on-the-floor awareness of the company's, the division's, the department's, the group's etc. purpose. An average worker in a company who is not aware of the company's *"raison d'être"* is less likely to understand why a change is needed and thus more likely to react with resistance to change. This is the *people* factor inhibitor for change.

2. Brittle business processes and information management. This is the *process* factor inhibitor for change.

3. Confusion about definitions. Simple questions like "what is a customer?" and "how do we make money?" should not have ambiguous answers. The definition confusion results in time wasted and suboptimal routines being formed. The cause of the confusion relates back to, and to some extent explains, reason number 1 above. This is the *information* factor inhibitor for change.

The list could of course be a lot longer, but these inhibitors are significant, especially when we look at a corporation from an information-processing perspective. Two cross-references between the different factors are mentioned above, but it is easy to see that in fact they are all much interconnected.

How do corporations and enterprises tackle the lack of readiness for change? Typically with a point solution:

– A BPM (Business Process Management) initiative. Tools for enabling flexible business processes solve the process flexibility, at least on the IT level. To some extent ERP-backed IT overhauls fit into this category as well, though you may argue that an ERP overhaul does not make ready for change, it rather imposes a time-static change and leaves the corporation in a new "snapshot" state. These initiatives address the *process* factor above.

– Some corporations have identified the need to straighten out the definitions used within the company and initiated the creation of a corporate semantic model, which serves as a common ground for definitions. The semantic model can take any form from a pile of more or less structured documents to a formal UML class diagram, E/R diagram or an ontology diagram. The semantic model project is an information management initiative that addresses the *information* factor above (see Chapter 8 about the Praxeme method).

– The *people* factor is the one that is usually hard to address by IT-related initiatives alone.

Before we go on to see how semantic integration can address the challenges posed by these change inhibitors, let us look at what Semantic Integration is.

14.3. Definition of semantic integration

Semantic integration is, first and foremost, "a way of thinking": we should be integrating concepts rather than just pure data. A simple example will clarify this.

If I want to integrate telephone numbers between two systems, I can find two fields in two systems' databases, and copy one to the other, installing integrity mechanisms by using an ESB or ETL tool. I will now be assured that all phone numbers associated with a certain employee will be transferred from system A to system B. Integration done, over and out? No, this approach will fail to take into account what the context and meaning of the telephone numbers are. The source system in this integration is an HR system that (among other phone numbers) included details on "in case of emergency" calls: a number to a spouse or family member. The target system is the corporate intranet where all contact details of the employees should be published. If the context and the meaning of the data that is integrated are not taken into account, we will end up publishing the number of spouses' phone numbers on the intranet, which was not the intent of the integration.

In this very simple example, we could say: well, just apply a little bit of intelligence and it will all work out. True, but real-life scenarios are a lot more complex. They encompass questions like:

– who is a customer?;

– what is the primary contact media in situation A or B?;

– who should get information about product updates for products that are marked end-of-life?;

– are customers ordering through all reseller channels equally entitled to the same price offers? the same service levels?,

and so on.

Semantically integrating real-world scenarios will call for the use of a *Common Information Model* (CIM). A CIM is a model that covers all concepts, terms and metadata in a given number of business processes and their supporting applications. For the purpose of semantic integration, the scope of the CIM should be extended to all aspects of the business to ensure that any business process and its supporting applications can be integrated. The model is typically described in UML, and can be viewed as a counterpart to what linguists call an ontology.

The CIM is the first critical part of semantic integration. It provides two essential benefits:

1. an abstraction layer that makes it possible to make any integration between two systems without being biased by a particular system (in the sense that for instance only the field names, table names and structures of the ERP system are used). This is a safeguard against application lock-in, and a significant risk-and-cost reduction for any future rip-and-replace project for one of the constituent systems. The abstraction aspect of the CIM enables it to be the "lingua franca" for the integration endeavors in a corporation;

2. a semantic model that starts with the meaning of data rather than technical necessities. In the first example above with the phone numbers, this means that we would have modeled the meaning of the communication (emergency alert) and the means of communication (telephone) as a context for the "in case of emergency" phone number. The semantic model nevertheless needs to drill down to all the technical necessities, such as country code, area code and number, but it will visualize them in their proper context.

To speed up the work with establishing a CIM, some companies choose to make use of an industry standard such as the TM Forum's Shared Information/Data (SID) model for telecommunications or ACORD[1] for the insurance industry.

The second critical component in semantic integration is tools to make use of a CIM in integration scenarios.

14.4. Parallel track information modeling

So far, we have only considered one information model. However, we need to look at information modeling at two levels: the business level and the IT level. The parallel track information modeling refers to how business and IT look at information modeling. In business, the need is typically to obtain the high level overview, to understand enough of other departments' business that smooth collaboration is possible. It stems from recognizing the waste of time in conversations like this:

– "Are the materials sent out to all customers?"

– "All the current ones. I just couldn't figure out what to do with the ones on suspension."

---

1. ACORD (Association for Cooperative Operations Research and Development) is a global, non-profit standards development organization serving the insurance industry and related financial services industries.

– "Well they are customers, but not paying customers – do we want to send the materials to them …?"

– "…and how about the ones pending service start. They have signed and will be customers soon but…. are they now?"

– "…and all the corporate customers – should we send one set of materials to the company or one for every individual user within the company…?"

This conversation quickly starts carrying an undertone of "what is actually a customer?" Companies with a large number of customers will tend to need a formal definition of what constitutes a customer. Yet, if such a definition exists, it is almost never a singular one. One company I worked for made an inventory and came up with 30 definitions – probably a more realistic number. And if we go on to define what is a partner, an employee, a core business process, a customer contract, you will likely find some sources of confusion, hence the need for a Business Information Model (BIM).

In IT, however, the need for semantic models also exists, stemming from a different need: the need to integrate information systems. If the ordering system and the logistics systems are to be integrated, they need to have a common definition of what an order is and the information that constitutes the order. Integration departments that have passed the early point-to-point integration stages will raise the question of what the common ground of the participating systems are. This can, for example, result in the use of a canonical format for information exchange between the systems. At this stage, some people will note the striking likeness of the canonical format and the semantic model. Both are information models. Both serve the need for a "common ground" definition. The semantic model is likely aimed primarily at being understandable, while the canonical format has to be complete and machine readable, therefore containing a lot more detail. Within the semantic integration paradigm though, we propose an information model without binding to a physical format. This is the Common Information Model (CIM).

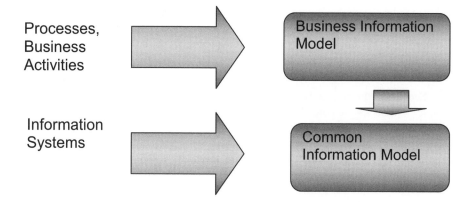

Figure 14.2. *Influences on the BIM and the CIM*

Now that we have two models – the BIM and the CIM – which are similar in nature – shouldn't the BIM and the CIM just be merged? Yes and no.

Let us look at the reasons for a yes first. There are good reasons why you should merge the information models from business and IT:

– Firstly, you will have common ground not only between different business departments or different IT projects, but you will have common ground between business and IT. For the long-lasting, cross-industry effort of bridging the business/IT gap, this would be at least a worthy step.

– Secondly, the models will act as quality control for each other. Putting the IT details into the business model makes sure that these definitions actually work. Normalizing the IT model to accommodate the business model makes sure that the integrations we make are sensible from a business perspective.

– Thirdly, you will be forced to accommodate change. The change will most likely be driven from the IT side of the model. This is not because change starts in IT (which it obviously does not), but because the changes in the business that drive change in IT will resurface as a change in the IT common model because it is needed for practical reasons, whereas a change in the business common model is more likely to be considered cosmetic and put in the queue for later treatment, or entirely forgotten.

Now, let us look at the reasons why we should *not* merge the business and IT models:

– Firstly, the model will contain more details than a business person should be expected to cope with. One of the drivers for the complexity of the CIM is the normalization which in turn is driven by extensibility requirements. The extensibility requirement on the CIM is – and should be – very commonplace. To make a model extensible, a large degree of normalization is required. Normalization, in turn, makes the model complex and less intuitive. For instance, a telephone number may be normalized to "contact medium" with the qualifier attribute "telephone"[2]. This will make the entity a little less intuitive to use, though it is more versatile and makes the model more extensible.

– Secondly, the manageability of the model will be impaired by making it too complex. Since we are considering change readiness, this is crucial.

A useful "best of both worlds" approach is to keep the models separate, yet establish a very clear relationship between them, by referencing the BIM entities from the CIM top-level entities. This is in line with the Praxeme approach method that encourages the use of MDA to manage dependency links between the semantic model (business view) and the logical model (IT view).

More importantly: where are all the semantic definitions of application data maintained in a consistent way? Remember, the CIM or the Master Data is not enough in itself. The meaning of each and every field in the application formats or database tables also have to be defined. For the sake of clarity, let us call this *semantic mapping*.

The necessity of semantic mapping calls for a tool for semantic integration. The semantic integration tool capabilities are more precisely:

– accommodate a variety of CIMs (expressed in UML, XML schema, DB schema, etc.);

– accommodate a variety of application formats;

– define and maintain the semantics of the application data, expressed as mappings to the CIM (semantic mapping);

– deal with master data in Master Databases, in canonical message formats or just in-memory.

14.5. Change inhibitors addressed with semantic integration

And how do the change inhibitors mentioned above relate to semantic integration? Very strongly. A semantic integration initiative, in fact, has the power to address all of the change inhibitors listed above:

---

2. See for example the prebuilt data models proposed by the MDM Alliance Group (http://www.mdmalliancegroup.com).

– The *people* factor is addressed by a BIM. A key factor for succeeding in a semantic integration initiative is getting all business people on the same page. This is achieved by modeling the concepts in use by business. As we will see later, it is preferable to make use of a formal notation such as a UML class diagram to make this model. The semantic model can when properly rolled out to the organization serve as a tool for raising the situational awareness of each employee.

– The *process* factor is addressed by enabling flexible integration between systems. Whether processes in a company's IT environment are controlled by an integration tool such as an ESB, by a BPM tool or by a workflow engine, the semantic integration engine will provide the last mile (or two!) of flexibility for these tools, enabling them to achieve true process flexibility.

– The *information* factor is at the heart of the semantic integration project. Ironing out confusion about the terms and concepts in use in the organization is the main purpose of the BIM. This is then refined to include IT-level details to form a CIM.

Now, you may ask: point solution with a business semantic model or BIM as a part of a semantic integration initiative – *What's the difference?* Well spotted! The difference is whether the model is *dynamic* or whether it will be *used*, two critical success factors for a BIM that go hand in hand. They go hand in hand due to the fact that if a model is used it will have to change as the business changes – it has got to be dynamic.

14.6. Putting it to work

To show how to put semantic integration to work, we use a case study from a telecom operator. Being in a period of change involving a number of acquisitions, the need for a semantic model was identified. And soon enough, it was discovered that a lot of system integration had to take place as well.

14.6.1. *Canonicalizing the BIM*

The first part of the project was to canonicalize the BIM. This was an effort led by an experienced modeler who carried out a number of workshops with the departmental directors and functional specialists. The BIM was approved by the senior management and accepted as the common business vocabulary. The structure was small enough to be printed on a tabloid (A3) sheet – it was comprehensible.

The entire project took roughly 3 months and laid good ground for further semantic integration.

14.6.2. *The quick win: a pilot project*

Towards the end of the BIM Project, this operator discovered some tools for utilizing model-driven tools in an integration environment: Progress DataXtend Semantic Integrator and Progress Sonic Enterprise Service Bus. To ensure the validity of these tools, a pilot project was carried out. In the pilot project, which ran less than 3 weeks, the key activities were:

– Identify two systems and a set of transactions to be tested with semantic integration. Systems that were more temporary in nature were chosen, which made the "loose coupling" benefit very clear – the temporary system could now easily be replaced.

– Initiate the modeling of the CIM, with some manageability and coherence principles in mind:

   - every top-level entity in the CIM should explicitly reference an entity in the BIM,

   - refining to accommodate the IT-level specifics was carried out in workshops,

   - while not covering the entire Business Information Model, it was recognized that this initial CIM was entirely reusable when working in a full-scale project.

– Integration of the systems was carried out using Progress DataXtend Semantic Integrator (DXSI) and Progress Sonic ESB.

14.6.3. *Using the CIM for integration*

The common model had a kernel from the pilot project. This kernel could successively be built upon so that the model was expanded for every integration performed. This meant that:

– each integration project could, if necessary, include an activity for adding to the CIM;

– the CIM did not grow "out of bounds" in terms of size, but rather kept at a pragmatic level where it corresponded to the reality of the information in the information systems it was to model;

– the borders and the direction for growth of the CIM were set. Due to the principle of reference to the BIM, the concepts and their relationships were not growing wild;

– the CIM was handled entirely in DXSI. One DXSI project artifact was kept for the CIM and one project artifact for the Exchange Model – the CIM and the application formats and their mappings to the CIM.

14.6.4. *Tools used*

The semantic integration tool had to be able to accommodate an exchange model (a metamodel for the CIM and the application formats). It also had to have the ability to expose Web Services or Java APIs from the runtime.

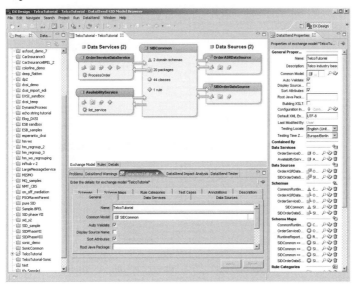

Figure 14.3. *The exchange model view*

The tool also had to have facilities for navigating and editing the models in network or hierarchical layout, while illustrating the relationships between the elements. It was expected that the common model could be created and maintained in the SI tool.

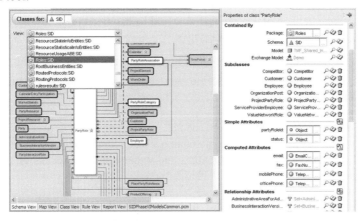

Figure 14.4. *The model explorer*

The import tool shows a difference view, highlighting each element to potentially be updated. In conjunction with the impact analysis feature, which shows the interconnections between all components in the interchange model down to the lowest level, this tool makes it possible to take full control over changes before they are committed.

Figure 14.5. *Differential import and impact analysis*

14.6.5. *Managing change and keeping the models alive*

The organic growth principle outlined above meant that there was some change (not only additions) to the CIM. This was handled by the change capabilities of the SI tool, which provided impact analysis for each element to be changed. Changes came in two flavors: changes to the CIM and changes to the application formats after e.g. a new version of a system. Both could be handled the same way:

– import the new format or CIM into the tool;

– use the import difference tool to analyze what elements are changed;

– use the impact analysis tool to see what these changed elements affect throughout the Exchange Model.

This meant that for any given change, immediate control over the resulting impact was achieved. At this step, no changes were committed yet. The same tools in DXSI were then used for automating and enhancing the process of rolling out these changes.

As an end result, this operator had overcome their current challenges with success and made the company ready for future change.

Conclusion

The system is mature enough to be implemented

An information system that quickly adapts its functions to different contexts would be used by many different types of companies. The idea of a *lego* information system has already taken off. This service-oriented approach is its basis. However, before starting to work on a large SOA project the maturity of the service-oriented approach has to be judged. How can this be done?

SOA integrates disciplines that have been worked on for several years, such as functional architecture (now known as enterprise architecture), process design, object-based approach and contract-based design. From this point of view, a sufficient level of maturity has been reached. From a technical point of view, the required tools are also available, e.g. modeling CASE (UML), programming languages (Java, C+, etc.), rules management systems, process engines, parameters and master data management, interconnections and administration between systems. The lack in terms of IS enterprise methods that are necessary for the identification of service requirements is compensated by Praxeme's open method and other contributions such as TOGAF created by the Open Group.

All of these assets are rich, operational and available. Companies can use them now. However, companies only really benefit from SOA if their staff understands its functioning. Understanding how SOA works takes time. This time does not include a delay before new methods or technical tools become available. The current assets are rich and reliable enough to introduce this kind of system. Consequently, it makes sense to introduce SOA now, to prepare software engineers for this new type of system and provide training on these assets (UML, IS enterprise method, solutions for interconnections, etc.). This time can be used to establish an adapted type of organization and present the benefits of a better integration of the process to the user.

It is a major risk for the information system if software engineers are not up to date with new developments. This delay of knowledge could lead to a complete failure in the implementation SOA. Do not wait for the next level of IT and methods maturity. This might be a risk, as SOA has already reached a good level of maturity. SMABTB's project of overhaul SOA has shown how difficult it is to train the respective members of staff. The future of information systems depends on an immediate change towards SOA. This action plan includes a time span of several years and includes different generations of computer engineers.

What is about to slow down this new trend?

Once an SOA business plan has been created, there are still different aspects that slow down the process. The person in charge will have to judge the capacity of the teams working on the project and has to correct the following issues before implementing SOA:

– Generation gap between older and younger members of staff. Teams have to include different age groups. This point is important when it comes to maintaining knowledge and distributing "modern" approaches of design to the entire company.

– Lack of understanding of the components used in logical architecture. Functional requirements and the development of the software are often too closely linked: each functional evolution brings heavy software modifications. SOA corrects this problem by introducing a supplemental effort of logical architecture that improves the IS sustainability level.

– Lack of coordination between different experts, architects, designers, analysts, etc. Everybody works on the same thing and the cycle of construction for information systems is no longer respected. For the implementation of SOA, different tasks and disciplines have to be separated. A "head architect" works with the chief information officer and ensures functional coordination, methods and techniques. Currently many CIOs lack operational knowledge in modern approaches to building systems. They launch projects they do not really understand and listen to young experts who are often promoted to the position of "technical architect" with only a few years of experience. Many CIOs no longer understand well the IT and marketing speak of software vendors, etc.

The head architect is the link between the CIO and the teams that work on modern approaches, mainly SOA. This position is also a link between the different generations of computer scientists from senior staff (those who created information systems that still function today) and younger members of staff without a lot of experience, i.e. they have worked in maintenance or projects that are not very strategic. None of this is their fault, but part of developments in the respective era.

– Not enough awareness of the benefits and limits of enterprise architecture. Some experts (e.g. functional enterprise architect) even state that the current state of information systems does not allow for the implementation of SOA. They do not understand the difference between cosmetic and overhaul SOA. This book has shown the difference between these two types of SOA.

SOA's capacity to correct weaknesses is very important and a decisive factor for companies. The question of *leadership* is most important and concerns the head architect. Issues that slow down SOA's introduction can be reduced if decision-makers have access to a methodological framework that has already been successful and shared between different users, i.e. open source. Praxeme's open method corresponds to these expectations.

Further information

This book goes hand in hand with the creation of a community that is based on the idea of *The Sustainable IT Architecture*. The members of this community share the ideas and principles explained in this book, especially when it comes to SOA's level of maturity (cosmetic, overhaul, extended), solutions such as BRMS, MDM and BPM, unified data formats, agility of services and Enterprise System Topology for Praxeme's open method.

To join this community, please go to: http://www.sustainableitarchitecture.com.

Weblinks

Agile Business Rule Development (ABRD):
http://www.eclipse.org/epf/openup_component/openup_abrd.php

ILOG: http://www.ilog.com/

MDM Alliance Group: http://www.mdmalliancegroup.com/

Praxeme Institute: http://www.praxeme.org/

Progress Software – Semantic Integration:
http://www.progress.com/dataxtend/index.ssp

Objecteering EA/Praxeme: http://www.objecteering.com/praxeme.php

Orchestra Networks: http://www.orchestranetworks.com/

Sustainable IT Architecture Community: http://www.sustainableitarchitecture.com/

Bibliography

[BLANC, 2005] BLANC X., *MDA en action, Ingénierie logiciel guidée par les modèles*, Eyrolles, 2005.

[BONNET, 2003] BONNET P., "Cadre de référence SOA," "Cadre de référence web services," http://soa.orchestranetworks.com.

[BONNET, 2004] BONNET P., "Gestion des variantes de services dans les architectures SOA," http://soa.orchestranetworks.com.

[BONNET and LAPETINA, 2007] BONNET P. and LAPETINA D., "Virtual Engine for Praxeme ," http://soa.orchestranetworks.com.

[BOOCH, 1996] BOOCH G., *Object Solution: Managing the Object-Oriented Project*, Addison-Wesley, 1996.

[CARLSON, 2001] CARLSON D., *Modélisation d'applications XML avec UML*, Eyrolles, 2001.

[CARR, 2004] CARR N. G., *Does IT Matter*, Harvard Business School Press, 2004.

[CASEAU, 2006] CASEAU Y., *Urbanisation et BPM*, Dunod, 2006.

[CHAPPELL, 2004] CHAPPELL D. A., *Enterprise Service Bus*, O'Reilly, 2004.

[DESFRAY, 1994] DESFRAY P., *Object Engineering – The Fourth Dimension*, Addison & Wesley, 1994.

[FOURNIER-MOREL X., GROSJEAN P., PLOUIN G., ROGNON C., 2006] *Le guide de l'architecture du SI*, Dunod, 2008.

[GAMMA, HELM, JOHNSON, VLISSIDES, 1994] GAMMA E., HELM R., JOHNSON R., VLISSIDES J., *Design Patterns, Elements of Reusable Object-Oriented Software*, Addison-Wesley Professional Computing Series, 1994.

[HAMMER and CHAMPY, 1994] HAMMER M. and CHAMPY J., *Le Reengineering, Réinventer l'entreprise pour une amélioration spectaculaire de ses performances*, Dunod, 1994.

[HERZUM and SIMS, 2000] HERZUM P. and SIMS O., *Business Components Factory: A Comprehensive Overview of Component-Based Development for the Enterprise*, John Wiley & Sons, 2000.

[KRAFZIG, BANKE, SLAMA, 2006] KRAFZIG D., BANKE K. and SLAMA D., *Enterprise SOA*, The Coad Series, 2006.

[LAPASSAT, 1997] LAPASSAT G., *Architecture technique informatique*, Hermes, 1997.

[LAPASSAT, 2003a] LAPASSAT G., *Architecture fonctionnelle des logiciels*, Hermes, 2003.

[LAPASSAT, 2003b] LAPASSAT G., *Urbanisme informatique et architectures applicatives*, Hermes, 2003.

[LARMAN, 2005], LARMAN G., *UML 2 et les Design patterns, Analyse et conception orientées objet et développement itératif*, Pearson Education, 2005.

[LONGÉPÉ, 2006] LONGÉPÉ C., *Le projet d'urbanisation du S.I.: Démarche pratique avec des cas concrets*, Dunod, 2006.

[MANOUVRIER and MÉNARD, 2007] MANOUVRIER B. and MÉNARD L., *Intégration applicative EAI, B2B, BPM et SOA*, Hermes, 2007.

[MEYER, 1990] MEYER B., *Conception et programmation par objet. Pour du logiciel de qualité*, InterEditions, 1990.

[MEYER, 2000] MEYER B., *Conception et programmation orientées objet*, Eyrolles, 2000.

[MONFORT and GOUDEAU, 2004] MONFORT V. and GOUDEAU S., *Web Services et Interopérabilité des SI*, Dunod, 2004.

[OASIS, 2006]: http://docs.oasis-open.org/soa-rm/v1.0/soa-rm.pdf.

[ROQUES and VALLÉE, 2002] ROQUES P. and VALLÉE F., *UML en action, de l'analyse des besoins à la conception en Java*, Eyrolles, 2002.

[ROSNAY, 2007] DE ROSNAY J., *2020 Les scénarios du futur*, Des idées & des Hommes, 2007.

[VAUQUIER, 1993] VAUQUIER D., *Développement orienté objets*, Eyrolles, 1993.

[VAUQUIER, 2003] VAUQUIER D., *Plan qualité du logiciel et des services Internet*, éditions Afnor, 2003.

Special Technical Note

Objecteering EA/Praxeme

All UML diagrams presented in this book were created with the Objecteering EA/Praxeme modeling tool. A downloadable version is available from this weblink: http://www.objecteering.com/praxeme.php.

Index